ASSUMED IDENTITIES

NUMBER FORTY-ONE:

The Walter Prescott Webb Memorial Lectures

ASSUMED IDENTITIES

The Meanings of Race in the Atlantic World

Edited by

John D. Garrigus and Christopher Morris

INTRODUCTION BY FRANKLIN W. KNIGHT

Contributors:

John D. Garrigus

Rebecca Goetz

Trevor Burnard

Sidney Chalhoub

Rebecca J. Scott

Jean M. Hébrard

Published for the University of Texas at Arlington by
Texas A&M University Press

Library of Congress Cataloging-in-Publication Data

Assumed identities : the meanings of race in the Atlantic world / edited by John D. Garrigus

and Christopher Morris ; introduction by Franklin W. Knight ; contributors: John D.

Garrigus . . . [et al.]. — 1st ed.

p. cm. — (The Walter Prescott Webb memorial lectures ; no. 41)

Includes bibliographical references.

ISBN-13: 978-1-60344-192-6 (cloth : alk. paper)

ISBN-10: 1-60344-192-1 (cloth : alk. paper) 1. America—Race relations—History. 2. Group

identity—America—History. 3. Eurocentrism—America—History. 4. Nationalism—

America—History. 5. Haiti—Ethnic relations—History—18th century. 6. Haiti—

History—Revolution, 1791–1804. 7. Virginia—Ethnic relations—History—17th century.

8. Ethnic relations—Religious aspects—History—17th century. 9. West Indies, British—

Ethnic relations—History—18th century. 10. Slave trade—Brazil—History—19th century.

I. Garrigus, John D. II. Morris, Christopher (Christopher Charles) III. Series: Walter Prescott

Webb memorial lectures ; 41.

E29.A1A86 2010

305.800973—dc22

2010002446

In memory of our colleague Evan (Buzz) Anders

1946–2008

Contents

Preface and Acknowledgments

Identity is a slippery concept. Everyone knows it exists. Everyone has it. But what is it? And—a question of special importance for historians—how does one document its existence? It presents a moving and shadowy target, always transforming, never fixed, never just one thing. As an object, it is seen differently depending on the subject's vantage point. Put another way, identity exists both as an object and as something subjectively understood within historical context, that is, within a social and political universe that moves through time. Identity is assumed.

Each of the essays in this volume assumes at least three identities: one taken by the subject, one given the subject by his or her contemporaries, one given to all by the historian. In the first and last essays, the subjects are individuals: Ogé and Rosalie. They bookend essays on groups and group identities: British West Indian planters, Chesapeake Anglicans, Africans in Brazil. Whether individual or group, the subjects of these essays, however they saw themselves and however they were seen by others, are assumed by the authors to have had racial identities forged within the early modern Atlantic world. That point is expressed in the volume's subtitle and discussed in the introduction.

The essays originated as lectures given during the 2007 Annual Webb Lectures, presented by the University of Texas at Arlington Department of History and, on this occasion, by the History Department's Graduate Program in Trans-Atlantic History. Trans-Atlantic history, which assumes a trans-Atlantic community and identity and projects it upon the past, has institutionalized an identity for our graduate program. The Trans-Atlantic field itself has been a way for scholars to escape some of the limits imposed by national histories. Yet with the election of Barack Obama, national conversations on identity are not so centered on the Atlantic as they once were, reminding us once again of the transitory nature of identity. The son of a black Kenyan and white Kansan, born in Hawaii and raised there as well as in Indonesia, Obama has an assumed identity, including his racial identity, that is surely more closely tied to the Pacific Ocean, even as he is assumed by some to be a more typical African American, from Southside Chicago, no less, an identity with roots in the nation's trans-Atlantic past and one that Obama himself in certain contexts seems to embrace.

But we need go no further than our own campus to witness the complex and transitory nature of identity. Within a mere decade or two the university has changed from a commuter campus, with a student body predominantly from the white suburbs and small towns around Dallas and Fort Worth, into a more residential university with a student body recently placed among the top 10 percent of national universities ranked according to racial diversity. For the Asians and Pacific Islanders, many of the Hispanics who trace their ancestry south to Mexico and Central and South America, and no doubt for others as well, the Atlantic Ocean does not figure into their identity, except to the extent that they, like President Obama, embrace an American identity that remains trans-Atlantic. In those moments, the historical identities explored in this volume are theirs too.

We would like to acknowledge several benefactors and friends of the Webb Lecture. C. B. Smith Sr., an Austin businessman and former student of Walter Prescott Webb, generously provided the original endowment that makes possible the annual presentation and publication of the lectures. Over the years the endowment has benefited from the additional support of Jenkins and Virginia Garrett of Fort Worth. President Robert Spaniolo supported our efforts by generously providing a reception in honor of the lectures, and providing additional support for publication costs from Rudolph Hermann's Endowment for the Liberal Arts. We also thank Beth Wright, dean of the College of Liberal Arts for supporting the cost of illustrations for this volume. Other thanks go to Bob Fairbanks, chair of the Department of History; Don Kyle, outgoing chair of the Department of History; Joyce Goldberg, chair of the Webb Lectures Committee; and our colleagues in History and elsewhere around campus who annually support the lectures.

ASSUMED IDENTITIES

Introduction

Race and Identity in the New World

FRANKLIN W. KNIGHT

R ace and identity constitute an important dimension of political discourse throughout the world in the twenty-first century. Both concepts are closely affiliated with ethnicity. This should hardly be surprising. The process of globalization has dramatically intensified in the past few decades and increasingly more people are on the move. At the same time, the increase in national boundaries has accentuated national designations as well as the identities of individuals. Presently national identities are proliferating as new nation-states are created. These newly designated states represent convenient labels for groups that simultaneously may already have had one or more other identities. Some of these identities may be racially derived. Some identities are based on ethnicity. Some are merely geographical.[1] Multiple identities assumed greater importance after the eighteenth century when language began to be more precisely defined. By then the number of nation-states was less but the problem of race and identity, as the contributors point out in this volume, became increasingly exacerbated.

It should not be surprising that problems of race and identity are extremely acute throughout the Americas.[2] The American experience created a sharp break in the history of the modern world, bringing into the European consciousness a vast productive region with diverse peoples never before identified by anyone. This was noted emphatically by the Abbé Raynal when he began his influential multivolume history in the eighteenth century: "No event has been so interesting to mankind in general, and to the inhabitants of Europe in particular, as the discovery of the New World, and the passage to India by the Cape of Good Hope. It gave rise to a revolution in commerce, and in the power of nations; as well as in the manners, industry, and governments of the whole world."[3] While Raynal and other of his admirers like Adam Smith focused on the commercial, epidemiological, botanical, and political revolutions that followed in the wake of the European expansion, they overlooked an equally important demographical revolution also taking place. Between the late fifteenth and the late eighteenth centuries several groups of Europeans, led by the Spanish and Portuguese, had established overseas colonies and empires throughout the Americas, destroying or pushing aside the indigenous inhabitants. Europeans moved overseas to these newly discovered locales in large numbers. But their numbers were dwarfed by the Africans transported to provide the greater proportion of the physical labor required to establish viable colonies. At the same time, both immigrant and indigenous peoples were overwhelmed by a newly created population of offspring that resulted from the mixing of all the groups.[4]

The gradual integration of the Americas into the European-Asian-African world systems had profound, long-term global consequences. The Europeans renamed the newly discovered hemisphere America; they called the indigenous inhabitants Americans. Without their knowledge and consent the original population obtained a new permanent identity. But the American experience was influential not only in the construction of new identities but also in the transformation of language as well as the cosmography of the Europeans.[5] The Americas would have reciprocal impact on the rest of the world. Eventually they developed an autonomous self-consciousness that started to manifest itself politically with the independence of the United States from Great Britain in 1776–1783 and the independence of Haiti from France in 1791–1804. Haiti and the United States of America represented pioneer forms of state formation. They also became models and catalysts for new political identities.

The United States currently manifests a virtual obsession with the hyphenated identity.[6] Many citizens want to reflect their origins in their identity and the simple term "American" is commonly being expanded. The result has been a plethora of "hyphenated Americans": Irish Americans, Anglo-Americans, Chicano Americans, Puerto Rican Americans, Cuban Americans, Mexican Americans, Black Americans, Afro-Americans, African Americans (these three representative of the same ethnic group), Arab Americans, Iraqi Americans, Indian Americans, Chinese Americans, Korean Americans, Vietnamese Americans, Italian Americans, and German Americans. The list seems inexhaustible. With the Census Bureau insisting on a baffling, inscrutable, and changing array of ethnic designations about every ten years, the country has become a veritable demographic alphabet soup. The result, however, does not necessarily clarify identity.

Nor is the United States alone. The disintegration of the Soviet Union unleashed the previously controlled and superficial consolidation of its more than 120 ethnic and national groups. From Lithuania, Estonia, and Latvia on the Baltic, to Moldavia, Georgia, Armenia, and Azerbaidzhan on the Black Sea and the Caspian Sea, a wave of ethnic consciousness has arisen along with the recovery of the previously autonomous states that had been swallowed up by the Soviet Union. In Yugoslavia, the convenient confederation administered by Marshall Tito foundered against the resurrected ancient ethnicities of Serbs, Croatians, Montenegrins, Macedonians, Bosnians, Kosovans, Herzegovinians, and Slovenes. The federal state collapsed into conflicting separate states, each with important, vociferous ethnic minorities refusing to be either absorbed or obliterated.

Nowhere is ethnicity rifer than in Africa. Given the relatively recent demarcation of its political boundaries, most Africa states represent a *potpourri* of ethnicities: Ghana with its Akan, Moshi-Dagomba, Ewe, and Ga; Angola with its Ovimbundu, Kimbundu, and Bakongo; Kenya, with its Kikuyu, Luo, Lubya, Kelenju, and Kamba. Tiny Benin—about the same size of the state of Delaware or the island of Cuba— has four major ethnic groups (Fon, Adja, Bariba, and Yoruba). The Cameroons have approximately two hundred distinct groups that may or may not represent distinct ethnicities.[7]

Throughout India and Asia ethnic groups are continually challenging the political order, peacefully when they can, and militarily when they must. Prime Minister Rajiv Gandhi's assassination resulted from ethnic Tamil hostility to Indian intervention in neighboring Sri Lanka where Tamil and Sinhalese have been sporadically engaged in civil war for years.

Wherever in the world one looks, ethnic invention is the order of the day.[8] Throughout the American continent, North as well as South, ethnic diversity is surprisingly common despite the reluctance of some local governments to uniformly acknowledge and document it. Every country reflects the inescapable ethnic consequences produced by time, colonialism, political circumstances, and the peripatetic nature of humans.

The Caribbean and circum-Caribbean states, including Mexico, Colombia, Venezuela, and Brazil, as well as the Andean countries of Ecuador, Bolivia, and Peru, have never denied their plural reality. The Jamaican national motto is "Out of Many, One People." Trinidad's motto: "Together we aspire. Together we achieve." And the indigenous populations everywhere on the continent have been very active in reasserting their identity—especially on the matter of the celebration of the Christopher Columbus quincentenary in 1992. Political competition is a great catalyst for ethnic consciousness, as the 1973 confrontation between Indians and the U.S. government at Wounded Knee in illustrated.[9]

Even countries that consider themselves to be ethnically homogenous disguise their kaleidoscopic ethnic variety.[10] Encouraged by the UN requirement for national recognition of minorities, ethnic groups are proliferating throughout Latin America and the Caribbean. About 15 percent of the Argentine population represents ethnic minorities of some sort. Uruguay lists 4 percent of its population as black, and 8 percent as mestizo. Paraguay notes that 5 percent of its population is "white or Indian."

Chile considers approximately 5 percent of its population to be "Indian" or "other." While the stated proportions may be the whim of some government official, the reality is inescapable: American communities are exceedingly diverse (though some are more diverse than others).

At the time that William Edward Burghardt Du Bois was writing, race and color were considered urgent and conflictive contemporary issues in the United States. The United States began to feel that what afflicted it also afflicted the rest of the world equally. Unlike most of his peers, Du Bois knew quite well that *race* was an insufficient and inconveniently imprecise designation of socio-cultural differences, but that these differences constituted an unavoidable and increasingly insolvable source of human conflict.[11] What exactly did he mean by race?

This militant flourishing of ethnic recognition represents exactly what Du Bois predicted long ago. "The problem of the twentieth century," he wrote in what he called the "The Forethought" to his illuminating book published in 1903, *The Souls of Black Folk*, "is the problem of the color line."[12]

Race is a widely used, and notoriously widely abused, term. Anthropologists and sociologists have spent much time examining the ways in which "race" may, or may not be applied. We need not be bogged down by their numerous definitions. *The New Columbia Encyclopedia* has as useful a definition as we are likely to need, and it anticipates some of the obvious anomalies of usage:

> One of the group of populations regarded as constituting humanity. The differences that have historically determined the classification into races are predominantly physical aspects of appearance that are generally hereditary. Genetically a race may be defined as a group with gene frequencies differing from those of the other groups in the human species, but the genes responsible for the hereditary differences between the traditional races are extremely few when compared with the vast number of genes common to all human beings regardless of the race to which they belong. Many physical anthropologists now believe that, because there is as much genetic variation among the members of any given race as there is between the groups identified as different races, the concept of race is unscientific and unsound and racial categories are arbitrary designations. *The term race is inappropriate when applied to national, religious, geographic, linguistic, or ethnic groups, nor can the physical appearances associated with race be equated with mental characteristics, such as intelligence, personality, or character.*[13]

Race can be, and has often been, employed with the most imprecise connotations and is therefore notoriously unreliable as a principal identifier. Moreover, as Julian Pitt-Rivers reminds us in his perceptive article, "Race, Color and Class in Central America and the Andes," the connotation can shift significantly when moved across cultural frontiers, or as it is frequently employed in various countries of Spanish America.[14] In Latin America, Pitt-Rivers writes, "the word *race* . . . clearly owes little to physical anthropology, but refers, however it may be defined, to the ways in which people are classified in daily life. What are called race relations are, in fact, always questions of social structure."[15]

In other words, "race" often becomes a synonym for "class" and even for social conditions across much of Latin America and the Caribbean. Race is undeniably an imprecise concept beyond its social and political application and varies tremendously across cultures and time, as historian Barbara Fields often points out.[16]

While "race" originates from the French language, "ethnic" comes from the Greek, *ethnos,* indicating community, such as a nation or people. As any survey of the term indicates, "ethnicity" is rather loosely used today to designate any group bound together by common ties of language, race, nationality, culture, or skin color who might feel themselves to be, or are considered by others to be, an ethnic group.[17] In Europe no group is defined ethnically as "white" or "European" or "Christian." These ethnic designations, however, frequently crop up in Africa, Asia, and South America.

In India, being Indian is not considered ethnically distinct. In Singapore, however, it is considered to be one of the principal ethnic groups. Nor, properly speaking, should "mestizo" and "mulatto" be considered especially useful ethnic terms. Nevertheless in Latin America they are so considered.

"Ethnicity," because it involves so many nuanced connotations, can be as elusive a term as "race." In some cases "ethnicity" is a synonym for "phenotype," or, as Harry Hoetink would prefer, "somatic norm image," that is, "the complex of physical (somatic) characteristics which are accepted by a group as its norm and ideals."[18] In some cases it represents class rankings; yet in other cases it is simply a convenient group identification.

What is important about these terms, as Oscar Handlin points out in *Race and Nationality in American Life,* is that they are historical, intellectual constructs, not rigid scientific definitions.[19] They are peculiar to time, place, and circumstances. Created by time, their definitions are altered by political or intellectual force. It should not be surprising, therefore, if the meanings attributed to these terms today should not be precisely the same ones that were intended by their users throughout modern history. In this these terms have a lot in common with terms such as "plantation," "Creole," or "maroon," that were transformed by transfer to the changing environment of the Americas.[20]

Race and ethnicity are closely related to what Donald Baker refers to as "identity, power, and psychocultural needs."[21] They are used by groups to define themselves or others, and to convey a variety of attributes simultaneously. This is clearly seen in the cases of slave societies where race, color, and ethnicity were emphasized as social signifiers, often to reinforce the superordination of a demographic minority group.

After the Enlightenment, language began to assume greater precision, and to reflect power relations more closely. It was further bolstered by the application of scientific rules to human societies. In short, race, ethnicity, and identity assumed ideological importance. As the Europeans expanded in the fifteenth and sixteenth centuries they left prodigious descriptions of the new peoples, places, flora, and fauna that they encountered in the wider non-European world. The resulting expansion of knowledge inevitably led to an increased consciousness of themselves and what demarcated their amorphous variety from the rest. Given their experience on the Mediterranean frontier, Europeans did not immediately assume that they were superior to non-Europeans, and they were painfully aware of many areas in which they were distinctly inferior.

Early European reports from the wider world, illustrated exceptionally well in the logs of Christopher Columbus, contain unrestrained admiration for the newly discovered peoples. Contempt and condescension toward unfamiliar cultures became a gradual acquisition after the Europeans began to dominate parts of the non-European world, especially after the "conquest" of the Americas.

Europeans, however, always felt themselves better than non-Europeans. Greeks considered non-Greeks to be barbarians, and Christians and Muslims had a number of impolite expressions for their adversaries. Jews were expelled repeatedly from a number of European states, but the fact of repeated expulsions indicates either that they never obeyed the orders or that they were allowed to return to their homelands.[22] European attitudes toward non-Europeans were often "paradoxical, shifting, ambiguous," as Anthony Pagden notes for criollo attitudes toward Indians in New Spain.[23] Those attitudes evolved through time from ethnocentricity to manifest racism.

The journals and letters of Christopher Columbus are typical of the genre in displaying the ethnocentricity of the early modern age. They tell us as much about the author as about the people described, and reveal open admiration for some of the natives: "The Kings and all the others went about as naked as they were born, and the women, too, without any shyness, and they are the handsomest men and women I have found up until now. They are exceedingly white, and if they wore clothing and were protected from the sun and the air they would be almost as white as the people in Spain ... In all Castile there is no land that can be compared to this in beauty and fertility ... All the people are strong and courageous and not feeble like the others I found before. They converse very easily and have no religion."[24]

In the spring of 1505 a Castilian adventurer named Martín Fernández de Figueroa joined a fellow native of Salamanca in a Portuguese-sponsored expedition that left for Sofala on the East African coast. After six years in the Portuguese Indies (during which time he served with Afonso de Albuquerque in India), he returned to Salamanca and eventually had his story written.[25] It is a simple story of chivalry and survival, demonstrating a sophisticated power of observation and the normal European obsession with gold: "From Sofala to the Strait of Mecca, three thousand leagues away, everyone is black. The inhabitants of Sofala are Kaffirs, who adore the sun and the stars. They wear colored cotton garments, and others cover only their shameful parts. There is no linen. The women wear nothing on their heads, and tin bracelets on their legs. They pierce their lips in six or seven places, which they consider very beautiful and elegant . . . And one hundred leagues inland, in a Kaffir kingdom called Monomotapa, lies the gold in which they trade very copiously in those parts."[26] The same observations could also be made of the account of Bernal Díaz del Castillo, the most articulate and possibly the most intrepid of the soldiers of Hernán Cortés, on the fighting at Tenochtitlán in June 1520, in what would become New Spain:

> As soon as the next morning dawned we sallied out with our whole force upon the enemy, being determined if we could not conquer, to make them fear us. The Mexicans came to meet us with their whole force, and both parties fought desperately; but as the numbers of our opponents were so immense, and as they constantly brought up fresh troops, even if we had been ten thousand Hectors of Troy, and as many Roldans, we could not have beaten them off; nor can I give any idea of the desperation of the battle; for though in every charge we made upon them we brought down thirty or even forty, it was to no avail; they came on even with more spirit than at first, nor could we, by our cannon or fire arms, make impression upon them. If at any time they appeared to give ground it was only to draw us from our quarters, in order to ensure our destruction. Then the stones and darts thrown on us from the terraces of the houses were intolerable. But I describe it faintly; for some of our soldiers who were in Italy swore, that neither amongst Christians nor Turks, nor the artillery of the King of France, had they ever seen such desperation as manifested in the attacks of those Indians. We were at length forced to retreat to our quarters, which we reached with great difficulty.[27]

In 1550 the aged Dominican friar, Bartolomé de las Casas, and the distinguished jurist Juan Ginés de Sepúlveda argued indecisively at Valladolid over whether the indigenous Americans should be considered natural slaves. The humanist position of Las Casas was that "all the peoples of the world are men," and that "mankind is one," and with typical hyperbole insisted that Spaniards were corrupting the American Indians rather than the opposite as his rival implied.[28] Sepúlveda presented the type of logic that racists much later would find convenient as explanations for their bigotry. He insisted, with Aristotelian logic, that Spaniards were more rational than Indians, and therefore were superior to the latter. Moreover, as God's elect, the Spaniards were natural rulers and the Indians natural slaves. But Las Casas had the moral force on his side since in 1537 the pope had conveniently ruled that the Indians of the Americas were rational, and therefore capable of being converted to what the Spanish called "the true faith."[29] This ruling meant that the Indians could not be regarded as natural slaves.

Diogo do Couto, after long service in Goa, left an unpublished chronicle—

Diálogo do soldado prático (Dialogue of the veteran soldier)—on his death in 1616, in which he commented critically on Portuguese, Dutch, and English conduct in the East Indies: "India has the most pure and excellent airs in the world, the finest and most salutiferous fruits, and spring and river waters on the face of the earth, bread, barley, every variety of pulse and vegetables, enough large and small cattle to sustain the world, and everything else about it is marvelous. The worst that there is there, is us, who came and ruined such a wonderful country with our lies, our deceits, our frauds, our chicaneries, our injustices and other vices which I forebear to mention."[30] The thread that connects all these early reports, spread over considerable time and geography, is the muted ethnocentricity of the early European narrators. That would not last for very long. As time passed, European self-confidence increased. By the end of the sixteenth century, Spanish arms, allied with newly imported diseases, created an empire throughout large parts of the Americas. Meanwhile the Portuguese created a magnificent trading-post empire that stretched from Lisbon through Brazil to Goa and Macao.[31] By the beginning of the eighteenth century, networks of trade and colonization integrally linked the Americas with Africa, Europe, India, and Asia.[32] The age of the great European empires reached perhaps their apogee. But the eighteenth century not only established political hegemony, it also revolutionized thought and consciousness. Part of this process involved new considerations of race, slavery, and identity. Race became hierarchically organized and affixed to colors that bundled a number of characteristics. Africans tended to appear at the bottom of this new classification. Slavery became sharply distinguished from other forms of servitude and in the Americas tended to be applied exclusively to describe Africans or their New World descendants. Under the aegis of the Enlightenment, a new rationality and an expanding scientific curiosity fundamentally affected attitudes toward society, politics, and the individual.[33] The confidence in the superiority of the natural sciences tended to obscure much that was ambiguous or false.

Modern racism and hierarchical ethnic classification assumed new importance with the Enlightenment—with the ideas of François Marie Arouet de Voltaire (1694–1778), Georges-Louis Leclerc de Buffon (1707–1778), Cornelius de Pauw, the Abbe Raynal, William Robertson, David Hume, and Adam Smith.[34] Those ideas were bolstered by scientific advances and the newly emerging concept of nationalism, as Peggy Liss points out in *Atlantic Empires,* where "by the 1760s in Europe, *nation,* long a component of *empire,* had begun to separate from and to succeed that concept as a preferable political organizing principle."[35] Neither "nation" nor "nationalism" could be easily defined, as many of the essays of this volume demonstrate.

While the rebellious North Americans avoided defining what exactly they meant in their grandiloquent declaration of 1776 that "all men are created equal," the French reformers in 1789 could not agree on what was France and who constituted true Frenchmen.[36] Indeed, the dilemma for the Colonial Committee examining the question at Versailles was whether nationality could be determined by race, color, nativity, or socio-economic class. The French Revolution never resolved the issue, but after that those concerns could never again be divorced from definitions of the state, or society, or the *conciencia de sí.*

The nineteenth century introduced the language of race into all political discussions, a little-explored legacy of the French Revolution that the essays by Rebecca Goetz, Trevor Burnard, John Garrigus, Sidney Chalhoub, Rebecca Scott, and Jean-Michel Hébrard explore from different dimensions. Racial identity was not the only concept propagated generally. The nineteenth century also produced what Charles Morazé called "the triumph of the middle classes," an intoxicating confidence in the unlimited resources of science, industry, and European values.[37] Those using the political language of the nineteenth century found it difficult to reconcile ethnic plurality and state formation. Nationalists tended to assume that a political state represented the congregation within a clearly defined geographical locale of people who shared certain common characteristics, including an identifiable ethnicity. None of the great organizing social principles of the nineteenth century—neither Comtian positivism nor Marxism nor Social Darwinism—accommodated the American reality of plural cultures and diverse ethnicities cohabiting harmoniously within a single organized state. Moreover, Europeans became narcissistically preoccupied with their own technical superiority over the rest of the world, and interpreted technical progress as indicative of human advance and social development. What is worse, Europeans defined nationalism in exclusionary, racist terms that denied the possibility of political independence to non-European populations. An inescapable irony accompanied this new attitude. For centuries Europeans had constructed global empires on the basis of inclusion of diverse peoples. Then, beginning in the late eighteenth century and throughout the nineteenth century, they gradually began to exclude them as being beyond the pale of their emergent nationalism or their notions of civilization.

The ideas of ethnic uniformity and national cohesiveness permeated the great social ideas that agitated political discourse during the nineteenth century. There were principal theoreticians in these debates. The French scholar, Auguste Comte (1798–1857), invented positivism and the science of sociology, and produced many enthusiastic disciples who would extend his work, especially throughout Latin America. The English naturalist Charles Darwin (1818–1882) published *On the Origin of the Species by Means of Natural Selection, or The Preservation of Favoured Races in the Struggle for Life* in 1859, and revolutionized evolutionary biology. The writings of the German Karl Marx (1809–1883) became the basis for socialism and communism. All three philosophers would be extremely influential throughout the Americas, especially among elites south of the United States.

For the elites of those Latin American states forging their political independence during the nineteenth century then, the non-European ethnic groups were considered handicaps to be overcome. Afro-Americans and indigenous Americans, despite their numbers and importance, were never recognized as integral components of the newly emerging polities. The plural society was never considered to be a viable option. The new states would nevertheless be constituted despite the inescapable presence of non-whites. That presence, however, had to be explained away. Positivists felt that the technical age would eventually eliminate "inferior races." Social Darwinists were confident that these would naturally fail to survive, or that miscegenation was indicative of a gradual transformation toward an acceptable European norm. Marxists felt that considerations of race should be subordinated to considerations of class, and thereby dissipated vital energies needed for the all-important class struggle. Clearly by the middle of the nineteenth century ideas about race had hardened, as well as perceptions of the wider world held by Europeans.[38] Indeed, all the essays included in this volume reflect the European preoccupation with racial and national identity and, in the examples of Garrigus, Scott, and Hébrard, attempts to push back against that rising tide of exclusion.

The prolific writings of José Antonio Saco, the great nineteenth-century Cuban nationalist, illustrate the point. A constant agitator for political independence for a country in which the European-derived component of the population was, at best, a slim majority, and when approximately 40 percent of the population were still African slaves, Saco had the temerity to write, "The Cuban nationality of which I spoke, and the only type that could occur to any intelligent person is that comprised of the white race, that by themselves amount to a little more than 400,000 individuals.[39]

By the end of the nineteenth century, Europeans talked arrogantly and exasperatingly of the "white man's burden," a phrase captured indelibly in verse by Rudyard Kipling:

Take up the White Man's Burden—
The savage wars of peace—
Fill full the mouth of Famine
And bid the sickness cease;
And when your goal is nearest
The end for others sought,
Watch sloth and heathen folly
Bring all your hope to naught.[40]

This was both a celebration of and a rationalization for imperialism, and it dominated European and American thought at least through the First World War. Europeans of that era, quite unlike their ancestors of the fifteenth and sixteenth centuries, imposed a static vision on the world in which lineal ascent ran from what they metaphorically called "darkest Africa" to the sublimity of industrialized Europe. The code words then were "civilization" and "progress," both enshrined in European culture.

As late as 1928 an expatriate Englishman who professed an abiding love for Jamaica wrote a revealing description of the social situation of the island. Among other things it demonstrated how confused both the writer and the situation were:

> The races inhabiting the West Indies today are a few native Indians, (British, Scotch [*sic*], Irish and Welsh and their descendants), French, a few Creole (i.e. born in the West Indies), Spanish, Creole, negroes, laborers from India, Chinese, who in Jamaica are rapidly developing as a trading class, and the Creole descendants of these Indians and Chinese, Portuguese, who originally came from Madeira, a few Syrians, who came as traders, and a large number of mixed race of negro and European in varying shades, from Sambo (three-quarter black) to those in whom the strain is imperceptible, and a small number the result of connections between negroes and coolies, Indians and negroes, and Europeans and Indians . . .
>
> The negro race has at present gone but a short way on the path to civilization. The individuals are still as children, childlike in belief and faith. Once gain their confidence and they will trust implicitly . . . Gratitude is, it is to be feared, not a strong point with many of them, although here and there pleasing examples to the contrary occur.[41]

Frank Cundall, the author, was still influenced by the ideas of the nineteenth century, and still oblivious to the profound changes taking place in his immediate Caribbean world as well as the broader Atlantic. His confusion of race, class, and nationality also masked his ignorance of the proletarian revolution taking place in the country of his sojourn. For by the late 1920s Marcus Garvey had had given the black people of Jamaica a different sense of their place in world history, and all across the Caribbean non-European groups were agitating for political and economic changes.

Within the broader American context race continues as a prominent political preoccupation. Unlike Latin America and the Caribbean, the United States has an unusual fixation on race. But even in relatively relaxed Brazil it generates much heated discussion. Although race matters appear in the political lexicon of other societies, the degree of concern is considerably less—elsewhere race is certainly less important than color. Indeed, despite the landmark U.S. Civil Rights Act of 1964—and it could be argued *because* of this Act—problems of race and ethnicity still pervade social, political, and economic relations across the United States. Virginia Dominguez illustrates in her brilliant study *White by Definition: Social Classification in Creole Louisiana* that as late as 1977 the New Orleans Bureau of Vital Statistics "employed two full-time clerk investigators to handle only cases concerned with racial designations, and the bureau spent some six thousand man-hours in 1976 exclusively on race cases."[42] That is the equivalent of 750 work days, or more than two years if the job were done by one individual, on defining race. As the traumatic experience of Hurricane Katrina demonstrated after

August 29, 2005, affairs in Louisiana are never attended with either required urgency or administrative efficiency, largely because of the element of race. While U.S. racial attitudes are neither static nor uniform across geography and generation, the furor generated by the publication in 1994 of a book, *The Bell Curve,* by the late Harvard psychology professor Richard Herrnstein and American Enterprise Institute political scientist Charles Murray, reflects a profound national preoccupation.[43] Despite the limited scientific skills of both authors, the book was a bestseller and generated extensive publicity and heated responses from both the scientific and popular communities.

The history and the social complexity of Latin America and the Caribbean create a different milieu for the perceptions and viability of race, class, and ethnicity, and that is reflected in notions of identity. It leads to what Pitt-Rivers calls "terminological inconsistency": "The problems of race relations in North America and Latin America are, therefore, fundamentally different. One concerns the assimilation of all ethnic groups into a single society; the other, the status distinctions between persons who have assimilated for hundreds of years, but who are still distinguished socially by their appearance . . . Assuming that the class structure of Latin America carries ethnic overtones, how is this structure affected by class differences being thought about largely in the idiom of 'race'? Such a view implies that classes are different in their essential nature. If the concept of 'social race' teaches us about race in terms of social structure, we should also have a concept of 'ethnic class' to remind us that class systems no longer function in the same way once class has phenotypical associations."[44] Because definitions of race, class, ethnicity, and identity are fluid, generalizations about the differences prevailing in Latin America and the Caribbean on the one hand and the United States on the other remain exceedingly complex. Moreover, the situation all across the Americas remains fluid. Despite the optimism cultivated by Barack Obama's election as president of the United States, a bedrock of bigotry and intolerance remains deep in the psyche of white America. Although the times are changing, the United States continues to manifest a tendency of toward mutually reinforcing social cleavages while in the other areas of the Americas the tendency is toward crosscutting social cleavages. Both types of societies produce discrimination and inequality, but the latter societies are more inherently democratic. The United States exercises enormous influence on the political discourse of the hemisphere. North Americans invariably see race in dichotomous terms of black and white despite their reality of a plural society. In the rest of the Americas, however, race represents a fluid spectrum, a sort of basket of crosscutting elements.

This does not mean that race is not important outside the United States. It is. But race is handled in a far more subtle way and it is seldom compartmentalized and polarized as it is in the United States. Notwithstanding, race, color, class, ethnicity, and condition seem destined to remain important considerations despite the far-reaching changes engineered by globalization and the changing fortunes of empires.

The protean complexity of any sort of identity constitutes an essential part of the history of every group because distinctions are expressed in languages that remain inherently dynamic. Captured verbal snapshots illustrate but never fully explain the important differences between the local, the region, and the global. Yet these contributors provide considerable food for thought.

John Garrigus provides a new angle for looking at the French and Haitian revolutions. His biography of Vincent Ogé, the most famous example of people of mixed African and European ancestry, poignantly illustrates the complication as well as novelty of those twin revolutions. Ogé was not only battling for recognition, for identity, but also battling against exclusion from French citizenship. That certainly was a time and an occasion in which the French, always so punctilious about language, found that a common language was not rich enough or expressive enough to accommodate the complex reality of the colonial condition

Rebecca Goetz deals with a critical moment in the rise of North American racism. She shows how the seventeenth-century colonial settlers along the Chesapeake began to redefine imported Africans and the indigenous inhabitants as incapable of truly understanding Christianity, and therefore assumed an eventual futility in religious proselytism. Among the implications was to sharpen the formerly ambiguous distinction between servants and slaves. By the beginning of the eighteenth century the term "servants" became associated with immigrants of European descent while the others became increasingly classified as slaves and treated as commercial commodities.

Trevor Burnard examines English colonists in a Caribbean territory where the idea of settlement had been largely abandoned and replaced by an aggressive, lucrative, exploitative settlement where the minority whites saw themselves as isolated islands of control in a sea of brutalized workers. The coercive conditions of sugar production in Jamaica in the eighteenth century affected both masters and slaves. But however they saw themselves, or however they imagined themselves, both groups remained symbiotically connected. Productive efficiency required the continuous negotiation of both parties to create a sort of environment of compromise.

If language proved inflexible within an empire it was even more limited in interimperial affairs as Sidney Chalhoub shows in his case study on nineteenth century Brazil. The international treaty between Portugal/Brazil and Great Britain in Vienna in 1815 precluded Portuguese involvement in the slave trade. In reality the trade continued with subsequent problems for the Brazilian police in the identification of recently enslaved Africans in light of the absence of any written record. The result was that the Brazilian police constructed an elaborate series of racial codes to help identify Africans suspected of being illegally imported to Brazil after 1815.

Rebecca Scott and Jean Hébrard trace the extraordinary saga of an enslaved West African woman in revolutionary Haiti, and the odyssey of her family as it moved from Haiti to Cuba to Louisiana to France around the middle of the nineteenth century.

With each move family members encountered new circumstances that affected their racial identity. In this case the family was moving across empires and languages, creating and altering identities even as they represent the existence of a revolutionary Haitian diaspora after the great revolution.

Many common threads tie these essays together. Race, ethnicity, condition, and nationalism represented factors that separately or collectively operated to shape how Europeans and non-Europeans saw themselves and each other. It was a complicated process that varied according to time, place, and circumstances.

Notes

1. For an insightful examination of this theme, see Livio Sansone, *Blackness without Ethnicity: Constructing Race in Brazil* (New York: Palgrave Macmillan, 2003).

2. This point may be followed in J. H. Elliott, *The Old World and the New, 1492–1650* (Cambridge: Cambridge University Press, 1970); Alfred W. Crosby, *The Columbian Exchange: Biological and Cultural Consequences of 1492* (Westport: Greenwood Press, 1972); Nicholas Canny and Anthony Pagden, eds., *Colonial Identity in the Atlantic World, 1500–1800* (Princeton: Princeton University Press, 1987); Ida Altman, *Emigrants and Society: Extremadura and America in the Sixteenth Century* (Berkeley: University of California Press, 1989); Ida Altman and James Horn, eds., *"To Make America" European: Emigration in the Early Modern Period* (Berkeley: University of California Press, 1991); D. A. Brading, *The First America: The Spanish Monarchy, Creole Patriots and the Liberal State, 1492–1867* (Cambridge: Cambridge University Press, 1991); Jack P. Greene, *The Intellectual Construction of America: Exceptionalism and Identity from 1492 to 1800* (Chapel Hill: University of North Carolina Press, 1993); David Abulafia, *The Discovery of Mankind: Atlantic Encounters in the Age of Columbus* (New Haven: Yale University Press, 2008); William J. Bernstein, *A Splendid Exchange: How Trade Shaped the World* (New York: Atlantic Monthly Press, 2008).

3. Guillaume-Thomas-François Raynal, *A Philosophical and Political history of the Settlements and Trade of the Europeans in the East and West Indies,* translated by J. O. Justamond (New York: Negro Universities Press, 1969 [1774]), 1. Raynal's work greatly influenced a number of European scholars including Adam Smith, as evident in his *An Inquiry into the Causes of the Wealth of Nations* (Dublin: Whitestone, 1776).

4. David L. Clawson, *Latin America and the Caribbean: Lands and Peoples* (Boston: McGraw Hill, 2006), 151–83.

5. Ann De León, "The Production and Reproduction of 'Aztec Bodies': Translating Pictorial and Textual Discourses on the Human Body from Sahagun's Florentine Codex (1579) to Antonio Peñafiel's Indumentaria Antigua Mexicana (1903)," PhD diss., Johns Hopkins University, 2007, 207.

6. Mary C. Waters, *Ethnic Options: Choosing Identities in America* (Berkeley: University of California Press, 1990); Frances Henry, ed., *Ethnicity in the Americas* (The

Hague: Mouton & Co., 1976); Paul R. Spickard, *Mixed Blood: Intermarriage and Ethnic Identity in Twentieth Century America* (Madison: University of Wisconsin Press, 1989); Barbara J. Fields, "Ideology and Race in American History," in *Region, Race and Reconstruction: Essays in Honor of C. Vann Woodward*, eds. J. Morgan Kousser and James M. McPherson (New York: Oxford University Press, 1982), 143–77.

7. See Map 2 in Phyllis Martin and Patrick O'Meara, eds., *Africa* (Bloomington: Indiana University Press, 1986).

8. Werner Sollors, ed. *The Invention of Ethnicity* (New York: Oxford University Press, 1989).

9. See Carol Talbert, "The Resurgence of Ethnicity among American Indians: Some Comments on the Occupation of Wounded Knee," in Henry and Spickard, eds., *Mixed Blood*, 365–83.

10. *Latin America Today: An Atlas* (Wellesley, Mass.: World Eagle, 1989), 52. Data assembled from U.S. Central Intelligence Agency, *The World Factbook*, 1988. Note that ethnicity has no consistent definition.

11. W. Burghardt Turner, "The Polemicists: David Walker, Frederick Douglass, Booker T. Washington, and W. E. B. Du Bois," in *Black American Writers: Biographical Essays, Volume I*, M. Thomas Inge, Maurice Duke, and Thomas R. Bryer, eds. (New York: St. Martin's Press, 1978), 47–132.

12. W. E. B. DuBois, *The Souls of Black Folk* (New York: New American Library, 1969), xi.

13. Paul Lagasse, et al., eds., *The New Columbia Encyclopedia* (New York: Columbia University Press, 2001–2007), accessed March 29, 2009, http://www.bartleby.com/65/ra/race.html, italics added.

14. Julian Pitt-Rivers, "Race, Color and Class in Central America and the Andes," *Daedalus* 96, no. 2 (Spring 1967), reprinted in John Hope Franklin, ed., *Color and Race* (Boston: Beacon Press, 1968), 264–81; and John J. Johnson, Peter J. Bakewell, and Meredith D. Dodge, eds., *Readings in Latin American History, Volume II, The Modern Experience* (Durham: Duke University Press, 1985), 312–27.

15. Pitt-Rivers, "Race, Color and Class," *Readings*, 313.

16. Fields, "Ideology and Race in American History;" and Larry Adelman, et al., *Race: The Power of an Illusion* (California Newsreel, 2003).

17. Pierre L. van den Berghe, *The Ethnic Phenomenon* (New York: Elsevier, 1981).

18. H. Hoetink, *Caribbean Race Relations: A Study of Two Variants* (Oxford: Institute of Race Relations, 1967), 120.

19. Oscar Handlin, *Race and Nationality in American Life* (Boston: Little, Brown, 1957).

20. See Franklin W. Knight, "El Caribe en la época de la ilustración, 1788–1837," in *Las Antillas en la era de las luces y la Revolución*, José A. Piqueras, ed. (Madrid: Siglo XXI de España, 2005), 3–26.

21. Donald G. Baker, "Identity, Power and Psychocultural Needs: White Responses to Non-Whites," *Journal of Ethnic Studies* 1, no. 4 (Winter 1974), 16–44.

22. D. van Arkel, "Racism in Europe," in *Racism and Colonialism: Essays in Ideology and Social Structure,* Robert Ross, ed. (The Hague: Nijhoff, 1982), 11–32. See also C. S. Holzberg, "Societal Segmentation and Jewish Ethnicity: Ethnographic Illustrations from Latin America and the Caribbean," in Henry, ed. *Ethnicity in the Americas,* 139–57.

23. Anthony Pagden, "Identity Formation in Spanish America," in *Colonial Identity in the Atlantic World, 1500–1800,* Nicholas Canny and Anthony Pagden, eds. (Princeton: Princeton University Press, 1987), 80. See also Anthony Pagden, *The Fall of Natural Man: The American Indian and the Origins of Comparative Ethnology* (Cambridge: Cambridge University Press, 1987).

24. "Sunday, 16 December, 1492," *The Log of Christopher Columbus,* Robert H. Fuson, trans. (Camden, Me: International Marine Publishing Company, 1987), 136–37. Columbus is on the northern shore of Hispaniola.

25. James B. McKenna, *A Spaniard in the Portuguese Indies: The Narrative of Martín Fernández de Figueroa* (Cambridge: Harvard University Press, 1967).

26. McKenna, *Spaniard,* 43.

27. Bernal Díaz del Castillo, *The True History of the Conquest of Mexico Written in the Year* 1568, Maurice Keatinge, trans. (London, 1800; La Jolla: Renaissance Press, 1979).

28. See Lewis Hanke, *Aristotle and the American Indians: A Study of Race Prejudice in the Modern World* (Bloomington: Indiana University Press, 1959), and Lewis Hanke, *The Spanish Struggle for Justice in the Conquest of America* (1949; Boston: Little Brown, 1965).

29. Bartolomé de las Casas, *An Account, Much Abbreviated, of the Destruction of the Indies,* Franklin W. Knight, ed., Andrew Hurley, trans. (Indianapolis: Hackett Publishing Company, 2003).

30. Quoted in C. R. Boxer, *Race Relations in the Portuguese Colonial Empire 1415–1825* (Oxford: Oxford University Press, 1963), 129.

31. J. H. Parry, *The Age of Reconnaissance: Discovery, Exploration and Settlement, 1450–1650* (New York: World, 1963); Elliott, *The Old World and the New 1492–1650;* Ralph Davis, *The Rise of the Atlantic Economies* (Ithaca: Cornell University Press, 1973); A. J. R. Russell-Wood, *The Portuguese Empire, 1415–1808: A World on the Move* (Baltimore: Johns Hopkins University Press, 1998).

32. Peggy K. Liss, *Atlantic Empire: The Network of Trade and Revolution, 1713–1826* (Baltimore, Johns Hopkins University Press, 1983).

33. Leon Poliakov, "Racism from the Enlightenment to the Age of Imperialism," in Ross, ed. *Racism and Colonialism,* 55–64.

34. See Canny and Pagden, eds., *Colonial Identity in the Atlantic World, 1500–1800.*

35. Liss, *Atlantic Empires,* 225.

36. Ira Berlin and Ronald Hoffman, eds., *Slavery and Freedom in the Age of the American Revolution* (Charlottesville: United States Capitol Society, 1983); Prosser Gifford, ed., *The Treaty of Paris (1783) in a Changing States System* (Washington: Woodrow Wilson Center, 1985); Franklin W. Knight, *The Caribbean. The Genesis of a Fragmented Nationalism* (New York: Oxford University Press, 1990), 195–217; Laurent Dubois and John Garrigus, *Slave Revolution in the Caribbean, 1789–1804: A Brief History with Documents* (New York: Palgrave Macmillan, 2006); Laurent Dubois, *Avengers of the New World: The Story of the Haitian Revolution* (Cambridge: Harvard University Press, 2004).

37. Charles Morazé, *The Triumph of the Middle Classes: A Political and Social History of Europe in the Nineteenth Century* (New York: World Publishing, 1966). Originally published in French as *Les Bourgeois Conquérants* (Paris: LeClerc et Cie., 1957).

38. See, for example, Philip D. Curtin, *The Image of Africa: British Ideas and Action, 1780–1850* (Madison: The University of Wisconsin Press, 1964); David Brion Davis, *Slavery and Human Progress* (New York: Oxford University Press, 1984).

39. *"La nacionalidad cubana de que yo hablé, y de la única que debe ocuparse todo hombre sensato, es la formada por la raza blanca, que sólo se eleva a poco más de 400,000 individuos."* Quoted in Eduardo Torres-Cuevas, *La polémica de la esclavitud: José Antonio Saco* (La Habana: Editorial de Ciencias Sociales, 1984), 82.

40. Rudyard Kipling, "The White Man's Burden" (1899), in *Collected Verse of Rudyard Kipling* (New York: Doubleday, 1910), 225.

41. Frank Cundall, *Jamaica in 1928: A Handbook of Information for Visitors and Intending Residents with Some Account of the Colony's History* (London: Published for the Institute of Jamaica by the West India Committee, 1928).

42. Virginia R. Dominguez, *White by Definition: Social Classification in Creole Louisiana* (New Brunswick: Rutgers University Press, 1986), 45.

43. Richard J. Herrnstein and Charles Murray, *The Bell Curve: Intelligence and Class Structure in American Life* (New York: Free Press, 1994). Taking their title from the normal distribution pattern for IQ, the authors appear to argue, but not consistently or unequivocally, that intelligence is partially linked to race and class. Even the American Psychological Association was drawn into the controversy. It established a special task force to investigate the claims made by the authors. The report supported some of the claims concerning IQ scores but failed to support specific statements linking IQ to racial or class differences.

44. Pitt-Rivers, "Race, Color and Class," 324–25. The phrase "terminological inconsistencies" is on page 316.

"Vincent Ogé Jeune Colon de St Domingue" (1790)
(Vincent Ogé the younger, colonist of St. Domingue)

"Thy coming fame, Ogé! Is sure"

New Evidence on Ogé's 1790 Revolt and the Beginnings of the Haitian Revolution

JOHN D. GARRIGUS

In August 1853, Georges Boyer Vashon, a free-born African American, wrote a 359-line poem entitled "Vincent Ogé," about an October 1790 revolt that tried to secure voting rights for property-owning free men of color in French Saint-Domingue.[1] Ogé, a wealthy merchant of one-quarter African ancestry, led this failed movement which was followed, ten months later, by the slave revolt that launched the Haitian Revolution. Vashon ended his poem with these stanzas:

> *Thy coming fame, Ogé! Is sure;*
> *Thy name with that of L'Ouverture,*
> *And all the noble souls that stood*
> *With both of you, in times of blood,*
> *Will live to be the tyrant's fear—*
> *Will live, the sinking soul to cheer!*

Yet Vincent Ogé has not achieved anything like the renown of Toussaint L'Ouverture; 150 years after Vashon's poem, we know far more about his death than about his life or the revolt that bears his name. On February 23, 1791, an executioner broke Ogé's body, and that of his colleague Jean-Baptiste Chavannes, and left them to die in the cathedral square of Cap Français, Saint-Domingue's most important city. Ogé's agonized public death made him a martyr for some contemporaries. Free men of color and their white allies in Paris described the execution as a terrible injustice, born of prejudice. White colonists and their European supporters, on the other hand, blamed Ogé for destabilizing Saint-Domingue, especially after the great August 1791 slave uprising that destroyed many plantations in this same part of the colony. The leaders of that slave revolt described the unfairness of Ogé's execution—not the hopes raised by his revolt—as a key motivation of their followers.[2]

In fact, the passions raised by Ogé's revolt and death were so great that in the two intervening centuries historians have never clearly established some of the basic facts about these events. One reason for this was that the colonial government tried Ogé secretly and prevented Saint-Domingue's press from publishing anything about it. Those contemporaries who did publish accounts of the revolt used it to address their political agendas. For colonial whites, Ogé's actions illustrated the danger of new humanitarian and abolitionist ideas. And Ogé's free colored colleagues in Paris described him in a way that protected their class from accusations of fomenting the slave uprising of August 1791.

Another reason why Ogé's "coming fame" never arrived is the difficulty of proving what Vashon, in 1853, believed was true: that Ogé's revolt launched the Haitian Revolution. In the mid-1840s, when Vashon came to Haiti from the United States, the mixed-race Haitian families who had ruled the country since independence in 1804 considered Ogé to be a martyr. For them, his tortured death showed that free-born people of mixed African and European ancestry, who made up about 5 percent of the colonial population, played as critical a role in the revolution as enslaved blacks, who made up about 90 percent of the colonial population. According to nineteenth-century historians from this "mulatto" class, Ogé began the revolution against racism and slavery, and was therefore as much a father of the Haitian nation as black generals like Toussaint L'Ouverture and Jean-Jacques Dessalines. Consequently, men who shared Ogé's mixture of European and African ancestry and his European education were authentic Haitians and suited to lead the nation.[3]

Vashon would have known and worked with members of these families during his years on the faculty of the national lycée (high school) in Port-au-Prince, from roughly 1848 to 1850.[4] He might even have seen a performance of a play about Ogé written by the school's director Pierre Faubert, which lycée students performed for the first time in 1841. But judging by his poem, Vashon does not appear to have understood how controversial it was to portray Ogé as a Haitian revolutionary. The French abolitionist Victor Schoelcher saw Faubert's play during a visit to Haiti and described it as an example of mulatto color prejudice against darker-skinned Haitians.[5] In fact, by the time Vashon had arrived in Haiti the image of Ogé as a glorious martyr was falling out of fashion. In 1847 the black general Faustin Soulouque had assumed the presidency, ending nearly thirty years of mulatto oligarchy.[6] He purged mulattos from the government, and in 1851 Faubert, the lycée director, went into exile in Paris. In France Faubert rewrote his Ogé play and finally published it, transformed into a statement about the absurdity of color prejudice.[7] But Ogé had already become a symbol of mulatto arrogance. To portray this wealthy freeborn man as a Haitian revolutionary became the equivalent of denying the achievement of the enslaved men and women who destroyed the French plantation system. Although mulatto presidents up to the 1940s tried to restore Ogé's reputation, since the early twentieth century Haitian historians have regarded him as "a flawed and minor revolutionary figure."[8]

Nevertheless, the Ogé revolt is part of nearly every narrative of the Haitian Revolution. The common elements found in most recent accounts are these: A wealthy free man of color from Cap Français, Saint-Domingue's largest port city, Vincent Ogé *jeune*—"the younger"—was in Paris on business in 1789. Inspired by the events of the French Revolution, he met with absentee planters and then joined a group of free people of color meeting in the offices of a French lawyer. He quickly became a leader in their unsuccessful efforts to win representation in the French National Assembly. In March 1790, after Parisian deputies approved an ambiguously worded colonial election law, Ogé secretly returned to Saint-Domingue. There, in October 1790, he met with Jean-Baptiste Chavannes, a noncommissioned officer in the colony's free colored militia. The two men wrote to the governor and the Provincial Assembly, demanding a literal interpretation of the new Parisian law: all financially qualified freemen should be allowed to vote, regardless of their ancestry. Refused, they gathered approximately three hundred free men of color in the mountains a dozen miles outside Cap Français. For its part, the city raised an armed group of about six hundred, including many militiamen and volunteers, and sent them into the hills to crush this assembly. But Ogé's men held their ground, and the first Cap Français force returned to the city. Several days later the Provincial Assembly sent out a second army, this time with fifteen hundred soldiers, many of them royal troops. This time, as the story goes, Ogé and his band were defeated. Ogé, Chavannes, and several dozen supporters fled into Spanish territory where they were arrested. Spanish authorities extradited them to Cap Français about a month later. Colonial authorities sentenced Ogé, Chavannes, and two others to a grisly public torture and death; each man performed a public confession and penance before the executioner strapped him to a wheel in the city's cathedral square and smashed his bones one by one, leaving him to die under the sun. When Ogé and Chavannes were dead, their heads were placed on pikes like those of rebel slaves.

This article relies on the often-ignored transcript of Ogé's January 1791 interrogation in Cap Français[9] to challenge or add to this "classic" version of the revolt in four principal ways. First, in six days of questioning by Bocquet de Frévent,[10] a prosecutor for the Cap Français royal court, Ogé provided a much clearer account of his social origins and motivations for traveling to Paris in the 1780s than that found in most summaries of his life. Second, Bocquet forced Ogé to reveal that he had been planning to mobilize free colored militiamen, probably colony-wide, for at least ten months before his revolt. Third, it shows that Ogé quickly grasped how events in Paris had heightened the political significance of militia service. He acquired the insignia of militia leadership in Paris with political rather than military ends in mind, know-ing they would galvanize Saint-Domingue's long-suffering free colored militiamen. Fourth, the interrogation suggests that although Ogé's political movement became an armed struggle it was never defeated by a French army. Bocquet and other colonial whites insisted that Ogé had always planned to mount a "revolt" and they encouraged the assumption that French troops had crushed the men of color, an image solidified by two centuries of historiography.

These new perspectives on Ogé point to four conclusions. First, Ogé's identity in colonial society was deeply ambiguous. Second, he viewed his alliance with free colored militiamen as a political, not military, movement. Third, he had good reason to believe that if his protest failed, he would be able to claim asylum on the Spanish side of the island and eventually return home. Fourth, white-led forces were unable to defeat Ogé in a conventional way. The hundreds of free colored militiamen who stood behind him held their ground against a larger force and then melted into the hills. The inconclusiveness of this encounter seems to have been what convinced French colo-nists to inflict a gruesome public death on Ogé and his lieutenants. This execution, far more than the revolt itself, pushed Parisian revolutionaries, colonial free people of color, and perhaps enslaved people of color to a new level of hostility against the plan-tation regime.

Ogé's identity, even his name, has been the subject of some confusion. The French officer Pamphile La Croix described him as the son of a wealthy Cap Français butcher and noted that his mother owned a coffee plantation.[11] The early Haitian historian Thomas Madiou said he was the son of a rich planter who had given him "the best education that it was possible for a mulatto to receive then in Saint-Domingue."[12] For the American Shelby McCloy, Ogé was "Jacques Vincent Ogé . . . educated at Paris."[13] None of these statements is completely incorrect, as it turns out.

Ogé identified himself to Bocquet as a freeborn man of color, the third son of Jacques Ogé and Angélique Ossé. One of Ogé's older brothers was named Jacques and historians have frequently confused the two because in 1793 Saint-Domingue refu-gees in Philadelphia published a document claiming to be "Ogé's confession." But this was a statement that the older brother Jacques made to colonial authorities just before his own execution.[14] Bocquet's interrogation provides little information about Ogé's father: Vincent Ogé said only that "his name was Jacques Ogé and he was white." It seems likely that Vincent *jeune* was named after a paternal relative, perhaps his father's brother, who may have been a merchant in Cap Français. In the interrogation Ogé told Bocquet that the family's true name was spelled with an "Au," presumably as Augé or even Auger.[15] This was a more common name in Saint-Domingue. Charles Auger, a Creole from Saint-Christophe, was governor of Saint-Domingue from 1703 to 1705 and had signed the first land grant in Ogé's native Dondon parish.[16] The Auger brothers Jean and Antoine were French merchants who sailed at least five slave ships to Saint-Domingue between 1736 and 1750.[17] In Cap Français "Auger frères" was the name of a merchant firm that dealt with Dutch smugglers from Curaçao in 1757 and 1758.[18] Though there is no direct proof, these may have been Ogé's uncles.

Ogé told Bocquet that his mother was Angélique Ossé, "*mulâtresse*, the legitimately born daughter of a white man named Joseph Ossé and a *négresse* whose name he cannot remember." This suggests that she and Ogé's father Jacques were also legitimately married, though he did not specify this. Lacroix was correct to describe Ogé as the son of a butcher, though the image of a cleaver-wielding shop owner is misleading; in 1780 his mother held a three-year contract to provide meat to the markets of Dondon parish where the family lived and owned a coffee plantation.[19] A widow Augé—who may have been Vincent's mother, or his uncle Vincent's widow—also owned considerable property in Cap Français in 1776 and 1787.[20]

Vincent Ogé *jeune* was born in Dondon parish in 1757. His oldest surviving sibling was named Joseph, presumably after Joseph Ossé, his mother's white father. In addition to Joseph and Jacques, Vincent had a younger brother named Jean-Pierre and an adopted brother, a foundling named Alexandre Conthia. There were also at least three girls, Françoise, Angélique, and an adopted sister.[21] The fragmentary church records of Dondon parish mention a Marie Magdelaine Ogé, dead by 1779, who may have been born between Joseph and Jacques.[22]

Dondon parish was located on Saint-Domingue's border with the Spanish colony of Santo Domingo. It was only nineteen miles away from Cap Français, the French colony's most developed city, but rugged mountains stood between them. Despite land grants by Governor Auger, up to the mid-1740s, when Ogé's oldest brother Joseph was born, Dondon was an isolated place with little wealth. The soil was fertile, but the parish was too mountainous and cool for sugar. Instead its free residents—French settlers, island-born whites, and ex-slaves—used their slaves to raise livestock and grow provision crops, tobacco, and indigo. This began to change in 1737, when Dondon became the first place in Saint-Domingue to grow coffee. Imported from Martinique, and newly favored by Europeans, the crop thrived on hillsides, and it appealed to small and middling planters because it did not require the elaborate mills and distilleries necessary to process sugar and indigo.[23]

In the 1750s, about the time Vincent Ogé *jeune* was born, coffee profits provoked a population explosion in Dondon. Hundreds of new residents brought in thousands of enslaved workers to tend their coffee bushes. In 1730, Dondon had only 524 slaves and 286 free people, working on farms, ranches, and 39 indigo plantations.[24] In 1771, the next year for which local census numbers are available, the parish had 6,037 enslaved people, and 551 free people. By this time Dondon had 192 coffee estates, so that many of its free inhabitants were no longer poor ranchers or hillside farmers. The population grew so dramatically that in 1773 authorities carved a new parish, Marmalade, out of Dondon.[25] Dondon's coffee planters were not as wealthy as the sugar barons of the Northern Plain, but they were close enough to Cap Français to buy enslaved Africans and market their crops far more easily than those located in more remote districts of Saint-Domingue, like Jérémie, where Ogé's interrogator Bouquet owned coffee estates.[26]

It is not clear how the Ogé family came by its coffee plantation. It is possible that Ogé's father Jacques was a coffee planter, but it is just as likely that Ogé's mother purchased the property or inherited it from her father Joseph Ossé, for land in Dondon was still cheap during his lifetime. A number of European immigrants to Saint-Domingue, like Jacques Ogé, married free women of color who had developed or inherited valuable colonial property.[27]

By 1768, the Ogé plantation was generating enough income for the family to send young Vincent to Bordeaux, where his sisters Angélique and Françoise were educated in the 1780s. He did not mention relatives in the city, but the colonial merchant Antoine Auger was one of the city's wealthiest men.[28] Ogé *jeune* was apprenticed to a goldsmith in Bordeaux from around 1768 to 1774 or 1775, perhaps in one of the workshops that had sprung up around the city's mercantile exchange during this time.[29] When he returned home, he worked in Cap Français, probably for his uncle Vincent, rather than return to Dondon. He described himself to Bocquet as a commission agent for coffee and as part owner of his family's coffee plantation.[30] Contracts he signed with royal notaries in the 1780s reveal that he owned a coastal schooner with three other partners, and had business deals with merchants in most of Saint-Domingue's major ports. They also show that he was quite active as a real estate broker in Cap Français, subletting prestigious addresses to whites.[31] In fact, in Cap Français, Ogé worked nearly exclusively with French clients and with notaries who never identified him in their documents as a man of color, although this was required by colonial laws.[32] When Bocquet asked Ogé if he had ever been insulted because of his race or color, the prisoner replied simply, "No."

As Stewart King and Dominique Rogers have shown, in the 1780s Ogé was by far the wealthiest merchant in Cap Français known to be of African descent.[33] But the records he left suggest that his social identity in that period was that of a white colonist. Like most of those men, he never married but kept a free mulatto *ménagère* or housekeeper named Marie Magdeleine Garette. In 1783 he paid her for two years of work by deeding over Rosette, an enslaved twelve-year-old child he had purchased from a ship's cargo.[34]

Although Ogé moved easily among whites in Cap Français in the 1780s, in rural Dondon the parish had begun building a road through his family's coffee estate. Ogé told Bocquet that work crews had cut down many of their coffee bushes, and had thrown down boulders, crushing the masonry huts where their slaves lived. Damages and legal expenses had cost his family six hundred thousand livres. So in 1788, Ogé explained, he left Saint-Domingue for France "to take a lawsuit that his mother had before the *conseil d'état du Roy* with Sieurs Poissac et Depuis about a road."[35] For a family with the Ogés' wealth and transatlantic connections, this was not unheard of; free people of color with far lesser means had appealed lawsuits to France and won.[36] He also planned to bring his two sisters Angélique and Françoise home from Bordeaux.

Yet there was another consideration behind Ogé's trip to France. He told Bocquet that he had advanced large sums to planters who had never reimbursed him. A troubled partnership with a merchant firm in Les Cayes, at the other end of the colony, dragged him further into debt. In 1788 he owed sixty to seventy thousand livres to creditors. In 1788, therefore, Ogé left Cap Français for Port-au-Prince, the colony's administrative capital and second port city. He assured Bocquet that he had published a notice of his departure in the city's newspaper. He took trading goods with him to Port-au-Prince: cloth, wine, some jewelry, and a few slaves. For about six months he collected debts in this new city, sold his goods, and helped a ship captain he knew liquidate his cargo, splitting the proceeds. When he left for France, he took with him some one hundred twenty thousand livres. Although he might have paid off his creditors, Ogé claimed that he intended to triple his capital by using it to buy goods in France for resale. At the same time he hoped to save the family plantation by resolving the road issue. He thought he could return home in three months.[37]

Ogé's apparent social ease in white urban society, his wealth, and the freedom with which he crossed the Atlantic have all made it difficult to classify him socially.[38] But historians have been far more divided about how to describe his political aims in 1790 when he returned to Saint-Domingue from revolutionary Paris. Was he a political figure bringing a new French law to the colony, or a military figure, rallying free men of color to fight the whites?

In 1914, Lothrop Stoddard, the influential writer and racial positivist, claimed Ogé was "convinced that he was destined to lead a successful rising of his caste."[39] Thomas Ott went further than most historians, asserting that Ogé intended to raise the slaves to fight for mulatto-white equality.[40] Writing from a Marxist perspective, C. L. R. James in 1938 described Ogé as a member of the bourgeoisie, "a politician, whose gifts were unsuited for the task before him."[41] For Robin Blackburn, Ogé was a lawyer who returned to Saint-Domingue from France with the help of Freemasons.[42]

Throughout Bocquet's interrogation Ogé denied that he had any military project for Saint-Domingue, insisting that his intentions were purely political. He was no rebel, only a man caught up in the general excitement of a larger group, whose members deferred to him because he had seen the revolution in France. However Ogé could not refute Bocquet's evidence that he had deliberately used military symbols and organizing techniques. The prosecutor showed that Ogé began to portray himself as a militia leader in October of 1789, in Paris. And Bocquet proved that in January of 1790

Ogé had attempted to return to Saint-Domingue with two dozen men of color. These revelations suggest that Ogé may have been planning to rendezvous with the hundreds of free colored militiamen that his brother Jean-Pierre and acquaintance Jean-Baptiste Chavannes were meeting with around this time in two separate parts of the colony.

Contemporaries and historians who portray Ogé as a military figure tend to interpret his interest in military symbols as evidence that he was preparing for war. They often report that he returned to Saint-Domingue in 1790 with arms he had purchased abroad, usually in the United States.[43] Indeed Bocquet interrogated Ogé about such arms shipments, but had no evidence with which to confront his denials. The idea seems to have come from absentee planters in Paris who were tracking Ogé's actions; they were convinced he was planning an attack on the colony. On June 19, 1790, they wrote to Saint-Domingue that Ogé and his colleague in Paris Julien Raimond were in London recruiting mercenaries, purchasing weapons and musical instruments for war, and that they had designed a uniform and were using maps to plan their campaign.

However, the interrogation suggests that Ogé acquired military gear in Paris for political reasons, to unify Saint-Domingue's free men of color around old symbols that had acquired new meaning in revolutionary Paris. Since the 1750s, colonists and administrators had been debating what "patriotism" should mean in Saint-Domingue. Imperial authorities argued that Saint-Domingue's primary function was military. From their perspective, a good colonist was above all a soldier, for whom patriotism meant sacrificing his plantation and wealth, if necessary, to defend French territory. For this reason, military officers governed the colony right down to the parish level. But many rich planters resented this authoritarian style. For them Saint-Domingue was primarily an economic engine for France, and "patriotism" meant developing the profitability of their estates. Without freedom from a "despotic" military government, the colony would never develop a "patriotic" population.[44]

There is no reliable evidence that connects Ogé with the military, or even the colonial militia, in which free men of color played an important part. But he was probably living in Cap Français in April of 1779, when imperial authorities had recruited free men of color to join a French expedition against the British in North America. If so, he would have seen the respect given to Captain Vincent Olivier, the reportedly 120-year-old free black veteran who had publically dined with the governor during those days. Olivier lived and owned land in Grande-Rivière parish, next to Dondon and was well known in Cap Français. Olivier's exhortations had helped gather over 900 free colored volunteers for that expedition; 550 of those men, including Chavannes, sailed with the French fleet in October 1779.[45] Ogé would have also seen the colonial newspaper article labeling such volunteers "unnatural" and proclaiming the moral superiority of those who donated money to the campaign, rather than risk their lives. Ogé was probably also on hand two years later when officials decided that free colored militiamen were such obedient and inexpensive troops that they would conscript all of them into a new army unit. And he would have witnessed the successful protest against that conscription and the repeated complaints by men of color in the 1780s against the degrading and abusive nature of their militia service.[46]

By the end of the summer of 1789, Ogé, living in Paris, already seemed to have been galvanized by revolutionary events. Sometime in late August or early September, he ran into Arteau, a white building contractor he knew from Cap Français.[47] Arteau invited him to the Hotel Massiac, a luxurious private residence where absentee planters had begun meeting to discuss how revolutionary events in France might affect their colonial properties. There is no evidence that Ogé was yet in contact with abolitionists, but when he appeared at the Hotel Massiac on September 7 he was naïve enough to inform these planters that he believed liberty should eventually be given to all men. It was a dangerous subject, he acknowledged. He claimed to have a plan that might tame "the storm that rumbles over our heads," and if they accepted him in their group and approved his idea, he promised to return to Saint-Domingue immediately to carry it out.[48]

Two days later, he recalled for Bocquet, he received a notice at his hotel advising him of a very different political meeting, in the offices of a Parisian lawyer named Etienne DeJoly. DeJoly, a early partisan of change who would serve as the revolution's Minister of Justice in 1792, had assembled forty to fifty free people of color to discuss how to get political representation in the French National Assembly for members of their class in the colonies. Although Julien Raimond would soon join this group, Ogé was by far the wealthiest man at the first meeting he attended, and the wealthiest to sign its *cahier de doléances,* or memorandum of grievances, on September 22. Significantly, militia reform was one of their most prominent grievances, occupying four places on a list of eleven immediate reforms that the free men of color were seeking. They wanted more than an end to a system of separate militia units organized by race, and a chance to compete for officers' positions in the militia. Because whites had monopolized all officer positions, they asked that all officers be ordered to step down, and that the new racially mixed militia units be ordered to elect new officers, chosen from among the men of color, until a later time when all men would compete freely for these leadership positions.[49]

As has been well documented, after the drafting of this *cahier,* Ogé became an important figure in the Parisian movement for free colored political representation.[50] But historians have overlooked his fascination with the way the French revolutionaries had redefined the militia, an institution that Frenchmen despised as much as colonial whites did. Citizen soldiers, like the Parisian National Guardsmen who had taken the Bastille fortress on July 14, were one of the most powerful symbols of the early revolution. They seemed to combine the military patriotism that colonial administrators and military reformers had long sought, with the individual freedoms colonial white "patriots" and their free colored neighbors claimed for themselves.

In Paris, Ogé was surrounded by men involved in the new revolutionary militia. DeJoly, who had first assembled the Parisian free people of color, had helped organize the National Guard unit of his Parisian section, Enfants Rouges. Sometime around October 22, 1789, Ogé and the other politically active men of color attended a dinner party for the visiting English abolitionist Thomas Clarkson, hosted by the Marquis de Lafayette, who had presented the Declaration of Rights of Man and of the Citizen to the National Assembly on August 26, and who had recently been elected commander of the Paris National Guard.[51] Ogé and his colleagues appeared at the dinner wearing Guard uniforms, which Lafayette had designed.[52] Two or three days later, on October 24, Ogé wrote his sisters in Bordeaux that he was a "Captain and Commandant in Saint-Domingue," and for the next several months he continued to allude to his military status. During the interrogation Bocquet presented these letters to Ogé, who claimed that he had only written them to impress his family. However, at about this same time he purchased an honorary colonel's commission and a medal from the Prince de Limbourg; this particular medal looked so much like the Cross of St. Louis worn by distinguished colonial militia commanders that in 1787 the colonial ministry had ruled that it could not be worn in Saint-Domingue.[53] The Cross, France's highest military honor, was so coveted by Saint-Domingue's colonists that in July 1790 it was rumored that the French crown was bribing planters to support its policies by promising to award them one of these medals.[54] Ogé also had his portrait engraved in silhouette, under the motto "il aime la liberté comme il sait la deffendre." He had four hundred copies printed and some of those that survive show him wearing a military uniform and a medal.[55] When Bocquet questioned him about the medal and portrait, Ogé claimed that these had nothing do with Saint-Domingue; the artist had devised the motto, and the colonel's commission was merely for vanity.

Bocquet's questions show that he was unconvinced by these explanations. Yet when colonists opened Ogé's luggage after the revolt they found no guns or maps. Among the books, papers, and pamphlets, however, they did find three uniforms with gold epaulettes and buttons bearing the arms of the city of Paris. Bocquet presented these to Ogé as proof that he had come to Saint-Domingue to lead an army. But what colonists did not realize was that in Paris in 1789 possession of a National Guard uniform advertised the wearer's political status; the uniform cost ten to thirty times as much as the minimum taxes required for voters; many National Guard members settled for just wearing the buttons cast with the Parisian coat of arms.[56] This was the full citizenship that Ogé had come home to claim.

In addition to the uniforms, colonial authorities also found a poem in Ogé's trunks, copied out of a Parisian gazette in his hand. The verses were originally dedicated to "M. de Lafayette," but Ogé had overwritten Lafayette's name with the words "M. Vincent Ogé." He had done this at a dinner to amuse his friends, he told Bocquet.[57] Lafayette was a member of the Friends of the Blacks, but the poem does not appear to have been about abolitionism. Rather, it was likely a paean to Lafayette's role as the leader of the National Guard. Ogé's rededication of the poem suggests that he himself aspired to represent the new revolutionary patriotism that Lafayette symbolized in Paris, the fusion of citizenship and militia service in Saint-Domingue.

By the end of 1789, Ogé claimed, he had spent almost two hundred thousand livres in France "for public affairs," borrowing money when he exhausted the sum he had brought from the colony.[58] At about the same time, apparently, he lost patience with the effort to seat free men of color in the National Assembly. Although the Assembly's Credentials Committee approved their admission, pro-colonial members of the Assembly raised an outcry that prevented them from joining its ranks. Ogé seems to have decided to take matters into his own hands. In December 1789 he passed several fraudulent bills of exchange, raising twenty-two thousand livres. Then in January he traveled to the port city of Le Havre to meet with a Captain Hebert who he knew had successfully evaded the British blockade of Saint-Domingue during the War of the American Independence. Ogé admitted to Bocquet that Hebert had agreed to carry him and a group of about two dozen men to Saint-Domingue. Hebert later backed out, claiming his ship was not ready.[59]

Although Parisian colonists were quite aware of these plans,[60] the story has been left out of nearly every account of Ogé's pre-revolutionary activities. The reason for this is that his Parisian colleague Julien Raimond, a wealthy indigo planter who, like Ogé, was of one-quarter African ancestry, was a major informant for a 1795 report on the slave revolution and its causes, commissioned by the revolutionary government.[61] Garran-Coulon, the left-leaning deputy who wrote the report, noted, "We only know about the Ogé affair from the accounts of his mortal enemies." So he sought out Ogé's Parisian colleagues, the most obvious of whom was Raimond. During the Terror white refugees from Saint-Domingue had accused Raimond of plotting the August 1791 slave uprising. Jailed in September 1793, he was not released until November 1794 and not exonerated until May 1795. Garran-Coulon was instrumental in that exoneration, for he was able to prove that colonists had altered and misrepresented Raimond's political career. Because he had worked so closely with Ogé in 1789 and early 1790, Raimond needed to convince Garran-Coulon that colonists' descriptions of Ogé's military preparations were lies, to protect his own reputation as an opponent of violence.[62]

It does appear that Raimond knew nothing of Ogé's actions, but the story Ogé told Bocquet—that his two dozen companions were poor men of color from Paris who hoped only to reestablish themselves in Saint-Domingue—is difficult to believe. Rather, the aborted voyage suggests that he was planning some action in the colony. It took approximately six weeks for letters from France to reach Saint-Domingue and this time period indicates one possible destination. Sometime in 1789, while Ogé was in France, a colonial court had convicted his younger brother Jean-Pierre of having insulted and struck whites. This same brother, Ogé told Bocquet, was later murdered in the Artibonite region of the colony. He did not describe the circumstances or the date.[63] But in mid-February 1790, roughly six weeks after Ogé had arranged to charter Hebert's ship, free men of color in the Artibonite began to protest their exclusion from parish elections; some two hundred armed men "presenting themselves with a spirit of insubordination and insurrection" met with Governor de Peinier. It is possible that Jean-Pierre Ogé was among them. The Artibonite free coloreds did eventually disperse, though only after a month of negotiations. The expectation that Parisian men of color would be arriving any day might explain why the assembly lasted so long. Yvan Debbasch describes the group as divided, which raises the possibility that Jean-Pierre Ogé was killed because of tensions between those who wanted to wait for Vincent's arrival and those who believed the prolonged situation was endangering them all.[64]

The interrogation, in combination with other sources, also suggests that Ogé was working with Jean-Baptiste Chavannes, his partner in the revolt, before he returned to Saint-Domingue. Chavannes[65] was from Grande-Rivière parish, the home of Vincent Olivier, and he was one of those who responded to the old black militia captain's call for volunteers in 1779. As a veteran of the free colored volunteer corps from the American revolutionary campaign, Chavannes had experienced the humiliating differences between imperial praise for free colored militiamen and the treatment they received at the hands of their white officers. In 1786, two years before Ogé left for Paris, seven men, including Chavannes' brother Hyacinth, had refused to appear for guard duty on a bridge in the region just outside Cap Français. They claimed that they had already served two weeks of uninterrupted guard duty and that their properties were suffering. That year Chavannes' widowed mother had to surrender her plantation, since she was unable to make the annual payments of fifteen thousand livres.[66] It was Chavannes and his connections to hundreds of frustrated free colored militiamen in Grande-Rivière and surrounding parishes that made it possible for Ogé to mobilize a small army within two weeks of returning to Saint-Domingue.

Ogé told Bocquet that Chavannes was merely a casual acquaintance. Before he left the colony, he had spoken with Chavannes in Cap Français at the home of Guillaume Castaing, probably Charles Guillaume Castaing, another French-educated free man of color. Castaing was Chavannes' maternal uncle, and both men were related to the wealthy free colored Laporte family of Limonade and Grande-Rivière parishes.[67]

But the timing of Chavannes' actions in Saint-Domingue and Ogé's work in Paris makes it possible that the two men may have been working together from 1789. Roughly eight weeks after the heady days of September 1789, when Ogé began to emerge as a "mulatto" spokesman in Paris, Chavannes submitted a petition to the Provincial Assembly. Dated November 10, 1789, it protested the discrimination and heavy duties borne by free colored militiamen.[68] Forty-two men signed this document, including many who would later rally around Ogé. Petitions like this were dangerous.

One of the first casualties of the revolutionary era in Cap Français was a free mulatto named Augustin Lacombe, from either Limonade or Saint-Suzanne parish, who was hanged on April 24, 1790, for submitting a petition that claimed the Rights of Man for free people of color.[69]

There is no evidence that Chavannes suffered for his petition. Nor is there evidence that he was preparing for anything in February 1790, after Ogé's failed embarkation in Le Havre. But Ogé admitted to Bocquet that on March 29, 1790, he had sent out a flurry of letters home. The day before this, on March 28, the National Assembly had approved an ambiguously worded set of voting instructions for Saint-Domingue, identifying financial and age requirements for voting, but saying nothing about race. The Parisian men of color and their French allies appear to have believed that the National Assembly intended to allow wealthy men of color to vote.[70] Ogé was so excited by this turn of events that he even sent a letter to Baptiste Fleury, a white militia officer and Dondon planter, who had two free sons of mixed ancestry.[71] He would not admit to writing Chavannes, but the free colored militia leader appears to have been waiting for him. About six weeks later, in mid-May 1790, Chavannes and his friends organized a large free colored assembly in Grande-Rivière parish, next to Ogé's native Dondon.[72]

Chavannes would probably not have known that planters in Paris had warned French port authorities not to allow free men of color to embark for the Antilles. Ogé could not book a direct passage home from France. Instead he did not leave Paris until May 19, arriving in London four days later and spending two weeks in Charleston, South Carolina.[73] Chavannes' free colored assembly broke up peacefully, like that in Artibonite six months earlier, but he was obliged to cross over into Spanish Santo Domingo when local authorities ordered his arrest. He had just returned home to Grande-Rivière in late October, when Ogé finally arrived from Paris, alone.

The fourth and perhaps most startling revelation from Bocquet's interrogation is that colonists never defeated Ogé or his troops in battle. The idea that Ogé fought twice against white troops and was crushed or routed the second time is present in much of what has been written about the revolt.

There is little debate about what happed before the armed clash. On October 21, Ogé and Chavannes had written strongly worded letters to Saint-Domingue's governor, following them up on October 28 with more letters, including one to the Provincial Assembly, demanding the right to vote in upcoming elections. Ogé insisted that when he used phrases like "we will resist force with force" he was merely setting down the ideas of an entire group of men who had come to Chavannes' home to hear about events in Paris. At the same time, he also wrote two letters to prominent free men of color in the West province, in Port-au-Prince and Mirebalais.[74] When twenty-six white dragoons came to Chavannes' house on Wednesday night, October 27, to arrest Ogé and Chavannes, Ogé said there had been about fifteen free people of color there.

They had sent the soldiers away without even waking Ogé up, when the leader of the platoon could not produce written orders.[75] But the soldiers' appearance so frightened the free men of color that they spread the word through the parish, and a large crowd, eventually more than three hundred free men of color, gathered at Chavannes' house. On Thursday, October 28, as these supporters came in, one group under Chavannes' leadership and another under Ogé moved out into the parish, disarming neighboring planters and the whites in the town of Grande-Rivière. At least one white was killed by Chavannes' group. Ogé's men held several whites prisoner overnight in the town's chapel and one of them, the landowner Louis-Francois René Verneuil, spoke to Ogé and saw a letter that Ogé had likely taken from the dragoons. In 1794 he testified, "I made renewed efforts to persuade him not to continue what he had started. I found him uncertain, indecisive. Having remained silent for a moment, he took a letter out of his pocket, gave it to me, and invited me to read it. This document was a letter from the provincial assembly of Le Cap, written to the municipality of Grande-Rivière, that said approximately the following: 'Ogé has just come from France, his destructive plans are only too well known. I ask you to do everything necessary to arrest him.' Having read the letter, I gave it back to him; as he took it, he said: 'You see perfectly well that I have nothing more to lose.'"[76]

On the subject of Ogé's armed clash with colonial troops, the historiography and the interrogation promote significantly different narratives. Perhaps the earliest account from Saint-Domingue comes from Mme. Larchevesque-Thibaud, who wrote her husband in France on November 5, 1790: "The mulattoes are still camped at Grande-Rivière. They fired on our armed men on the first day, after which they placed themselves on a high crest. The troops still hope to capture them.'"[77] The author of a letter dated November 18, 1790, from Port-de-Paix, west of Cap Français, described an inconclusive pursuit of the rebels. "The Cap decided to form an army of three thousand men with artillery and it marched on these rebels to crush the revolt; they retreated into the mountain but they were closely followed and there were small battles with deaths and wounded on both sides; however the mulattos had the most casualties."[78]

The account most historians have relied upon is found in Garran-Coulon's 1795 *Report*. Garran-Coulon was disturbed by the fact that colonial newspapers were forbidden to print anything about this entire affair and by colonists' testimony in Paris "that very small forces were able to disperse the men of color, without combat."[79] His final description, confirmed and amplified by the nineteenth-century Haitian historian Thomas Madiou, described a failed attack by a General Vincent with six hundred to eight hundred men who were unable to break the ranks of some three hundred men of color.[80] As Vincent pulled back, Cap sent a larger more professional force under Colonel Cambefort. Cambefort took command from Vincent and led the combined force of fifteen hundred back to encounter the men of color. For Garran-Coulon it was Cambefort who "finally scattered Ogé's troops, and took [prisoner] several of those who had fought for him."[81] Madiou portrays a more decisive encounter in which Cambefort vigorously attacked Ogé, who pulled his men back to the summit of a nearby hill that Cambefort again attacked. "After this second failure, Ogé could no longer hold his companions under his flag. Desertion spread in their ranks and only 24 remained around him."[82]

Many subsequent historians have followed Madiou's lead, crediting colonial forces with a successful second battle. Gabriel Debien and Ralph Korngold use passive voice to leave the question of "victory" open.[83] For Korngold, "General Cambefort took the field with 1,500 men and artillery. Against such an overwhelming force Ogé and Chavanne could not hold out. Their force was scattered and many prisoners fell into the hands of the whites."[84] C. L. R. James suggests an even more aggressive free colored stance: "The Mulattoes all over the country were prevented from concentrating by heavy rains and floods. But the impetuous Ogé threw himself and his few hundred men on Le Cap. He was defeated, and with a few companions fled into Spanish territory, whence he was extradited."[85] For Thomas Ott, "Ogé lacked the genius of organization, and the whites under the command of Mauduit quickly drove the mulatto conspirators in the vicinity of Le Cap François into the nearby mountains."[86]

Bocquet's interrogation portrays a different scene: a force of well-trained free colored militamen, interrupted by Vincent's attack as they organized themselves into military battalions and elected officers at a farmhouse, fought and repelled this larger force. Almost immediately they began to fortify their position, reflecting their degree of military training and experience. Then, perhaps rethinking their situation, the free colored troop appears to have dissolved. The interrogation suggests that Cambefort's men found the empty Poisson farmhouse with half-constructed fascines, a kind of improvised rampart.

By this point of the interrogation, Ogé was insisting that he did not want bloodshed. He claimed his men disarmed the whites of Grande-Rivière to prevent violence, but it is clear that the entire free colored group felt it needed to defend itself. Denying that he or Chavannes were establishing an army, Ogé admitted that on Saturday, October 31, their supporters had mustered in ranks before the farmhouse where they had camped after disarming the local planters. They elected officers, melted lead for balls, and made musket cartridges.[87] He himself had started to write a list of these units and their leaders, which authorities found. But as this was happening, a platoon in a banana grove near the river saw troops approaching from Cap Français and began to fire on them. The main free colored force formed battle lines before the farmhouse.

Beyond this point, significantly, Bocquet posed no questions about the battle between Ogé's men and the forces from the city. Rather, his next question was about what happened when the Cap Français force, presumably Vincent's, pulled back. Ogé replied that some men of color with military experience began to erect fascines, large bundles of sticks lashed together to provide cover in a coming battle, around the farm-house. But the majority retired into the woods for the night, so they would not be caught on open ground if the troops returned.

The next day, Sunday, November 1, a mulatto detachment skirmished with a group of white dragoons from Grande-Rivière who were holding free colored pris-oners. Word came from neighboring Dondon that whites there, who had taken Ogé's mother and sisters hostage, had released the women, who were unharmed. In response the men of color freed some of the white hostages they had taken. But other men of color brought in five more. Then on Sunday afternoon, Ogé and a group of about two dozen men moved up into the mountains to the farm of Lucas, a member of the group who had signed Chavannes' militia petition in November 1789.[88]

Neither Bocquet nor Ogé said anything about Cambefort's second, larger force, which allegedly dispersed Ogé's men into the mountains that Sunday afternoon. Instead Bocquet asked Ogé why he and his colleagues had left the Poisson farm, a question that proves there was no second battle. He answered that the site was too exposed, that they were not safe there, and that Lucas's farm was on higher ground and more difficult to reach.[89]

From this point on, Ogé claimed to know even less about military events than before. On Saturday, he said, he had taken charge of cooking in the group. While on Lucas's farm he saw a mulatto slave named Hyacinthe from the Bonamy plantation in the room where the white prisoners were kept, but he did not ask him why he was there.[90] Similarly he claimed to know nothing of the activities on the various detach-ments of men who came and went from the Lucas house. One of the officers elected on Saturday, a free quadroon named Tessier,[91] seems to have been spying on troop movements in Cap Français for Chavannes and bringing food to the Lucas farm. Bocquet showed Ogé notes that Chavannes had written to Tessier describing Ogé as "Général" and "Colonel." Ogé insisted he did not take these titles, though he admitted to wearing his uniform and medals throughout this period.[92]

They stayed at chez Lucas from Sunday to the following Thursday, sending out scouting parties to acquire food and watch for attackers. When troops from Cap began to approach, the group released its white prisoners. Ogé, Chavannes, and sev-eral others went to Chavannes' home and spent Thursday night there while the main group proceeded to a second farm in the hills. On Friday the leaders caught up with this main group and went to a third farmhouse to spend Friday night, getting lost on the way. Finally on Saturday twenty-four men crossed into the neighboring colony.[93] Chavannes told Spanish authorities that this had been Ogé's idea, not his, more evi-dence that Ogé had never envisioned a military campaign.[94] Thomas Madiou's sources reported that Chavannes and others had urged Ogé to bring slaves into the rebellion but that he consistently refused.[95]

They entered the Spanish town of Saint-Raphael on Sunday, November 7, relinquishing their twenty-four muskets and two cartridge boxes to Spanish authorities. Then they split into three groups to travel to the Spanish capital of Santo Domingo. Ogé traveled to the border town of Attalaye, to meet his mother, whom his adopted brother Conthia had brought there for safety. In the town of Bannik, on November 12, Ogé wrote a four-page letter to the Spanish authorities explaining what had happened. Understanding that they had stirred up a hornet's nest in Cap Français, Ogé appears to have been asking for political asylum. And in the town of Hinche, he met with his brother Joseph, who carried a letter from the leading free men of color of Port-au-Prince and Mirebalais, in Saint-Domingue's western province.[96] They were not convinced that the National Assembly's March 28 instructions justified pushing the colonial government to allow them to vote. Moreover, they believed that Ogé's letters to the governor were "written in imprudent terms and may have a bad effect." They invited him to visit them and show them proof that the French National Assembly intended to give them voting rights.[97]

Although he had admitted earlier in the interrogation to sending Joseph to Mirebalais and Port-au-Prince, Ogé now denied he had given his brother letters to carry there. This was probably because the Mirebalais free men of color addressed him, in the letter held by his interrogators, as "Commander of the North Province, presently in Grande-Rivière." He also denied having written to the southern port city of Les Cayes.[98] Nevertheless, in late October 1790, as men were gathering around Ogé and Chavannes in Grande-Rivière, between six hundred and eight hundred free men of color rallied in the hills of Torbec parish, just outside Les Cayes. They successfully repulsed an attacking force of about five hundred colonial militiamen. Then they negotiated a truce with royal authorities and stood down on November 13.[99]

Ogé's interrogators possessed no evidence linking him to this Torbec revolt, one of whose leaders was the free man of color André Rigaud. Like Chavannes, Rigaud was a veteran of the 1779 Savannah campaign and like Ogé he had trained as a goldsmith in Bordeaux. Bocquet believed that Ogé must have succeeded in bringing with him some of the twenty-eight men who had accompanied him to Le Havre in January of 1790, but Ogé steadfastly denied this.[100]

In the border town of Hinche, the Spanish arrested both Vincent and Jacques Ogé, and they eventually captured all twenty-four of the men who had crossed the border. Their list of prisoners illustrates how intimately Ogé's core supporters were interconnected. Four different groups of brothers made up 13 of the 24-man troop; three Angomar brothers from Grande-Rivière, including a farmer and a mason; three members of the Chavannes family, Jean-Baptiste, Hyacinth, and Joseph; three members of the Jouvert family, a mason, a carpenter, and a coffee planter; and the Ogés: Vincent, Jacques, Joseph, and their adopted brother Alexandre Conthia.[101] All of the men except Vincent Ogé lived in the countryside. Ten of the twenty-four were farmers or coffee planters; five were carpenters but three of these artisans worked primarily as farmers too. Three were bricklayers or masons, one was a constable, one was a baker, one sold cloth and animals, and another sold salt fish and crude rum. Of the nineteen men whose home parishes were named, fifteen—that is, all but the four Ogés—were from Grande-Rivière. One of the Grande-Rivière residents was originally from the Dutch smuggling center at Curaçao, and another was originally from Bayaxa, on the Spanish side of the border.[102]

By late November 1790 a new French governor, de Blanchelande, had assumed office. He pressed Spanish officials to extradite the rebels, but they were divided over what to do. Santo Domingo's Governor Garcia wanted to cooperate with the French, but the Spanish had given asylum to other refugees from Saint-Domingue, white and free colored. Pedro Catani, the doyen of the Audiencia de Santo Domingo, believed the mulattoes should be welcomed in Spanish territory and used as troops after consulting with royal authorities in Spain. The royal attorney Antonio Vicente de Faura believed that Ogé should only be extradited after formal judicial proceedings. Meeting ten months later, the Cabildo of Santo Domingo criticized Garcia for sending Ogé back to Cap Français before getting advice from Madrid.[103]

While his colleagues, especially Catani, viewed Ogé's group in military terms, Governor Garcia seems to have understood that Ogé represented something potentially more dangerous: Parisian abolitionists' political attack on racial labels. Nevertheless, his attitude toward Ogé was more sympathetic than that shown by the French colonists. He had the prisoners returned to Cap Français in late December with the request that Blanchelande treat Ogé with compassion. The Amis des Noirs in Paris also misread how deeply the whole affair had threatened Saint-Domingue's whites. By January 1791 Brissot knew Ogé had been arrested, but assumed he would be sent back to France for trial.[104]

The extradition was likely also a surprise to the prisoners. They knew Saint-Domingue had executed Augustin Lacombe in Cap Français in April 1790 for demanding the application of the Declaration of the Rights of Man. But Chavannes had twice organized assemblies of free men of color in Grande-Rivière and both times he had taken refuge across the border, eventually returning home. At least some of Ogé's supporters who remained on the French side expected clemency, for they too surrendered voluntarily. On November 18 Garnier from Port-de-Paix wrote his father in Marseilles that French troops had arrested more than 115 of Ogé's supporters."[105] And in December 1791 the rebel slave leaders Jean François and Georges Biassou wrote to French colonial officials that their followers "fear[ed] ... being treated like those involved in the Ogé affair, who after having surrendered voluntarily and thinking themselves in complete safety on the word of the leaders of Le Cap, were partially sacrificed! You would not believe, sirs, how they are struck by what they call this treason."[106]

In fact, rumors may have exaggerated how many of Ogé's supporters were arrested. After receiving the twenty-four prisoners from Santo Domingo, the colony publicly broke four men on the rack, hanged twenty-one others, and sent thirteen to serve in the galleys for life, which suggests that only fourteen were captured locally. The judges had to sentence forty-five men in absentia, hanging some in effigy. They submitted fifty-three more names to the royal attorney for investigation.[107]

Ogé and the other men who had turned themselves over to the Spanish suffered the full weight of French colonial anger. For colonists, this was not another militia protest, like those Chavannes had mounted earlier in 1790. By crossing the Atlantic, Ogé brought to Saint-Domingue the connection between militia service and citizenship that the colony had resisted for so long. Colonists refused to acknowledge the distinction between political and military action, seeing Ogé's epaulettes, printed portraits, medal, and ersatz colonel's commission as military tools. To a degree that has been obscured in the historiography of the revolt, colonists in Saint-Domingue and Paris had ample reason to believe that Ogé's revolt had been planned for nearly a year. Moreover the contents of Ogé's baggage proved to colonists that he was indeed affiliated with abolitionists. In his valise, his captors found "two small ceramic medallions in bas-relief representing a chained negro," presumably a Wedgwood abolitionist medallion, perhaps a gift from Clarkson or another antislavery activist in London. His baggage also contained Benjamin Sigismond Frossard's 1789 book *La cause des esclaves nègres,* an attack on the slave trade.[108]

Aside from the question of Ogé's intentions, colonial whites were probably frightened by his supporters' ability to avoid outright defeat. On Saturday, October 30, men of color had held their ground against a colonial militia that may have been twice as large. Then they had denied whites a clear triumph that could offset this defeat. In Torbec, in the South, André Rigaud and his eight hundred men had not disarmed whites, or taken white hostages the way Ogé and Chavannes' men had. After a two-week standoff, the southern free coloreds had turned over their weapons to a royal officer, and six or seven of the leaders had agreed to be arrested.[109]

The story colonial partisans publicized in France underlined that Ogé had been defeated, but only by regular troops. The message to Paris was that Saint-Domingue needed more French soldiers. The exemplary punishments meted out to the captured men sent another message, one that makes more sense in view of the fact that Ogé's tiny army was neither crushed, nor disarmed.

It made no difference to colonists, but the evidence contained in Bocquet's interrogation suggests strongly that Ogé did not want an outright revolt, or at least not prolonged combat. If he and Chavannes had melted into the population instead of crossing the border, they might have survived to fight another day. But Ogé was no guerrilla. His aims had been political, not military.

This article has not tried to rescue Ogé's outmoded nineteenth-century reputation as one of Haiti's founding fathers. But the evidence from Bocquet's interrogation contradicts the notion that he was either an idealistic lawyer or a man determined to wage war on white colonial society. As a merchant who had lived and worked in Bordeaux and Cap Français, he saw that the new Parisian definition of the militiaman-as-citizen would be especially explosive in Saint-Domingue, where imperial authorities relied on militia service that white colonists refused to provide. For this reason he seems to have understood that if he could bring this definition across the Atlantic, Saint-Domingue's leaders would either have to extend citizenship across the color line, or bring in more professional soldiers to take the place of free men of color. We don't know what Ogé told the men who gathered around him in Grande-Rivière in October 1790, but he would likely have argued that events in France authorized him to assume the role of a colonial militia commander, complete with his faux Cross of Saint Louis. This was patriotic and revolutionary precisely because he was not a soldier, but a merchant and a volunteer.

What has not been understood about Ogé, then, is the degree to which his attempt to connect "patriotism" and armed service in Saint-Domingue was successful. Though he failed to bring a platoon of supporters from France to spread his ideas, it does appear that even in absentia he inspired a standoff in the Artibonite valley and another in Grande-Rivière. When he did finally arrive, he and Chavannes not only mobilized the area around Grande-Rivière, but stimulated five hundred men of color in the South province to pick up arms and confront the idea that citizenship was *pour les blancs seulement.*

Notes

This paper would not have been possible without the ideas and research advice David Geggus has generously provided over the years. My research into Ogé's early life was guided by the published and unpublished work of Stewart King and Dominique Rogers, which they graciously made available.

1. George Boyer Vashon, "Vincent Ogé," in *Autographs for Freedom,* ed. Julia Griffiths (Wanzer, Beardsley & Co, 1854). Vashon was Oberlin's first black graduate and valedictorian in 1844. He left the United States for Haiti after Pennsylvania refused to allow him to practice law because of his race. Paul N. D. Thornell, "The Absent Ones and the Providers: A Biography of the Vashons," *The Journal of Negro History* 83, no. 4 (Autumn 1998): 290–291.

2. French National Archives, Paris; [henceforth CARAN] DXXV 1 folder 4 #14;

for a translated version, see Laurent Dubois and John D. Garrigus, *Slave Revolution in the Caribbean, 1789–1804: A Brief History with Documents* (New York: Bedford St. Martin's Press, 2006), 102.

3. This is the major theme of David Nicholls, *From Dessalines to Duvalier: Race, Colour and National Independence in Haiti* (Cambridge: Cambridge University Press, 1979).

4. Thornell, "The Absent Ones and the Providers," 291.

5. Anna Brickhouse, *Transamerican Literary Relations and the Nineteenth-Century Public Sphere* (Cambridge: Cambridge University Press, 2004), 227–30.

6. Vashon's parents had given him the middle name "Boyer," after Jean-Pierre Boyer, Haiti's strongest and most color-conscious mulatto president, who ruled from 1820 to 1843.

7. Pierre Faubert, *Ogé ou le préjugé de couleur, drame historique [Port-au-Prince, lycée national, 9 février 1841], suivi de poésies fugitives et de notes* (Paris: C. Maillet-Schmitz, 1856); Brickhouse, *Transamerican Literary Relations,* 231.

8. Brickhouse, *Transamerican Literary Relations,* 231; Léon-François Hoffmann, "Haitian Sensibility," in *A History of Literature in the Caribbean,* ed. Albert James Arnold, Julio Rodríguez-Luis, and J. Michael Dash (Philadelphia: John Benjamins, 1994), 368.

9. Martin-Ollivier Bocquet de Frévent, "Extrait des minutes du Conseil Supérieur du Cap," CARAN DXXV58/ 574, January 1791, is the unpaginated handwritten transcription of Ogé's interrogation, held from January 20 through January 25, 1791 in Cap Français. I count 149 pages in the manuscript; the page numbers given are mine, based on my digital photographs of the entire document.

10. Blanche Maurel, *Cahiers de doléances de la colonie de Saint-Domingue pour les États Généraux* (Librairie E. Leroux, 1933), 383, identifies Bocquet de Frévent' as "royal councillor, in 1789 acting lieutenant of the royal *sénéchaussée* court of Cap Français."

11. Pamphile Lacroix, *La Révolution de Haïti (1819),* ed. Pierre Pluchon (Paris: Karthala, 1995), 68.

12. Thomas Madiou, *Histoire d'Haiti* (Port-au-Prince: Impr. de J. Courtois, 1847), I:72.

13. Shelby T. McCloy, "Negroes and Mulattoes in Eighteenth-Century France," *Journal of Negro History* 30, no. 3 (July 1945), 279.

14. Jacques Ogé, T*estament de mort d'Ogé et adresse de Pinchinat aux hommes de couleur, en date du 13 décembre dernier: avec la réfutation de cette adresse par un habitant de Saint-Domingue: suivi d'un un récit des journées des 9 et 10 novembre dernier, à Saint Marc* (Philadelphia: Chez Parent imprimeur rue Vine au coin de la troisième Nord no. 85, 1793).

15. Bocquet de Frévent, "Extrait des minutes," 6.

16. M. L. E. Moreau de Saint-Méry, *Description topographique, physique, civile,*

politique et historique de la partie française de l'isle Saint Domingue, Nouv. ed. (Paris: Société de l'histoire des colonies françaises, 1958), 251, 1446.

17. "French slave ship owners with the name 'Auger,'" *The Trans-Atlantic Slave Trade Database,* http://www.slavevoyages.org/tast/database/search.faces?yearFrom =1514&yearTo=1866&anyowner=Auger&natinimp=10.

18. Richard Pares, *War and Trade in the West Indies, 1739–1763* (London: Cass, 1936), 380, 382.

19. Thanks to Dominique Rogers for sharing this reference with me. Archives d'Outre-Mer, Aix-en-Provence [henceforth CAOM] SDOM 1088, 12/9/1780.

20. CAOM DPPC G¹495a and G¹495b. Stewart King assumes this is Ogé's mother and that these are the joint property held by Vincent and Angélique. However the Cap Français cadastre of 1776 does not mention him. In fact the 1788 document says that a Sieur Picard represented all three of the widow's houses, which had multiple tenants. By this time, however, Vincent Ogé had left Cap Français. King calculates the value of the "Augé" property listed in this document at one hundred twenty-seven thousand livres, perhaps working backwards from the rental sums recorded by city officials. King, *Blue Coat,* 208.

21. Bocquet de Frévent, "Extrait des minutes," 3, 6, 41.

22. See the November 2, 1777 entry in the Dondon parish registers in Latter Day Saints microfilm #1094188 and CAOM, 55 MiOM 4.

23. Moreau de Saint-Méry, *Description,* 253, 264; Michel-Rolph Trouillot, "Motion in the System: Coffee, Color, and Slavery in Eighteenth-Century Saint-Domingue," *Review* 5 (1982): 344, 347.

24. CAOM G509¹ No. 20

25. Moreau de Saint-Méry, *Description,* 271.

26. Maurel, *Cahiers de doléances de la colonie de Saint-Domingue pour les États Généraux,* 383, says that Bouquet owned coffee estates in Jérémie worth two hundred fifty thousand livres.

27. The best-documented example of this is the family history of Ogé's colleague, the indigo planter Julien Raimond. See John D. Garrigus, *Before Haiti: Race and Citizenship in Saint-Domingue* (New York: Palgrave Macmillan, 2006), 45–48.

28. Paul Butel, *Les négociants bordelais, l'Europe et les îles au xviiie siecle* (Paris: Aubier, 1974), 281.

29. Stephen Auerbach, "'Encourager Le Commerce Et Répandre Les Lumières:' The Press, the Provinces and the Origins of the Revolution in France, 1750–1789" (PhD diss., Louisiana State University, 2000), 163; André Rigaud, who would support Ogé in November 1790 by helping to lead a simultaneous revolt in Saint-Domingue's southern peninsula, was also apprenticed as a goldsmith in Bordeaux at around the same time. There is no evidence the two men knew each other. C. L. R. James, *The*

Black Jacobins: Toussaint L'ouverture and the San Domingo Revolution, 2nd ed. (New York: Vintage, 1963), 96.

30. For the preceding biographical information, see Bocquet de Frévent, "Extrait des minutes," 2 and 3.

31. I first became aware of these documents thanks to Stewart R. King, *Blue Coat or Powdered Wig: Free People of Color in Pre-Revolutionary Saint Domingue* (Athens: University of Georgia, 2001) CAOM SDOM 191 14 juillet, 15 juillet, 26 juillet, 30 juillet and 15 septembre 1785; CAOM F³91, feuille 162; CAOM SDOM 187, 1 juillet 1784.

32. Ogé returned from Bordeaux in 1775 and by 1778 colonial laws were requiring that all legal deeds involving free people of color identify their race and cite documents proving that they were not slaves. M. L. E. Moreau de Saint-Méry, *Loix et constitutions des colonies françoises de l'amérique sous le vent* (Paris: Chez l'auteur, 1784), 5: 767, 807; Dominique Rogers has shows that notaries in Cap Français applied some of these regulations far more erratically than their colleagues in Port-au-Prince. Dominique Rogers, "Les libres de couleur dans les capitales de Saint-Domingue: Fortune, mentalités et intégration à la fin de l'Ancien Régime (1776–1789)" (PhD diss., Université de Bordeaux III, 1999), 300–301.

33. This is partly based on the value of properties in Cap Français that Stewart King describes as the joint property of Vincent Ogé and his mother. However the Cap Français cadastral records of 1776 and 1787 [CAOM DPPC G1495a and G1495b] do not mention Vincent Ogé but only the widow "Augé." King calculates the value of this "Augé" property at one hundred twenty-seven thousand livres, perhaps working backwards from the rental sums recorded by city officials. King, *Blue Coat,* 208. For Rogers's discussion of free colored merchants in Cap Français, see Rogers, "Les libres de couleur," 199–200.

34. CAOM SDOM Reg 182 Bordier jeune, 27 février 1783.

35. Bocquet de Frévent, "Extrait des minutes," 5.

36. Rogers, "Les libres de couleur" cites three cases: CAOM SDOM 774, ancienne côte Gérard, 8/8/1777; CAOM SDOM 920, 17/6/1786; and CAOM SDOM 73, 10/6/1789.

37. Bocquet de Frévent, "Extrait des minutes," 10–11.

38. King, *Blue Coat,* 207–208, has difficulty making Ogé fit into his schema of economically conservative free colored planters and poorer but more entrepreneurial urban free coloreds.

39. Lothrop Stoddard, *The French Revolution in San Domingo* (Boston: Houghton Mifflin, 1914), 111.

40. Thomas O. Ott, *The Haitian Revolution: 1789–1804* (Knoxville: University of Tennessee Press, 1970), 37.

41. James, *The Black Jacobins,* 68.

42. Robin Blackburn, *The Overthrow of Colonial Slavery, 1776–1848* (Verso, 1988), 179, 182; I am unaware of any documentary evidence that Ogé was a Freemason.

43. See, for example, James, *The Black Jacobins*, 73; Laurent Dubois, *Avengers of the New World: The Story of the Haitian Revolution* (Belknap Press, 2004), 87. Shelby McCloy even wrote that Ogé "served for a time in the French army abroad, rising to the rank of lieutenant colonel." McCloy, "Negroes and Mulattoes in Eighteenth-Century France," 279.

44. Garrigus, *Before Haiti*, 111–14.

45. CAOM F³189, "Extrait mortuaire dudit Vincent Olivier Negre libre dit Capitaine Vincent agé de 120 ans 14 mars 1780."

46. John D. Garrigus, "Catalyst or Catastrophe? Saint-Domingue's Free Men of Color and the Savannah Expedition, 1779–1782," *Review/Revista Interamericana* 22 (1992): 109–25.

47. Bocquet de Frévent, "Extrait des minutes," 8.

48. Vincent Ogé, *Motion faite par M. Vincent Ogé, jeune, à l'Assemblée des colons, habitans de S.-Domingue, à l'Hôtel de Massiac*, vol. 12, La révolution française et l'abolition de l'esclavage (Paris: Editions d'histoire sociale, 1968), 7.

49. De Joly et al., *Cahier, contenant les plaintes, doléances and reclamations des citoyens-libres and proprietaires de couleur, des isles and colonies françoises* (Paris, 1789), 3–4.

50. Gabriel Debien, *Les colons de Saint-Domingue et la Révolution: Essai sur le club Massiac (août 1789–août 1792)* (Paris: A. Colin, 1953); David P. Geggus, "Racial Equality, Slavery, and Colonial Secession during the Constituent Assembly," *American Historical Review* 94, no. 5 (1989): 1290–1308.

51. Françoise Thésée, "Autour de la Société des Amis des Noirs: Clarkson, Mirabeau et l'abolition de la traite (août 1789-mars 1790)," *Présence africaine* 125 (1983): 48.

52. Ellen Gibson Wilson, *Thomas Clarkson: A Biography* (New York: St. Martin's Press, 1990), 58, cites Clarkson's 1830 *History*.

53. CAOM F³278, feuille 329; see Berault and Antoine Valentin de Cullion, *Adresse à l'Assemblée nationale : conspiration découverte* (Saint-Marc: Imprimerie de l'Assemblée générale, 1790), 5, 12.

54. Ibid.

55. For the civilian version of this image, see Marcel Châtillon, ed., *Images de la Revolution aux Antilles* (Basse-Terre: Société d'histoire de la Guadeloupe, 1989), fig. 21.

56. Dale L. Clifford, "Can the Uniform Make the Citizen? Paris, 1789–1791," *Eighteenth-Century Studies* 34, no. 3 (2001): 368, 269, 373.

57. Bocquet de Frévent, "Extrait des minutes," 133–34.

58. Ibid., 10.

59. Ibid., 14–17.

60. CARAN Dxxv 86, dossier 827, pièce 6, "Extrait des registres de la société correspondante de colons français séante à Paris," letter dated January 30, 1790.

61. Garran-Coulon, *Rapport sur les troubles de Saint-Domingue, fait au nom de la Commission des colonies, des Comités de salut public, de législation et de marine, réunis* (Paris: Imp. nationale, 1797) II : 56, and Garran-Coulon, *Débats entre les accusateurs et les accusés, dans l'affaire des colonies* (Paris: Imp. nationale, 1795), 9 vols.

62. John D. Garrigus, "Opportunist or Patriot? Julien Raimond (1744–1801) and the Haitian Revolution," *Slavery & Abolition* 28, no. 1 (2007): 1–21.

63. Confirming this idea that Jean-Pierre Ogé was involved in political affairs, Julien Raimond wrote that he thought colonial whites had hired Ogé's brother's slave to kill him, in exchange for manumission. Julien Raimond, *Réponse aux considérations de M. Moreau, dit Saint-Méry, député à l'assemblée nationale, sur les colonies* (Paris: Imprimerie du patriote françois, 1791), 32.

64. Yvan Debbasch, *Couleur et liberté. Le jeu de critère ethnique dans un ordre juridique esclavagiste* (Paris: Dalloz, 1967), 171, cites Governor Peinier, letter of March 14, 1790 [CAOM F³195].

65. This is how the name is spelled in the historiography. But throughout the interrogation, the spelling is consistently "Chavanne."

66. King, *Blue Coat*, 63, 221.

67. Castaing had been educated at Montauban, in southern France, and raised in Saint-Domingue's Limonade parish. During the revolution he traveled to France, married Josephine Beauharnais' divorced daughter and became part of the extended Bonaparte family. Erick Noël, "Le sang noir des Castaing, ou l'insolite ascension d'une famille des Isles," *Bulletin du centre d'histoire des espaces atlantiques* 7 (1995): 171–82. Some whites suspected Castaing of being involved in the Ogé revolt. See the extract from a November 12, 1790 letter of M. Debarras, a white colonist in CAOM F³196, p. 125; on the Laporte family, which King describes as "among the upper ranks of the planter elite in the 1780s," see King, *Blue Coat*, 144; for Chavannes, see King, 156, 163, 208.

68. Mémoire from Chavannes and others November 10, 1789: Messieurs le Président et membres de l'assemblée générale et provinciale de la partie du Nord; property of Dr. Marcel Chatillon, personal communication with the author.

69. *M.L.E. Moreau de Saint-Méry, Considérations présentées aux vrais amis du repos et du bonheur de la France, á l'occasion des nouveaux mouvemens de quelques soi-disant Amis-des-noirs* (Paris: l'Imprimerie Nationale, 1791), 22; also Lacroix, *La Révolution de Haïti* (1819), 50.

70. Raimond, *Réponse aux considérations de M. Moreau, dit Saint-Méry, député à l'assemblée nationale, sur les colonies*, 36–37.

71. Bocquet de Frévent, "Extrait des minutes," 33, 34.

72. Émile Nau, *Réclamation par les affranchis des droits civils et politiques. Ogé et Chavannes* (Port-au-Prince: T. Bouchereau, 1840), 32.

73. Bocquet de Frévent, "Extrait des minutes," 28–29.

74. Ibid., 51–53.

75. Ibid., 55, 56.

76. Translated by Jeremy Popkin in *Facing Racial Revolution: Eyewitness Accounts of the Haitian Insurrection* (Chicago: University of Chicago Press, 2007), 47.

77. Cited in ibid., 43.

78. Blaise Garnier, *Combats affreux, arrivés a l'isle St. Domingue: et dont l'aristocrate Damas est l'auteur* (Marseille: J. Mossy pére & fils imprimeurs de la nation du roi & de la ville, 1791), 1.

79. Jean-Philippe Garran de Coulon, *Rapport sur les troubles de Saint-Domingue, fait au nom de la Commission des colonies, des Comités de salut public, de législation et de marine, réunis* (Paris: Imp. nationale, 1797), 2:49.

80. Ibid.

81. Ibid.

82. Madiou, *Histoire d'Haiti,* 1:79.

83. Gabriel Debien's careful account seems to preserve the ambiguity of the situation: "The people of color were dispersed . . . after a clash in which they held the battle order. Ogé and Chavannes with about 60 followers were able to attain Spanish territory close to Dondon." Gabriel Debien, *Études antillaises: XVIIIe siècle* (A. Colin, 1956), 155.

84. Ralph Korngold, *Citizen Toussaint* (New York: Hill and Wang, 1944), 48–49.

85. James, *The Black Jacobins,* 68.

86. Ott, *The Haitian Revolution,* 37.

87. Bocquet de Frévent, "Extrait des minutes," 93.

88. Ibid., 95.

89. Ibid., 96.

90. Ibid., 100, 104.

91. Jacques Ogé mentioned both Lucas and Jean-François Tessier in *Ogé, Testament de mort d'Ogé.*

92. Bocquet de Frévent, "Extrait des minutes," 98–100, 103.

93. Ibid., 105.

94. Melania Rivers Rodríguez, "Los colonos americanos en la sociedad prerrevolucionaria de Saint Domingue. La rebelión de Vicente Ogé y su apresamiento en Santo Domingo (1789–1791)," *Memorias: Revista Digital de Historia y Arquelogia desde el Caribe* 2, no. 2, http://www.uninorte.edu.co/publicaciones/memorias/memorias_2/articulos/articulomelaniariverscorregido.pdf, cites "Testimonio del expediente de la aprehansión del Mulato Francés Juan Bautista Chavanne, su esclavo, sus bienes, y papeles hecha en San Juan por el comandante interino Teniente de Dragones, Don Manuel de Ayban, AGI, Audiencia de Santo Domingo, 1.029, Expediente de la revolución y guerra en la colonoia francesa, 1791.

95. Madiou, *Histoire d'Haiti,* 1:76.

96. Bocquet de Frévent, "Extrait des minutes," 116–17, 147–48.

97. Dubois and Garrigus, *Slave Revolution in the Caribbean*, 76.

98. Bocquet de Frévent, "Extrait des minutes," 129–30.

99. For a more detailed analysis of this event, including its relation with the slave revolt that occurred in the same parish six weeks later, see Garrigus, *Before Haiti*, 248–52.

100. Bocquet de Frévent, "Extrait des minutes," 130.

101. Rivers Rodríguez, "Los colonos americanos."

102. Ibid.

103. Ibid. See pages 12 to 14 of this unpaginated article.

104. See Brissot's preface to Julien Raimond, *Observations sur l'origine et les progrès du préjugé des colons blancs contre les hommes de couleur* (Paris: Belin, 1791), viii.

105. Garnier, *Combats affreux*, 4.

106. Dubois and Garrigus, *Slave Revolution in the Caribbean*, 102.

107. CAOM 87 Miom73 [CAOM Receuil Col. 2e série 18 ; biblio MstM 18] "Arrêt de Conseil Supérieur du Cap Contre le nommé Ogé jeune & ses Complices Du 5 Mars 1791 Extrait des registres du Greffe du Conseil-Supérieur du Cap."

108. Bouqet de Frévent, 44, 126. The full title of Frossard's book was *La cause des esclaves nègres et des habitants de la Guinée, portée au tribunal de la justice, de la religion, de la politique ; ou histoire de la traite et de l'esclavage des Nègres, preuves de leur illégitimité, moyens des les abolir sans suite ni aux colonies ni aux colons.*

109. CAOM F^{3}196.

"The Child Should Be Made a Christian"

Baptism, Race, and Identity
in the Seventeenth-century Chesapeake

REBECCA GOETZ

Late in September 1667, Virginia's burgesses passed legislation governing a serious matter of bondage and freedom, and of religious inclusion and exclusion. The act, titled "An act declaring that baptisme of slaves doth not exempt them from bondage," stipulated the following:

"Whereas some doubts have risen whether children that are slaves by birth, and by the charity and piety of their owners made pertakers of the blessed sacrament of baptisme, should by vertue of their baptisme be made free; *It is enacted and declared by this grand assembly, and the authority thereof,* that the conferring of baptisme doth not alter the condition of the person as to his bondage or freedome; that diverse masters, freed from this doubt, may more carefully endeavour the propagation of christianity by permitting children, though slaves, or those of greater growth if capable to be admitted to that sacrament."[1] The burgesses thus closed a legal loophole and clarified a widely accepted tenet of Christian practice that had formerly awarded freedom to enslaved converts. This law allowed the English to accomplish the grim goal toward which they had been marching—a Christianity in which the traditional privileges of an Englishman, most notably freedom, were denied to Africans and Indians.

Historians have long acknowledged the existence of this law, and have placed it in a larger historical conversation about the legal institutionalization of slavery. Baptism and Christian conversion it conferred had been an accepted route to freedom in the sixteenth and early seventeenth centuries.[2] Treatments of the 1667 law generally integrate it into a suite of other laws enacted between 1660 and 1705 that, as Winthrop Jordan argued, constituted an "unthinking decision" to legally enslave Africans.[3] Historians' treatment of the baptism law thus fits into an existing narrative about the parallel developments of slavery and freedom, but this approach to the 1667 law sub-sumes it into a context that distorts its unique place in the history of Christianity in the Chesapeake and in the construction of race in the early South.

While recognizing that the law is crucial to the historical understanding of the transition from African indentured servitude to permanent, hereditary slavery, this ar-ticle explores baptism's singular role in defining the English understanding of human difference. Although the law did not prevent the baptism of Africans (indeed, it prob-ably meant to encourage it), it had the practical effect of discouraging English slave owners from baptizing their slaves. The law did not apply to Indians and was not intended to alter Indian policy, but it probably had a chilling effect on Indian baptism as well, since Anglo-Virginian masters probably still feared that Indian indentured servants (who served terms much longer than English servants) could successfully sue for their freedom based upon their baptisms. Thus, the ambiguities of the law shaped the servitude and freedom of Indians and Africans in ways the burgesses probably had not anticipated. The law also had other critical unintended consequences. It engaged competing ideas about the nature of baptism that transformed how Anglo-Virginians thought about the sacrament. The law also allowed Anglo-Virginians to assess the "capability" of individuals for genuine baptism, allowing them to flout centuries of Christian custom to argue that some, if not all, Africans might not be capable of Christian conversion at all. In the two generations following the passage of the law, Anglo-Virginians manipulated the meaning of baptism and controlled access to bap-tism to redefine their own Christian identities and to create racialized, specifically non-Christian identities for Indians and Africans.

The term "identity" has many loose meanings; here it is used to describe processes of identification and categorization. "Identity" explains the various ways in which English people characterized themselves as Christians, and indicates the method by which the English categorized others they defined as non-Christians incapable of conversion through baptism.[4] Passing the 1667 law was an exercise in self-definition and in racial categorization for the English; Virginia's legislature thus accomplished a legal redefinition of what it meant to be Christian. It was a crucial step in the En-glish quest to comprehend and regulate human difference by establishing racialized identities for Indians and Africans while simultaneously defining their own Protestant Christian identity.

Baptism was a certainty in the life of almost every European child born into a Christian family. But despite its inevitability, Europeans strongly and sometimes even violently contested the meaning of baptism. Should only infants be baptized? Or should one be baptized as an adult capable of understanding the Christian faith? Was baptism the primary route to salvation, or did it signify only a covenanted relationship with God? In the early modern European world, questions about baptism took on enormous cultural, social, and theological significance. The fundamental differences in the ways Catholics and the emerging Protestant denominations viewed baptism fueled bitter controversies about the nature of the Christian community and how one became a member of it. The result was endemic and acrimonious debate about who was Christian, how one's membership in the Christian community was properly designated, and indeed, to what extent baptism conferred an undeniable Christian identity. Even more puzzling for Europeans was the question of what rights and responsibilities baptism conferred on its recipients.

English Protestants argued variations on all these Continental themes, and English colonists carried the ambiguities and various understandings they had of baptism with them to the Chesapeake. In Virginia and Maryland, as in other parts of the New World colonized by Europeans, controversies over baptism took on even more ambiguity, but the stakes were even higher than they had been at home, for in the Chesapeake the English encountered American Indians who had never been baptized and seemed to show little inclination for accepting the ceremony and all its attendant meanings and responsibilities. Then the English imported African slaves who also had not been baptized in the Church of England, though many were Kongolese Catholics. By the middle of the seventeenth century, the key questions for English Virginians were, first, did baptism in the Church of England make a person properly English? And, second, did baptism make a person free?

Early in the Reformation, Protestants upset what had been a universally accepted baptismal culture when they began to question baptism's efficacy in both fighting sin and in incurring eternal salvation. Animated debaters argued whether baptism was essential to salvation (as Catholics believed), and when it should take place: shortly after birth as a matter of course, or whether some education in Christian doctrine or even a profession of faith were necessary predecessors to baptism (as some Protestants began to insist). The baptism debate between Protestants and Catholics and, indeed, among different groups of Protestants, centered on one overriding controversy: did baptism result in salvation and faith, or did salvation and faith result in baptism? Catholics held the former position and Protestants usually held the latter position, with varying degrees of radicalism. Some radical Protestants even denied the necessity of baptism.

The English waded into the resulting theological quagmire with enthusiasm, but ultimately the Church of England sailed carefully between the Scylla of Catholic belief and the Charybdis of radical Protestant belief. The Church of England, with a monarch at its head rather than a pope, functioned as a state church designed to make the religion of the people and the government of the people a single entity. The theology was an ambivalent mixture of Continental reforms and residual Catholic folk practice, but the government prized conformity with the doctrines and practices of the new, national church, punishing those who remained Catholic and those who wished to further reform Church of England practice with varying degrees of severity. In the

English church, secular and spiritual loyalties were indivisible: to be English was to worship exclusively in the Church of England and to accept its tenets. Those who were outside the established church were generally deemed to be outside the English polity as well. An Englishman could not simultaneously serve two masters—monarch and pope.[5] This expectation led to hostility towards Catholics on the one hand and, on the other hand, radical Protestants, Presbyterians, and, by the 1650s, Quakers. Those who refused to participate in Anglican services faced certain legal strictures, social censure, and a decrease in their rights as Englishmen. By attaching rights within the English polity to support of and participation in the English state church, the English were implicitly excluding those who were outside the church either by choice or by circumstance—a state of affairs that had a great deal of influence on the religious and legal status of Africans and Indians in the New World.

The Church of England steered a delicate middle course specifically on baptism, retaining the infant rite and mandating it for all children born in the country. For the English, baptism was both a sign and seal of a covenant with God, a Protestant belief characteristic of Continental divines, and a sacrament that eased faith and salvation, a nod to residual Catholic belief and practice. In other words, Anglican baptism had something for everyone, reluctant Anglicans and budding Calvinists alike. For the faithful of the Church of England, baptism of infants allowed these children to join the spiritual community of Christian believers. But certainly people who rejected baptism were feared in England: among the Christian sects active there and in the Chesapeake, only Quakers refused infant baptism, which earned them at best contempt and at worst criminal prosecution and even execution. Even Puritans generally allowed their children to be baptized, although they rejected the traditional language of godparent-hood in favor of "witnesses," "guardians," or "sureties." As one historian has noted, "the cultural pressure to baptize newborn babies was overwhelming," and refusal to baptize a child or delaying baptism were both legally condemned.[6] But not to be baptized was a spiritual "mark of difference" that signaled exclusion from the Christian community.[7] In other words, baptism was a crucial cultural component of early modern English culture—it defined communities of Christians in both the temporal and spiritual worlds and cast suspicion on those who did not partake in the ritual.

While successfully negotiating the difficulties of baptismal theology in the Reformation by adopting the most appealing notions about baptism from all sides of the debate, the English satisfied traditionalists and reformers alike. But the very flexibility that allowed the English state to survive the tumults of the Reformation in the sixteenth and early seventeenth centuries relatively unscathed eventually led to diverging ideas about what being both English and Christian meant in a world that the English perceived to be threatened both by unreformed Christians as well as infidels and heathens (Turks and other Muslims as well as Africans and Indians). The English viewed their church as a beacon for the rest of the Christian community, as a role model to be emulated. In that sense the English saw themselves as leaders of a universal church that anyone who professed faith could join—even Catholics and other heathens. But increasingly the English also saw that there was a connection between the overwhelming rightness of their religion and church and the liberties that they enjoyed as Englishmen.[8] The unified vision of the church came into conflict with the contradicting vision of the English as a particularly blessed nation of the elect. A sense of superiority warred with the sense of universality in ways that had profound consequences in the Chesapeake.

From the start of the English colonial adventure in North America, Christian baptism was a tool of conquest. Baptizing the Indians they encountered would allow the English to number the Indians in the Christian community; it was generally believed that conversion would bring the Indians to civility—a term that indicated to English ears the acceptance of English language, land tenure, agriculture, animal husbandry, and clothing, as well as religion. But in additional to being a tool of salvation and assimilation, baptism also meant inclusion in the English political community. For baptism had political as well as theological implications; as one historian has put it, the baptized were members "not only of the local and national congregation of worshippers, but also engaged with the wider spiritual community of Christians in all times and places."[9]

In Virginia as in England, this cultural pressure to baptize English infants translated into a legal necessity as well. Virginia's General Assembly condemned the "new fangled conceits" and "hereticall inventions" of those Virginians who refused to baptize their children (most likely Quakers who had begun to enter the colony in small numbers) and leveled the hefty fine of two thousand pounds of tobacco for each offense.[10] In 1665, the Northampton County Court fined Ambrose London (probably a Quaker) at least that much for not baptizing his children.[11] There was at least one acceptable reason for not baptizing a child. In 1690, Christopher Blith was summoned before the Surry County Court for not baptizing his children but "now makeing it appeare that he was soe bare of Clothes that he could not, & that as soon as he could gett any he Carried his s[d] Childe to be baptized . . . he is discharged from the s[d] presentment paying his fees."[12] In Blith's case, extreme material poverty, not spiritual poverty or nonconformity, excused his failure to baptize his children.

The actual ceremony of baptism as performed in Virginia had been in use almost continuously since 1552 and was adapted from the previously used Catholic version of the rite. Virginians seem to have taken the ritual seriously; numerous court records show the purchase and maintenance of fonts in churches. In 1672, Surry County accounts noted a payment of eleven hundred pounds of tobacco to a Mr. Caulfield, reimbursing him for expenses incurred acquiring a "bason" for the church in which to baptize newborns.[13] The ritual of baptism, in addition to welcoming a new member to the community, was an opportunity to establish secular social ties for children through the selection of godparents. In the Chesapeake, godparents often provided livestock—usually cows or pigs but sometimes a horse—to godchildren in their wills. Some godparents even gave their godchildren gifts of livestock before their deaths, as John Wilkins did when he gave his godson Fisher a cow in 1639.[14] John Broch gave his two godsons a more unusual gift, deeding to brothers Joseph and Benjamin Croshaw "a stocke of bees" in 1646.[15]

In the Chesapeake, godparents also took on the role of caring for orphaned godchildren—although often these children were not actually blood kin. This was a common arrangement throughout the seventeenth century. In 1648 Stephen Gill took custody of his orphaned godson John Foster, promising to keep him for nine years and to teach him to read. Elizabeth Lang's godmother successfully sued in Northampton County Court in 1677 to gain custody of her goddaughter by promising to care for and educate Elizabeth. In a similar case, when Hannah Harlow insisted in orphans' court that she be placed with her godfather John Tatum, Tatum readily agreed to assume his social and spiritual obligations. Sometimes wills even explicitly stated that godparents should assume guardianship of their godchildren upon the death of the parents. In 1672, worried that after his death his wife would marry a "cross man" who would abuse his daughter Anne, Jarrett Hawthorne specified that Anne's godmother Margaret Wyld would have custody of her.[16] Godparents incurred serious social and spiritual obligations, and they were important threads that helped knit Chesapeake society together. The traditional rituals of baptism held together a sense of family even in the face of appalling mortality in the Chesapeake.[17]

Godparents also reinforced the Protestant English identities of their godchildren. In 1691, when Peter Blake, "a professed Papist & contemner & slighter of ye Publick worship of God," won custody of the orphan Christopher Homes in Nansemond County, Christopher's godfather protested vigorously. He wished to have custody of Christopher so that he might "better performe those duties doth become him as a Godfather, Christian & a friend to ye afore^{sd} Childe, y^t hee may be brought up in ye Knowledge and feare of God, & in ye true principells of Christian Religion." Blake had already taken Christopher into Maryland, and his recovery to true Protestantism would be all but impossible to achieve.[18] Most godparents viewed their obligations in less drastic terms. Godparents who wished to be involved in their godchildren's education as English Christians left them Bibles and other religious tracts in their wills.[19] In other words, the English used baptism as one means of creating and reinforcing their own identities in a colonial world. But they also used baptism as a tool for converting Indians and Africans, as a means of forcing diplomatic exchange with Indians, and for exercising control over their new lands.

The kidnapping and subsequent conversion of Powhatan's married daughter Metoaka (better known to posterity as Pocahontas) in 1614, illustrates the connection between baptism and colonization. Though the English hoped that Powhatan would be willing to negotiate an end to a desperate Anglo-Indian war of attrition in exchange for Metoaka's release, Powhatan remained obdurate. The young woman, however, proved susceptible to English missionary efforts. "Powhatan's daughter I caused to be carefully instructed in the Christian Religion," bragged Virginia leader Thomas Dale, "who after she had made good progresse therein, renounced publikely her Countrey Idolatry, openly confessed her Christian Faith, was, as shee desired, baptized, and is since married to an English Gentleman [John Rolfe] of good understanding."[20] Metoaka received her instruction—and a new name, Rebecca—from the Puritan minister Alexander Whitaker, who had come to Virginia expressly to convert the heathen Indians. The English took Metoaka's baptism as proof that the Indians could in fact be converted and take on English identity. Her conversion was a great victory in what for the English had not only been a war for survival but also a bid to preserve and extend their own Christianity.

Metoaka's own conversion and baptism were the exception rather than the rule in early Virginia, and after the ferocious Anglo-Indian violence in 1622, Indian converts remained few and far between. Yet baptism and the Christian conversion it signified seem to have granted some rights to Africans and Indians living as servants or slaves in Virginia after 1622. The muster list taken in January 1624 recorded not only the number of able-bodied men and the number of weapons that could be used against the Indians, but also recorded interesting tidbits about the denizens of Virginia. Of the two Indians listed as living with the English, one of them lived on [William] Tucker's plantation and was listed as "William Crashaw an Indian baptized." (William Crashaw was also the name of an evangelizing minister who vigorously supported the conversion of Virginia's Indians from his London parish, suggesting a connection between the minister's efforts and the Indian's conversion.) Another Indian lived on Thomas Dunthorne's Elizabeth City plantation and was listed as "Thomas an Indian Boaye."[21] That the muster listed a baptism for the Indian William Crashaw but not for little Thomas suggests that Indian baptism remained exceptional but that those who underwent the ritual gained some rights and a new identity from the process, otherwise the Virginia Company's census takers would not have recorded it. Unfortunately, neither Thomas nor William appears in any Virginia record again, making it impossible to assess their success or failure in living among English Christians.

William Crashaw's baptism was not the only post-1622 Indian baptism. To facilitate more Indian baptisms, London merchant Nicholas Ferrar provided £300 for a college for the conversion and instruction of Indians.[22] Although the Anglo-Indian agricultural utopia of the college never materialized, the Ferrar endowment supported Indian children who lodged with English families and were thereby converted. In 1641 George Menifye presented to the general court an Indian boy who had been "christened and for the time of ten years brought up amongst the English" by Menifye and William Perry, who apparently served in godfatherly capacities by undertaking the religious education of their charge. The court questioned the Indian boy closely and was satisfied that the boy was sufficiently familiar with Christian doctrine. Menifye went home that day with £15 for his troubles.[23] This is quite possibly the only recorded situation in which a godfather benefited materially from his godson—not the other way around. Other sources mention Indian conversions as well, including the Bible of the Bass family of Surry County, in which the minister John Bass recorded his marriage to "Keziah Elizabeth Tucker dafter [daughter] of Robin the Elder of ye Nansimuns [Nansemond's] kingdom, a Baptized Xtian [Christian]" in 1638.[24]

Almost all relationships between the Indians and the English were geared toward converting Indians to Christianity, at least from the English point of view. In 1655 and 1656, in exchange for killing wolves, the English gave the Indians cows, which was to "be a step to civilizing them and to make them Christians."[25] Since the cow-to-Christian progression did not work out as well as the Assembly hoped (possibly because rather than raising dairy cattle, Indians used cows almost exclusively for meat), the burgesses passed laws to enable Indian parents to send their children to live with English families, where the children would learn about English religion, language, and other customs. Not all English families were as scrupulous about their Christian responsibilities as the general court had anticipated. Instead, in 1657 the court had to reiterate that Indian children thus adopted were to be freed at twenty-five.[26] Some English planters found conversion programs an easy way to acquire slave labor.

Although the Anglo-Indian violence of 1622 and 1644 halted most of these kinds of relationships on the mainland, they were more common on the Eastern Shore, where violent interactions remained less common. There, Indian children were brought before the Accomack County Court. Their ages were judged, and ceremoniously their Indian names were recorded along with new English names. Renaming implied a godparent-like relationship between English masters and Indian adoptees, since one of the godparent's responsibilities was to name his godchild. Assigning an English—Christian—name implied that baptism was the intent, if not the actual outcome, of this ritual renaming. Renaming assigned a fresh identity to Indian children—which they likely welcomed, since Algonquians often took new names during certain life transitions—and from the English perspective it brought them into the Christian spiritual community. In 1667 at least thirteen Indian children were presented before the Accomack court and renamed—the same year as the baptism law.[27] The English settlers of the Eastern Shore were slower to abandon this interaction with Indians than were their counterparts on the mainland. Nevertheless, adoption of Indian children waned after 1680. Thereafter, Indians who appear in court records were identified not by proper English Christian names but by the diminutives increasingly also common among African slaves: Jenny Indian, Dick Indian, and Charley Indian, for example.[28] Even in the relative absence of Anglo-Indian violence, English people on the Eastern Shore repudiated baptism for Indians.

The muster list of 1624 also recorded the existence of twenty-two people of African descent: ten men, ten women, and two children (the list identifies them variously as "negroes" or "negars"). Of these men, women, and children, only seven are named, and all of these have English names, which indicates they were probably Christian. It is likely that the unnamed Africans did not have English names, or any record of their conversion, and therefore might have been held even at this early date as slaves for life. Those with English names probably had some previous experience with the English or other Europeans and were able to take advantage of that knowledge. Certainly at least three came in ships from England.[29] But the baptism of only one—a child—is recorded. The list of people at Captain William Tucker's plantation in Elizabeth City includes "Antoney Negro Isabell Negro and William theire Child Baptized."[30] Perhaps William, Antoney and Isabell's son, was named for his master William Tucker. And since English practice urged that godparents bestow their own names on godchildren, it is possible that William Tucker was little William's godfather. The recognition in the muster list of a baptized black child suggests that that baptism meant something to both the English master and to the child's African parents. Antoney and Isabell knew that baptism and a godfather secured some rights and protections for their son. And it seems that William Tucker was the kind of master who encouraged these kinds of arrangements for his non-English servants. As the infant William's situation suggests, Africans in Virginia knew that baptism granted membership in the established church, and that most Englishman believed that being Christian brought freedom and certain liberties. They could not fail to see the advantages of baptism, especially in the emerging hardscrabble world of the English Chesapeake, where most of the first African slaves were almost certainly people who were familiar with European languages, cultures, and religions. Historian Ira Berlin has called these people Atlantic Creoles—people who successfully navigated the merging of African, European, and American worlds around the Atlantic littoral.[31]

The correlation between baptism and rights was clear in the experience of one African baptized in the Church of England who came to Virginia in 1624. John Phillip, "a Negro Christened in England twelve yeers since," was permitted to testify in court about the improper seizure of a Spanish ship by the English ship in which he was traveling.[32] In recording his testimony, the clerk was careful to note Phillip's baptism and Christian conversion, suggesting that had Phillip not been able to demonstrate his Christianity, his testimony would not have been accepted. Phillip was brought before the court three years later on charges of fornication with an English woman. But probably owing to his free Christian status, he was punished in the traditional English church court fashion: he and his paramour wrapped themselves in white sheets and held white rods in a ritual of Christian penance at church for three Sundays in a row.[33] A non-Christian would likely have been whipped rather than undergoing ritual punishment, penance, and forgiveness.[34]

Those Afro-Virginians living as Christians in early Virginia commonly made sure their children were baptized and used godparenthood as a way of building community networks. The experience of the Johnson clan demonstrates this admirably. Anthony Johnson arrived in Virginia in 1621, numbering him among the first Africans to arrive in the colony (Africans had probably first been sold in the colony in 1619 from Dutch ships).[35] He was known only as "Antonio a Negro" and resided, probably as a servant, on the Surry County plantation called Wariscoyack. In 1622 an African woman named Mary came to the plantation. At some point, Antonio married Mary, gained his freedom, anglicized his name to Anthony Johnson, and acquired property on Virginia's Eastern Shore. Johnson established himself as the patriarch of a large family.[36]

Johnson and his family were not the only free, property-owning, moderately prosperous blacks on the Eastern Shore. The families of Francis Payne, Emmanuel Driggus, William Harmon, King Tony, and Philip Mongum joined the Johnsons on the Eastern Shore in a close-knit black Christian community held together by bonds of marriage and of spiritual kinship. With the exception of King Tony, all of these men have "Christian" first names as well as surnames, which indicate a conversion to Christianity. Indeed, some of these men might already have been Christian on their arrival in Virginia: "Antonio" is an Iberian name, and Emmanuel Driggus's name could have been a corruption of "Rodriguez." Johnson and Driggus had contacts at some point with the Spanish or the Portuguese, and probably the English as well, in the Caribbean before their arrival in the Chesapeake. This might explain why these families became so adept at moving in the English legal world. The court records of Accomack and Northampton County are full of lawsuits, criminal cases, debt actions, and other materials such as wills and notices of lost livestock generated by these families. But through these documents, it is possible to see how connected these families were by bonds of spiritual kinship. Their practices continued long after the 1667 baptism law, indicating that that law had little effect on Afro-Virginians who had already learned to use English religion to their advantage.

When Francis Payne died in 1673, his will was a testament to his Christianity:

"I bequeath my Soule to my lovinge ffather my creator and to Jesus Christ whereby his blood and passion suffered for my Sinns & all ye world trustinge through his merits to injoy that heavenly portion prepared for mee and all true believers and as for my body I bequeath it unto the ground from hence it came there to receive xpian [Christian] burial."[37] Payne's pious phrases in the preamble reflect more devotion than the usual formulaic sentences that precede most English wills of the time. More importantly, he went on to oblige his wife to "give unto each of our godchildren a Cow calfe a peece when they attaine to lawfull age."[38] Payne observed the time-honored Virginia tradition of providing godchildren with the means of corporeal as well as spiritual sustenance, adopting the English practice with ease. But one godchild had done something to anger Payne: "But as for Devrax [Devorax] Dregus [Driggus] hee is to have nothing by this Will."[39] By naming the black sheep of his spiritual family, Payne help-fully tells us that the Paynes and the Drigguses were joined by bonds of spiritual kin-ship. Probably other Drigguses and possibly Johnsons as well were numbered among Payne's other godchildren. But the Drigguses did not limit themselves to kinship with the Paynes. When King Tony's will was probated in March 1678, he left his godchild Sarah Driggus a cow.[40] These two wills demonstrate that these Afro-Virginian fami-lies were committed to reciprocal spiritual and social obligations, just as English fami-lies were. They had embraced English Christianity in its full meaning, even as English Christians rejected the possibility of spiritual kinship with and among African slaves in the baptism law of 1667.

Their Christianity also allowed the Eastern Shore's black families to participate in the broader English political community. But Christian ties to English people also allowed Africans to protect themselves and their families in times of trouble. In 1645, Emanuel Driggus signed an indenture with his master Francis Potts consigning his two daughters Elizabeth and Jane to indentured servitude. Although the length of their service was uncommon (Elizabeth had to serve until she was sixteen and Jane until she was thirty), the indenture specified that the girls were to be brought up "in the feare of god and in the knowledge of our savior Christ Jesus."[41] Such long indentures were unheard of in England, but what is clear is that Potts had a clientage relationship with the Drigguses which might explain why the indenture made spe-cific religious references and why Potts was assigned a role in the girls' lives that looks remarkably like that of godfather. Emanuel Driggus later "bought back" the younger girl Jane, whose indenture had been the longest. In essence, Potts protected the two girls in the same way an English godfather might look after his goddaughters if their natural parents were unable to do so. Emanuel Driggus had learned to use an English institution to his and his family's advantage.[42]

Nevertheless, the Afro-Virginian families of the Eastern Shore were exceptional. By 1677 free blacks made up 16 percent of Northampton County's population.[43] No counties on the mainland ever saw such a flourishing of free black planter families. Possibly Northampton County's distance from the mainland allowed for other cus-toms to develop, since there are no other examples of black families so entwined. But gradually the fortunes of these families fell, probably as a direct result of legislation in the general court that continually chipped away at the privileges enjoyed by free blacks all over Virginia. Late in the century, the Johnson family moved to Maryland. Their Christianity had ceased to be a protection, even far away from the center of political power in Virginia.

By the time the baptism law passed in 1667, English Virginians lived in a world in which Indians and Africans alike both comprehended the many meanings of baptism and took advantage of them to both build their own communities and identities and also to gain a place in English society. Yet Virginia instituted a law barring baptized slaves from gaining their freedom, and it was not the only colony to do so. Maryland first considered such a law in 1664, when some legislators asked for legislation stating that baptized slaves did not get their freedom, "they thinking itt very necessary for the prevention of the damage of such Masters of such Slaves may susteyne by such Slaves pretending to be Christened."[44] The danger as Marylanders saw it was not from actual Christian slaves but those who pretended conversion for their own nefarious purposes. No law was passed in Maryland until 1671 explicitly stating that baptized slaves could not gain their freedom, and unlike the Virginia law, Marylanders did not even bother to encourage planters to baptize their slaves.[45] The Caribbean colonies followed suit with similar laws later in the seventeenth century. The Virginia planters innovated legally with their law of 1667, even if they were anxious about the idea of holding Christian slaves.

The text of the 1667 law implied both that African slaves demanding their post-baptismal freedom was a common occurrence prior to the law's passage, and that many English Virginians must have been expressing doubt about the wisdom of baptizing their slaves. The burgesses began their new law by acknowledging the delicate question of Christian conversion and slavery: "Whereas some doubts have risen whether children that are slaves by birth, and by the charity and piety of their owners made pertakers of the blessed sacrament of baptisme be made ffree...."[46] The burgesses were eager to show both their own Christianity and their commitment to converting their slaves by illustrating the fact that slaves converted frequently enough to cause comment. Their own "charity and piety"—two key Christian attributes—were undeniable. The preamble to the law also underscored the ongoing importance of baptism as both a social and a religious marker of Christian identity in Anglican belief and practice. But it also betrayed a budding sense of discomfort within English planters' Christianity: while they were committed to their spiritual obligation to convert the heathen, they also recognized that the act of baptism essentially depleted their captive workforce.

But did baptism frequently result in freedom for slaves? The available evidence suggests a much more complicated picture of the role of baptism in pre-1667 emancipations. Cases were highly individual, often reacting to specific sets of circumstances, and most emancipations seem to have been the result of careful negotiation between slaves, masters, masters' heirs, and the courts. Slaves sometimes sued for their freedom but were more likely to negotiate for it within carefully formulated networks of masters, overseers, ministers, lawyers, and godparents, and sometimes slaves even arranged for some sort of monetary compensation for their masters. Baptism was usually just one of many criteria for freedom that slaves advanced, and only one of the strategies they used. But it also seems that very few slaves were actually attempting to gain their freedom in ways that involved the courts at all. Some of the records that indicate emancipation were presented to the court only for record-keeping purposes, not because the court had any role in emancipation. Instead, the surviving records reveal the ingenuity of slaves who negotiated freedom for themselves and their families, using English attitudes toward conversion and baptism as an important way of differentiating themselves and gaining advantages. But it is almost certain that large numbers of slaves were not single-mindedly pursuing freedom through baptism. Instead, baptism functioned as both a mechanism of freedom and as a consequence of it; there was no explicit causal relationship between the two concepts that led directly from baptism to freedom. The correlation between the concepts was too complicated for the simple statement forbidding the freedom of slaves based on their baptism at which the burgesses finally arrived.

In 1641, for John Graweere, the freedom and subsequent baptism of his child were intimately connected events. Graweere, a black man who was either a slave or an indentured servant, who had a child with an unnamed black woman from a neighboring plantation, told Virginia's general court that "he desired [the child] should be made a Christian and be taught and exercised in the church of England, by reason whereof he . . . did for his said child purchase its freedom."[47] The court duly noted this arrangement, acknowledging that "the child shall be free . . . and remain at the disposing and education of the said Graweere and the child's godfather who undertaketh to see it brought up in the Christian religion aforesaid."[48] Although the godfather is not identified in this record, it is clear that Graweere truly understood the religious underpinnings of English society in the Chesapeake: a godparent served the dual purpose of helping to educate the child and providing him with access to the Anglo-Virginian Christian community. There is no evidence that Graweere's child was freed because of its incipient baptism and acceptance into the wider Christian community. Baptism was not a precondition for freedom, but rather a consequence of it—one that Graweere probably understood would confer status and opportunity on his child. And perhaps Graweere's English co-conspirators were more likely to accept Graweere's purchase of freedom for his child once they understood that Graweere intended the child be brought up in ways familiar to the English. And perhaps the threat of freedom was less disturbing to the English since Graweere apparently made no attempt to free himself or his child's unnamed mother.

Graweere's case is interesting precisely because of its ambiguities. There was an implied link between baptism and freedom, although one did not flow directly from the other. In a time when the status of Africans was contingent on a number of factors and unclear legalities, religion and not physical appearance (skin color, for example) was a more powerful and evocative way of categorizing people and of moving through the malleable barriers between slavery and freedom. For John Graweere, the baptism and godparenthood was part of a process of acculturation in which Christianity was open to all and religion was a possible way to avoid bondage.

Graweere apparently did not need to sue either to gain his child's freedom or to enforce it; his was an arrangement carefully negotiated, in which his child's baptism and incipient Christianity were decisive factors. Graweere was not unique; Mihill Gowen made an arrangement similar to John Graweere's for his own child in York County in 1657. Gowen had been granted his freedom by his master Christopher Stafford's will, which required him to serve only a further four years after Stafford's death. Stafford's heirs honored the agreement and had Gowen's bill of freedom entered in the county court records (possibly to prevent his reenslavement at a later date). At the same time, Stafford's niece Anne Barnehouse also recognized the freedom of Gowen's son "borne the 25 Aug 1655 of the body of my Negro Posta being baptized by Edward Johnson 2 Sept 1655 & named William & I the said Anne Barnhouse doth bind my selfe . . . never to trouble or molest . . . or demand any service of the said Mihill or his said sone William." As in John Graweere's case, Gowen seems to have made no effort to secure Posta's freedom, but he did use the ecclesiastical establishment to secure notice of the freedom of his child. Edward Johnson, the minister who had baptized William two years before, was the signed witness on William's bill of freedom. While this notation does not list a godfather for the child, as Graweere's did, Gowen used Johnson similarly to how Graweere used his son's godfather as a guarantor of freedom. Again, there is no evidence to suggest that William Gowen was freed on the basis of baptism; rather, his baptism was one of a number of factors that allowed his father to negotiate his freedom among Christopher Stafford's heirs and the local minister.[49]

Networks of religiously based freedom of the kind Graweere and Gowen set up for themselves and their sons could also protect their baptized children from illegal or unfair servitude. While this case might simply indicate the easy malleability of status for blacks in the early years of settlement, it is telling that each child's clear Christianity played such a visible role in his freedom. An unbaptized child, with no network of protectors connected through the ancient traditions of baptism followed by most English Virginians, might not have fared so well.

Slaves who failed to negotiate such contractual arrangements with their masters sometimes availed themselves of the courts and governing institutions of Virginia. In 1654, when Elizabeth Key, who was probably the daughter of an English father and an African mother, sued for her freedom partly on the basis of her baptism, her English godfather was a crucial witness. Shortly after her reputed father Thomas Key's death, Elizabeth and her brother John Key found themselves sold to the estate of Colonel John Mottrom. Initially in court documents deponents called Elizabeth a "Negro," and then later "Molletto," indicating confusion about Elizabeth's status and parentage. Elizabeth's paternity became crucial to her case for freedom. One deponent claimed that Thomas Key could not be her father, since "a Turke of Capt. Matthews was Father to the Girle." Another deponent noted that she had heard that Thomas Key had been fined for fornication with an African woman in another parish, and that Elizabeth was the product of that relationship. But the deciding factor in Elizabeth's suit for freedom was her Christianity. A Colonel Humphrey Higginson claimed that he had an agreement with Thomas Key to look after Elizabeth and take her back to England with him and give her a portion of her father's estate when she came of age: "That shee hath bin long since Christened Col. Higginson being her God father and that by report shee is able to give a very good account of her fayth." In essence, Higginson accepted the obligation of being Elizabeth's godfather and affirmed her Christian ties. She gained her freedom, but instead of sailing to England with Higginson, she married the lawyer who argued her case.[50]

Slaves also used Christianity in the courts to gain their freedom when, presumably, careful negotiation with their masters and a network of kin and contacts had failed them. In 1644 a mulatto slave named Manuel sued successfully before the Virginia Assembly in Jamestown to be "adjudged no Slave but to serve as other Christian Servants do." Manuel made an explicit connection between his Christianity and his right to serve a lesser term as an indentured servant, not as a slave for life. His master William Whittacre was not pleased with the deal, however, writing in 1666 that he had purchased Manuel "as a Slave for Ever," and that he eventually had freed Manuel in September 1665 (making Manuel's term of service still significantly longer than that of most English servants). Whittacre maintained that Manuel had been sold to him under false pretenses and petitioned the governor and his council for "satisfaction from the Levy being freed by the Country and bought by your Petitioner at £25 Sterling." The Assembly denied Whittacre's petition to be reimbursed for the loss of his slave; the Council of Virginia—an institution dominated by the wealthiest and most powerful planters in the colony—did not acknowledge "any Reason why the Publick should be answerable for the inadvertancy of the Buyer or for a Judgment when justly grounded as that Order was." The entire sequence—Manuel's suit for freedom, Whittacre's response to it, and the Assembly's reaction to Whittacre's petition—all suggest that even slaves who did not work within their network of contacts and used the courts instead were able to use evidence of their Christianity to gain their freedom, and that the Council (whose members stood to lose the most from allowing a precedent for freeing Christian slaves) recognized claims to Christian freedom as just—even when the original order was over two decades old. Only two years before the Assembly passed the baptism law, the Council of Virginia upheld a precedent that freed Christian slaves, obligating them to serve their masters as would an indentured servant.[51]

Indians who found themselves unexpectedly in servitude for life also used baptism as a justification for freedom. In 1661, an Indian boy was able to gain his freedom in a manner reminiscent of John Graweere's strategy. Metappin, called a Powhatan Indian in court documents, was ordered freed, "he speaking perfectly the English tongue and desiring baptism." Technically it was illegal to enslave Tidewater Indians, but the circumstances of Metappin's enslavement were peculiar. Surry County documents there show that an Indian identified as "a Kinge of the Waineoakes" sold Metappin, "a boy of his nacon … untill the full terme of his life" to Elizabeth Short, accepting a horse as payment.[52] Metappin's sale into slavery did not resemble George Menifye's earlier experiment with Indian servitude and conversion. Under what pretense the King of the Waineoakes sold Metappin (also called Weetoppin in Surry records) is unclear, but Metappin fought back almost immediately, bypassing the Surry court and suing for his freedom directly in the General Assembly. But his status as an Indian was not what explicitly resulted in his freedom; his promise of conversion as well as his proficiency in English accomplished that task. In other words, it was his status as a proto-Englishman that allowed his freedom. Even the planters of Surry County, a prosperous and chronically labor-short tobacco-growing area on the south side of the James, had to acquiesce to the freedom of an Indian who could be bound to them by ties of conversion.[53]

The experiences of Manuel, Metappin, and their predecessors were soon to become the exception rather than the rule. In 1667 the Lower Norfolk County Court was not interested in entertaining the free, Christian aspirations of a black man. At that court, "Fernando a Negro" sued his master Captain John Warner for his freedom. Fernando cleverly amassed a series of arguments in favor of his freedom: he claimed he was Christian, that he had lived in England, and he produced documents to support his claim. One can imagine Fernando's impassioned pleas before the court. But Lower Norfolk County's judges were unconvinced. To them, Fernando merely was "pretending he was a Christian and had been severall yeares in England." The qualifications that had served Africans from John Phillip to Mihill Gowen well were now cause for doubt. Additionally, the magistrates noted that Fernando's documents were "in Portugell or some other language which the Court could not understand." The judges rejected Fernando's appeal, and declared "the Court could find noe cause wherefore he should be free but Judge him a slave for his life time."[54]

There are many reasons the court ruled against Fernando. Perhaps he overwhelmed the court with his protestations, which combined several different avenues of argument for his freedom. It is also possible that by claiming Christianity and by providing documentation in an Iberian language, Fernando left the inadvertent impression that he was Catholic—an affiliation unlikely to win him any privileges in Protestant Virginia. And after all, from the judges' perspective, anyone could claim to have been in England and therefore be subject to the English customary law regarding the limited term of indentured servitude. But Fernando did not give up. He appealed his case to the general court of Virginia. Unfortunately, the destruction of most seventeenth-century general court records in 1865 make it impossible to know the outcome of Fernando's case. Whether or not the court freed Fernando, though, Anglo-Virginians were increasingly wary of blacks who pressed for freedom based in whole or in part on their Christianity.

It seems likely that Fernando's case, whatever its outcome, was one of the precipitating factors in the passage of the 1667 law. Faced with the tenacity of slaves like Manuel and Fernando and the increasing reluctance and fear of masters like William Whittacre, Anglo-Virginians faced the tension between their beliefs and obligations as Christians and their need to maintain control of a captive labor force. In one swift stroke, the Virginia legislature undid centuries of English and Christian custom. A close reading of the language the burgesses used in the law reveals two innovative threads in their thinking about the sacrament of baptism: that they ought to take more care to determine that only sincere converts receive baptism, and that many enslaved people might not be capable of baptism at all. Virginians were to "more carefully endeavour the propagation of Christianity," which might in this instance mean that slave owners should more "discerningly" determine who among their human property should receive baptism, rather than offering the sacrament to all comers without regard to the possible consequences. The burgesses suggested that children might be appropriately targeted for instruction and baptism while at the same time questioning the capability of adult black slaves to adequately comprehend Christianity and therefore be completely converted. "[T]hose of greater growth," meaning adult enslaved people, should in the burgesses' new legal formulation only be baptized "if capable to be admitted to that sacrament."[55]

What precisely did the burgesses mean when they referred to who was "capable" of receiving baptism? Contextually, the burgesses explicitly meant that children might be able to learn about and accept Christianity, but adults would not likely be receptive. Yet "capable" also indicated in seventeenth-century usage a legal or moral qualification or ability.[56] This usage then implied that adult enslaved people were morally incapable of learning about and accepting Christianity, and thus excused planters from pursuing Christian education and baptism for those individuals. For most planters, though, this situation was not limited to adults; there is little evidence suggesting that planters pursued baptism for enslaved children in the latter half of the seventeenth century. Having been "freed from this doubt" that baptism equated freedom, slave owners chose not to baptize their slaves but to systematically exclude them from this rite of Christian initiation and membership. Indeed, slave owners began to assign their slaves a new identity that suggested that Africans were innately and irrevocably non-Christian, an attitude that the law unintentionally fostered.

Ministers trained in England but serving in Virginia found this state of affairs puzzling. Reverend Morgan Godwyn, who preached at a parish in York County until his departure for Barbados in 1670, tried very hard to baptize slaves while in Virginia, but found the task difficult simply because many slave owners thought their slaves lacked the ability to become Christian. Godwyn did not believe those assertions: "As to their [slaves'] (alike pretended) *Stupidity*, there is as little truth therein."[57] Yet when he tried to baptize African slaves, even in the wake of the 1667 law that should have permitted such baptisms, he ran into stubborn opposition. One woman informed Godwyn that he "might as well Baptize a Puppy, as a certain young *Negro.*" Another slave owner was even more hostile, telling Godwyn that baptism "*was to one of those* [slaves] *no more beneficial than to her black Bitch.*"[58] Applying bestial characteristics to African slaves was a convenient mechanism for Virginia planters to protect their property from baptism—after all, dogs could not be baptized, having no ability to comprehend any sacrament. Godwyn later lamented the "Hellish Principles, viz. that *Negroes* are Creatures destitute of Souls, to be ranked among Brute Beasts."[59] "Creatures destitute of Souls" had no ability to be included in the community of Christians, even as slaves. The planters Godwyn encountered upped the ante by suggesting that slaves were not human beings at all. The very language of capability, which Virginia's burgesses perhaps thought would mitigate the issue of freedom by encouraging slaveholders to baptize at least children, encouraged planters to think of their slaves as completely incapable of ever being Christian—as hereditary heathens. Thus this law, despite its evangelical intent, encouraged the opposite approach.

Morgan Godwyn was not the only Englishman to encounter Virginia's peculiar attitudes about baptizing slaves. In 1699, the Bishop of London's personal representative in Virginia, the Reverend James Blair, fumed that "little Care is taken to instruct the Indians and Negroes in the Christian faith."[60] Blair also penned a longer treatise on the state of the Church of England in Virginia, to which he appended "A Proposition for encouraging the Christian Education of Indian, Negroe, and Mulatto Children." In this short addendum, Blair proposed evangelization through baptism and education, aimed at young children of Indians and Africans, thus echoing the supposition of the baptism law of 1667 that conversion would be more easily accomplished with children. ("The old ones that are imported into the Countrey," would be more difficult to convert, Blair surmised, "by reason of their not understanding the Language, being much more indocile.") Blair wisely added a significant financial incentive to his plan to encourage planters to allow their slaves to receive religious instruction. Under Blair's plan, masters or mistresses whose slave children were baptized, attended church regularly, and could give a public account of their faith would not have to pay taxes on those children until they reached the age of eighteen. Planters who did not allow their young slaves to be catechized would still have to pay levies.[61] It was a smart plan, but it had no chance of passing the Virginia legislature. Virginia's planters, as another minister dedicated to the conversion of Indians and Africans noted almost a generation later, "disapprove of it [conversion]; because they say it often makes them [enslaved people] proud, and not so good servants."[62]

Even at the turn of the century, slaves were still using baptism as one among many reasons for freedom, despite the fact that many of their masters did not believe in baptizing or instructing them in any way. Court records from 1695 described William Catillah, a mulatto, as "servant to Mrs Margrett Booth," and it seems, from the terms described in his lawsuit, that he had been indentured to Booth as a small child. Having turned twenty-four, he demanded his freedom because he was "the son of a free woman & was baptized into the Christian faith." Booth was unable to prove to the court why she continued to hold Catillah and he gained his freedom. The court probably did not regard Catillah's Christianity as a reason for his freedom; more likely the court freed him on the basis of an indenture guaranteeing his freedom. Nevertheless, it is significant that Catillah himself considered his baptism and his Christian identity as a contributor to his freedom.[63]

Baptism was probably a factor that protected some mulattoes—people, like William Catillah, of English and African descent—from perpetual servitude. In 1683, for example, Elizabeth Banks, an English indentured servant to James Goodwin, was whipped for "bastardy with a Negroe slave." Nineteen years later, her daughter Mary (probably the child for whom Elizabeth was whipped) made indenture arrangements for her own bastard child Hannah Banks to another member of the Goodwin family. Hannah had to serve until the age of twenty-one, and Peter Goodwin was required to "see the child baptized into the Christian faith & (as soon as she comes to majority) to teach or cause her to be taught the creed the Lords Prayer & the Tenne Comandments in the Vulgar tongue if she be capable to attaine unto the same." Peter Goodwin had duties similar to those of a godfather according to this indenture; even if he was not Hannah's actual godfather it still fell to him to educate her in the Christian faith. Unlike most other servants and slaves of African descent, Hannah would be brought up Christian, perhaps because she was also of English descent. Claiming that descent entitled the Banks children to baptism and its privileges—privileges that slaves did not get. But Hannah's indenture also reflected another growing assumption about the ability of blacks and mulattoes to become Christian; it mandated that she ought to be taught the catechism only if she proved herself "capable." Implicit in that requirement is the acknowledged possibility that Hannah Banks, mulatto indentured servant, might not have the innate capability to understand her catechism and truly be Christian. Only her English blood gave her the opportunity to try.[64]

Other mulatto servants' indentures also specified education. In 1703 John Bayly specified in his will that his "Mulatta Boy named William" be given both his freedom and fifteen pounds sterling. Bayly ordered that William stay with a Major Buckner "untill he Arrives at the Age above named [twenty-one] and also requested that the said Major to take care that the sd Boy be kept to School and brought up in the feare of God and Protestant Religion." At twenty-one, William was to use the money to leave the colony.[65] Like Hannah Banks, William's master allowed for his education, although he did not seem to doubt that William would be capable of learning "Protestant Religion." Like Hannah Banks and William Catillah, William's knowledge of Christianity served to include him in the Christian community, not exclude him. William's status as a mulatto was helpful rather than harmful. Not every mulatto servant's indenture specified education in the Christian religion as a requirement of the agreement. Abraham Royster, a mulatto bastard whose mother had apparently left York County while her son remained, signed a standard seven-year indenture to learn the trade of boatwright without any religious education at all.[66] Mulattoes, in other words, fit into a liminal space in which they sometimes could call upon their English heritage and their Christian ties for some protection, even after the 1667 baptism law discontinued the connection between baptism and freedom.

Slaves who were Christian seem to have had some other privileges, or at least their masters noted it as important. Anne Trotter left a slave to her godson Richard Dixon, identifying the slave as a "Negroe Girle named Elizabeth And Christned in Charles Parish Church to him and his heires for ever."[67] It seems likely that Elizabeth was intended to be a personal servant for Richard or eventually for his wife, suggesting that slaves who were actually part of the household were more likely to be baptized or accorded some Christian education. (It is also possible that Elizabeth was mulatto, though a slave, which might explain why she was baptized so readily.) Nevertheless, by the beginning of the eighteenth century, Elizabeth's experience was by far the exception rather than the rule. By then, not only had the English rejected the connection between baptism and freedom, they also had rejected the notion that baptizing Indians and Africans was necessary.

By denying the connection between baptism and freedom for Africans and Indians, English people were doing more than just perfecting the law of slavery. By questioning the ability of Africans to become Christian, settlers defined both their own religious and cultural identity and the identities of the Indians they lived beside and the Africans they owned. The 1705 Law of Servants and Slaves stated clearly that servants "of Christian parentage" who were themselves Christian could not serve past the age of twenty-four—a strong restatement of the idea of hereditary Christianity and how it still contributed to definitions of slavery. Yet a few paragraphs later, this law reiterated that baptism of "servants" could not result in freedom at any age.[68] "Christian" had come to mean white, English, and free. Only the English could be truly Christian—a New World innovation that would have profound consequences. In this sense, the 1667 law and its successor legislation was a crucial step in the English quest to comprehend and regulate human difference, by identifying themselves as Protestant Christians and their slaves as heathens incapable of Christian conversion.

Notes

1. William Waller Hening, ed. *The Statutes at Large: Being a Collection of All the Laws of Virginia,* 13 vols. (New York: R. W. G. & Bartow, 1819–1823), II, 260. Italics in original.

2. Oscar and Mary Handlin, "Origins of the Southern Labor System," *William and Mary Quarterly,* 3rd Ser., 7, no. 2 (April 1950), 211–12. Edmund Morgan argued in 1975 that the 1667 law seemed to encourage slave owners to instruct their slaves in

Christianity but actually removed all incentive for slaves to express interest in English religion. See Edmund Morgan, *American Slavery, American Freedom: The Ordeal of Colonial Virginia* (New York: W. W. Norton, 1975), 331–32. Other historians have also discussed the baptism law in this context, discussing it as part of the problem of slavery and freedom, and attributing its passage to fears generated among Virginia's gentry about changing demographic patterns: in other words, as African slaves became a greater percentage of the population, the English imagined the threat of more free, baptized blacks. See Warren Billings, "The Cases of Fernando and Elizabeth Key: A Note on the Status of Blacks in Seventeenth-Century Virginia," *William and Mary Quarterly*, 3rd Ser., 30, no. 3 (July 1973), 467–474; Edward Bond, *Damned Souls in a Tobacco Colony: Religion in Seventeenth-Century Virginia* (Macon, Ga.: Mercer University Press, 2000), 196–203. This demographic explanation, though, is unconvincing, since the real explosion of African slaves did not occur until after 1680; in 1667 there were only about two thousand Africans and as many as thirty-eight thousand English settlers in Virginia. When Anglo-Virginians shut the door on Christian baptism as a route to freedom, they still lived in a society with slaves, not a slave society fully dependent on bondage for economic stability, rendering the historical argument that the English were threatened by legions of free Christian Africans premature.

3. See, for example, Winthrop Jordan, *White Over Black: American Attitudes towards the Negro, 1550–1800* (Chapel Hill: University of North Carolina Press, 1968), 71–82, which discusses the statutory enactment of slavery in the Chesapeake, and Kathleen Brown, *Good Wives, Nasty Wenches, and Anxious Patriarchs: Gender, Race, and Power in Colonial Virginia* (Chapel Hill: University of North Carolina Press, 1996), 135–36. Anthony Parent has argued that Jordan's formulation of an "unthinking decision" is inaccurate; see Parent, *Foul Means: The Formation of a Slave Society in Virginia, 1660–1740* (Chapel Hill: University of North Carolina Press, 2003), 105–34.

4. On the uses and abuses of identity as a category of analysis, see Rogers Brubaker and Frederick Cooper, "Beyond 'Identity,'" *Theory and Society* 29, no. 1 (2000), 1–47; see especially 14–17 for the meaning of identity I have employed here.

5. John D. Krugler, *English and Catholic: The Lords Baltimore in the Seventeenth Century* (Baltimore: Johns Hopkins University Press, 2004), 13. Krugler goes on to argue that the fact that Lords Baltimore, the English Catholic founders of Maryland, were able to openly profess their Catholicism and still be in the service of the Crown indicates that the Protestant English suspicion of Catholics was not absolute. Nevertheless, it is fair to say that Catholics with less wealth and influence than the Calvert family would not have had an easy time of it.

6. David Cressy, *Birth, Marriage, and Death: Ritual, Religion, and the Life-Cycle in Tudor and Stuart England* (Oxford: Oxford University Press, 1997), 101.

7. "27th Article of the Faith," *Book of Common Prayer* (London, 1687), n.p.

8. Rebecca Anne Goetz, "From Potential Christians to Hereditary Heathens:

Religion and Race in the Early Chesapeake, 1590–1740" (PhD diss., Harvard University, 2006), 29–32.

9. Cressy, 108.

10. Hening, *The Statutes at Large*, II, 165–66.

11. Northampton County Court Records, 6 September 1665, fol. 11 (hereafter cited as NCCR).

12. Surry County Court Records, 7 January 1690/91, fol. 776–777 (hereafter cited as SCCR).

13. SCCR, 4 September 1672, fol. 7.

14. Susie Ames, ed., *County Court Records of Accomack-Northampton, Virginia, 1632–1640* (Washington, D.C.: American Historical Association Publications, 1954), 28 April 1639, 144.

15. York County Court Records, II, 25 July 1646, fol. 160 (hereafter cited as YCCR).

16. For John Foster see YCCR, II, 24 August 1648, fol. 400; for Elizabeth Lang, see NCCR, IX, 28 January 1677/78, fol. 225; for Hannah Harlow see NCCR, IX, 28 January 1667/78, fol. 225–226; for Jarrett and Anne Hawthorne see YCCR, V, 26 February 1671/72, fol. 8.

17. Historian Lorena Walsh first noted this practice in Maryland. See Lorena Walsh, "'Till Death Do Us Part:' Marriage and Family in Seventeenth-Century Maryland," in Thad W. Tate and David L. Ammerman, eds., *The Chesapeake in the Seventeenth Century* (New York: W. W. Norton, 1979), 147.

18. William P. Palmer, ed., *Calendar of Virginia State Papers and Other Manuscripts*, 11 vols. (1875–1893; New York: Kraus Reprint Corporation, 1968), 31.

19. See, for example, Accomack County Court Records, II, Will of Anne Browne, 16 September 1665, fol. 137a (hereafter cited as ACCR).

20. "A Letter of Sir Thomas Dale, from James Town in Virginia," 18 June 1614, in Samuel Purchas, ed., *Hakluytus Posthumus or Purchas his Pilgrimes, Contayning a History of the World in Sea Voyages and Lande Travills by Englishmen and Others*, vol. 19 (Glasgow, 1906; reprint from 1625 edition), 102.

21. Virginia M. Meyer and John Frederick Dorman, eds., *Adventurers of Purse and Person in Virginia 1607–1624/25*, 3rd ed. (Richmond: Dietz Press, 1987), 51, 62.

22. Susan Myra Kingsbury, ed., *Records of the Virginia Company of London*, 4 vols. (Washington, D.C.: Government Printing Office, 1906–1935), III, 117.

23. H. R. McIlwaine, ed., *Minutes of the Council and General Court of Colonial Virginia 1622–1637, 1670–1676* (Richmond: Virginia State Library, 1924), 31 March 1641, 477–78. (Hereafter cited as MCGC.)

24. "Nansemond Indian Ancestry of Some Bass Families," in Albert D. Bell, *Bass Families of the South* (Rocky Mount, N.C.: Privately printed, 1961), 12. For more on the Bass Family, see Helen C. Rountree and E. Randolph Turner III, *Before and After*

Jamestown: Virginia's Powhatans and their Predecessors (Gainesville: University Press of Florida, 2002), 151–52.

25. Hening, *The Statutes at Large,* I, 395.

26. Hening, *The Statutes at Large,* I, 455.

27. ACCR, II, 16 August 1667, fol. 33b and 35a; 25 October 1667, fol. 35a; 25 October 1667, fol. 40b-41a; 17 December 1667, fol. 44a-44b. See also 17 August 1668, fol. 62b for another case that looks similar to the 1667 renamings.

28. See, for example, ACCR, VII, 1 January 1683/84, fol. 28a; 6 August 1684, fol. 47; 2 December 1684, fol. 53a.

29. "Angelo a Negro Woman in the *Treasuror*" (no date), "Mary a Negro Woman in the *Margrett & John* 1622," and "John Pedro a Negar aged 30 in the *Swan* 1623." See *Adventurers of Purse and Person in Virginia 1607–1624/25,* 31, 48, 64.

30. Ibid., 51.

31. Ira Berlin, *Many Thousands Gone: The First Two Centuries of Slavery in North America* (Cambridge, Mass.: Belknap Press of Harvard University Press, 1998), 17. James W. Sweet agrees that those Africans in Virginia prior to 1630 had been exposed to Christianity and that allowed them to be more fully "integrated into the day-to-day affairs of English colonial life," but he questions the validity of the category of Atlantic Creoles. See James W. Sweet, "African Identity and Slave Resistance in the Portuguese Atlantic," in Peter C. Mancall, ed., *The Atlantic World and Virginia, 1550–1624* (Chapel Hill: University of North Carolina Press, 2007), 246.

32. MCGC, 30 November 1630, 33.

33. Ibid., 11 October 1627, 155.

34. Goetz, "From Potential Christians to Hereditary Heathens," 126–30.

35. On the early African population of Virginia, see Engel Sluiter, "New Light on the '20 and Odd Negroes' Arriving in Virginia, August 1619," *William and Mary Quarterly,* 3rd Ser., 54, no. 2 (April 1997), 395–398; John Thornton, "The African Experience of the '20. and Odd Negroes' Arriving in Virginia in 1619," *William and Mary Quarterly,* 3rd Ser., 55, no. 3 (July 1998), 421–34. On the ongoing questions of when and how Africans first came to the English colonies, see also Michael Guasco, "'Free from the Tyrannous Spanyard?' Englishmen and Africans in Spain's Atlantic World," *Slavery and Abolition* 29, no. 1 (January 2008), 1–22.

36. T. H. Breen and Stephen Innes, *"Myne Owne Ground": Race and Freedom on Virginia's Eastern Shore, 1640–1676* (New York: Oxford University Press, 1980), 8–10; Berlin, *Many Thousands Gone,* 29–31.

37. NCCR, IX, 29 September 1673, fol. 220.

38. Ibid., fol. 221.

39. Ibid.

40. NCCR, X, 11 March 1678/79, fol. 247.

41. NCCR, III, 27 May 1645, fol. 82.

42. Brent Tarter and John T. Kneebone, eds., *Dictionary of Virginia Biography*, vol. IV, s.v. "Emanuel Driggus," by Rebecca A. Goetz (forthcoming).

43. Breen and Innes, *Myne Owne Ground*, 68.

44. William Hand Browne, Hall, Clayton Colman, and Steiner, Bernard Christian, et al., ed., *Archives of Maryland*, 72 vols. (Baltimore: Maryland Historical Society, 1883–1972); I, 526, September 1664.

45. Ibid., III, March/April 1670/71, 272.

46. Hening, *The Statutes at Large*, II, 260.

47. MCGC 477.

48. Ibid.

49. YCCR, III, 26 January 1657/58, fol. 16.

50. Warren Billings, ed., *The Old Dominion in the Seventeenth Century: A Documentary History of Virginia* (Chapel Hill: University of North Carolina Press, 1075), 165–69. In 1654 Virginia did not yet have a law that explicitly made slave status hereditary through maternal lines (such a law passed in 1662). Thus the question of Elizabeth Key's parentage would have been very important. On the 1662 law, see Goetz, "From Potential Christians to Hereditary Heathens," 105–41.

51. Petition of William Whittacre to the Honourable Sir Wm. Berkeley Kinght Governor &c. And the Honourable Council of Virginia, ca. 24 October 1666, Randolph Mss, Virginia Historical Society. For a printed version of the petition, see Warren Billings, ed., *The Papers of Sir William Berkeley, 1605–1677* (Richmond: Library of Virginia, 2007), 297–98.

52. SCCR, I, 2 July 1659, fol. 82.

53. Hening, *The Statutes at Large*, II, 155. Surry County, writes Kevin Kelly, "was tobacco's child." See Kelly, "Economic and Social Development of Seventeenth-Century Surry County, Virginia" (PhD diss., University of Washington, 1972), 210.

54. Lower Norfolk County Order Book, 1666–1675, fol. 17. (Library of Virginia Microfilm.)

55. Hening, *The Statutes at Large*, II, 260. I am grateful to Chris Morris for suggesting that "more carefully" as used here might be plausibly interpreted to mean "more discerningly."

56. *Oxford English Dictionary*, s.v. "capability."

57. Morgan Godwyn, *A Supplement to the Negro's & Indian's Advocate* (London, 1681), 9.

58. Morgan Godwyn, *The Negro's & Indians' Advocate, Sueing for Their Admission into the Church* (London, 1680), 38.

59. Morgan Godwyn, "A Brief Account of Religion, in the Plantations," in Francis Brokesby, *Some Proposals towards Promoting of the Gospel in Our American Plantations* (London, 1708), 3. (Godwyn's piece was probably written, along with his other missives, in the early 1680s.) For more on Godwyn's biography, see Alden T. Vaughan,

"Slaveholders' 'Hellish Principles': A Seventeenth-Century Critique," in *Roots of American Racism: Essays on the Colonial Experience* (Oxford: Oxford University Press, 1995), 55–81.

60. Michael G. Kammen, ed., "Virginia at the Close of the Seventeenth Century: An Appraisal by James Blair and John Locke," *Virginia Magazine of History and Biography* 74, no. 2 (April 1966), 141–69; quotes on 166–67.

61. Samuel Clyde McCulloch, ed., "James Blair's Plan of 1699 to Reform the Clergy of Virginia," *William and Mary Quarterly*, 3rd Ser., vol. IV, no. 1 (January 1947), 70–86; 85–86.

62. Hugh Jones, *The Present State of Virginia: From Whence Is Inferred A Short View of Maryland and North Carolina*, ed. Richard L. Morton, (London, 1724; reprint Chapel Hill: University of North Carolina Press, 1956), 99.

63. YCCR, X, 6 April 1695 fol. 138; YCCR, X, 24 May 1695, fol. 153.

64. YCCR, VI, 24 June 1683, fol. 498; YCCR, XII, 24 November 1702, fol 67; YCCR, XII, 24 February 1703/04, fol. 181.

65. YCCR, XII, 24 May 1703, fol. 136.

66. YCCR, XIII, 25 February 1706/07, fol. 51.

67. YCCR, XI, 24 December 1700, fol. 401–402.

68. Hening, *The Statutes at Large*, III, 447–62.

West Indian Identity
in the Eighteenth Century

TREVOR BURNARD

What is a British West Indian? Moreover, what is a West Indian identity?[1] In the West Indies, identity has always been associated with race and with colonialism and with postcolonial legacies. We can see the importance of both topics in imaginative writings on West Indian identity (or lack of it) by the most important British West Indian authors.[2] We can also see it in the work of historians, for whom the question of identity, and its connection in the West Indies with the issue of race, is a central concern.[3]

I am particularly interested in this essay in how white West Indian identity was defined in the eighteenth century—an age when national identity came to be a subject of philosophical and historical discussion. I want to concentrate on these attempts at self-definition by white West Indians in the middle to late eighteenth century. At the same time I want to show how these ideas of a collective self were contested, principally by metropolitan Britons who increasingly disbelieved white West Indians' insistence that white West Indians were essentially British. They were also contested by black West Indians, who had little reason to accept that being West Indian was necessarily to accept the values and behaviors of white West Indians.[4] A collective sense of self is only partly determined by how a people define themselves. It is defined as much by other people, often, as in this case, in order to clarify their own collective identities. It was the peculiar difficulty of white West Indians that they came to be seen by the people that they most wanted to emulate—Britons—as being emblematic of troubling aspects of the British collective self. Much of this essay will revolve around white West Indian attempts to counter pervasive denigration from Britons and from North Americans, such as Benjamin Franklin, that white West Indians were not really as "British" or "English," as they claimed to be. As such, this essay is as much about the representation of identity and the acceptance of that representation by others as it is about the reality of identity itself.

White British North Americans and British West Indians aspired to a British identity, more specifically to be English, which was often a synecdoche for "British." They wished to be seen to be English enough in habits, behavior, and ideology to be in fact, and in English opinion, considered the equal of metropolitan Britons. They were insistent that their methods of governance and their institutional structures were so British as to be close to equivalent to those enjoyed in the mother country. Both British North Americans and British West Indians were to be disappointed in the refusal of metropolitan Britons to take their self-declared assertions of "Englishness" seriously. For British North Americans, British refusal of American claims to "Englishness" contributed greatly to their sense of abandonment in the political and constitutional crisis of the 1760s and to their eventual decision to break with Britain in 1776. Colonial North Americans were angry at metropolitan Englishmen who did not see colonists as they saw themselves. Their resentment was heightened by the fact that by the mid-eighteenth century British North America had achieved a significant resemblance to Britain in standard of living, in political and social institutions, and in material prosperity.[5]

The British West Indies, on the other hand, did not become anywhere near as Anglicized as did British North America, despite the efforts of Creole elites to insert English social and cultural patterns into the West Indian cultural dynamic. As Kathleen Wilson notes, "the West Indies retained in experience, imagination, and representation an ineffable otherness. Literally and figuratively islands of slavery, exploitation and physical and social death, they seemed to promise obliteration for the enslaved, the penurious, and the prosperous alike."[6] In short, the West Indies were places of radical instability. This was not only because of colonists' relentless push for wealth. British Caribbean slave society also allowed men to indulge their innermost desires, including sexual excess, ready violence, and social and cultural abandonment.

In the seventeenth century, all of Britain's American colonies were places of exotic barbarism, where European conventions were routinely flouted. By the mid-eighteenth century, however, British North America had moved beyond its early settlement phase.[7] Its residents could legitimately claim that they lived in civilized societies. When West Indians made such statements, as we shall see, they were not believable. Savagery lay very close to the surface in their colonies, because of the particular horror and violence of West Indian slavery.[8]

Some of the discomfort Britons felt about West Indian society was rooted in unease over manifestations of modernity. The slave plantation was the most advanced form of capitalism of the eighteenth-century. What some observers saw as planters' excessive individualism and indulgent self-expression was the "narcissistic self" often identified as a feature of twentieth-century Western society.[9] James Ramsay, an Anglican missionary to St. Kitts in the 1760s, became an abolitionist partly in revulsion at planters' self-involved and anti-religious behavior.[10] He scorned planters as belonging to "the kingdom of I." But this was not the most common criticism of white West Indians in the last quarter of the eighteenth century. Rather, contemporary observers believed that the British West Indian whites were reverting into barbarism.

It was Benjamin Franklin who most clearly articulated the idea that a chasm existed between British West Indian and British North American colonial societies. In his *Observations on the Increase of Mankind,* published in the middle of the Seven Years' War, Franklin argued that North American settlers had adapted remarkably well to the challenges of the New World, transforming a wilderness into a replica of the Old World. Moreover, he maintained that their society had the potential to become ever more important to Britain as a nation and to Britishness as a cultural ideal. This thesis rested on an argument that he had first rehearsed as early as 1729, that "the riches of a country are to be valued by the quantity of labor its inhabitants are able to purchase and not by the quantity of silver and gold they possess."[11]

By 1750, Franklin had become convinced that the only labor worth cultivating was free labor, and white labor in particular. Writing during the mid-eighteenth century heyday of West Indian prosperity and power, he offered a radically contentious proposition: that the population of Britain's northern mainland colonies, mainly white and mostly of British descent, was increasing at such a rate that before long it would surpass that of Britain. Moreover, these rapidly growing provinces with relatively few slaves would soon become more valuable to Britain than the more obviously wealthy southern colonies and West Indian islands. They were valuable precisely because their source of wealth was their ability to produce white people, "Britons" who "tho' a Hundred Years transplanted, and to the remotest part of the Earth, may yet retain . . . that *Zeal* for the *Publick Good,* that *military Prowess,* and that *undaunted Spirit,* which had in every Age distinguished their Nation."[12]

Franklin advanced a proposition that was to haunt American society for the next two centuries: that whiteness was "natural" and "American," while blackness was "foreign" and "un-American." Yet his idea of Northern whiteness, which pretended that African Americans had virtually no presence in the north, could not exist without a contrasting image of southern and West Indian blackness, just as Englishness needed non-Englishness to illustrate the particular advantages of English character.

Franklin's essay concluded with a plea to "whiten" North America by growing the English and English-descended population in the northern provinces rather than increasing the slave populations of the southern and especially the West Indian colonies: "Why increase the Sons of *Africa,* by planting them in *America,* where we have so fair an Opportunity by excluding all Blacks and Tawneys, of increasing the lovely White and Red?" The future of American prosperity, he argued, was in those places where the population was most clearly white (and by "white," he meant English or possibly British: he lamented the fact that Pennsylvania was filling up with German "Boors" rather than with Anglo-Americans, and he was not much more complimentary to the Scotch-Irish).

Franklin framed this argument with a critique of the British West Indies. He maintained that slavery, on which West Indian prosperity was based, was a bad investment in 1750, when interest rates were high in the colonies, and wages for manufacturing work were low in Britain. Moreover, slavery was inherently bad, he thought, "every slave being *by Nature* a *Thief*." Arguing that the most important economic value of a laborer was his or her character, he asserted that the character of Africans was uniformly bad. The author of *Poor Richard* lambasted Africans as dreadfully hopeless people with no work ethic. If Americans could "see and know, the extreme slovenliness of the West Indian slaves in making Molasses, and the Filth and Nastiness suffered to enter it, or wantonly thrown into it, their Stomachs would turn."[13] Slaves took spaces that could be profitably occupied by white immigrants, whose industry and frugality would eventually lead to greater prosperity.

Moreover, importing large numbers of enslaved Africans "infected" West Indian whites with African values and behaviors. When whites owned slaves, "the white Children became proud, disgusted with Labour and being educated in Idleness, are rendered unfit to get a living by Industry."[14] West Indians, in short, surrounded by Africans, dependent upon Africans, unable to grow their populations sufficiently to counteract African tendencies, were themselves turning into Africans, or into barbarians. Meanwhile the northern mainland colonies were becoming ornaments to British civilization, and eventually might surpass Britain itself in population and civility.[15] Franklin's sense of a virtuous America thus rested on a sense of northern difference from degenerate West Indian planters. Indeed, Franklin's disdain for West Indian slaveholders was designed to convince Britons that Americans were indubitably and provably British. The white West Indian was a convenient "other" for Franklin. This was a proposition that white West Indians increasingly encountered from Britain itself as the eighteenth century wore on.

Despite the efforts of Franklin and others, the British refused to accept American self-definitions of themselves as essentially English. As the American Revolution approached, more North Americans denounced the way Britons associated America with the West Indies. In Massachusetts, James Otis fulminated that settlers in the Caribbean were a "compound mongrel mixture of English, Indian and Negro," thereby implying in the language of the day that they were like Spanish Americans. In contrast, northern colonists were "free born British white subjects," as truly British as Britons themselves.[16]

In fact the British did share this low opinion of West Indians. In the phrase Britons used about American soldiers in southern England during World War II, West

Indians were "overpaid, oversexed and over here." Their prodigal spending attracted more condemnation than admiration. Part of this was jealousy; the West Indian absentee planter was a new social type that would become a stock figure of fun during Britain's nineteenth-century empire: the returning colonist as nouveau riche semi-foreigner of dubious origins and vulgar taste.[17] But there was more than envy. Not only were white West Indians having more fun than they ought but the pleasures they most enjoyed were especially sinful, because they involved transgressing civilized boundaries, especially the boundaries that separated the black body from that of the white body.

Samuel Foote presented this stereotype in his popular farce of 1761, *The Patron.* The character Sir Peter Pepperpot is a ludicrous figure, "a West Indian of overgrown fortune, who dreams of a woman who is as sweet as sugarcane, strait as a bamboo, and [with] teeth as white as a Negro, a plantation of perfection."[18] One plausible model for Pepperpot, William Beckford, a Jamaican-born former planter who had become a leading London merchant and the crusading Lord Mayor of London, was regularly denounced as "the Negro-whipping Beckford."[19] Despite all the economic benefits of the plantations and despite the clear value of the West Indies to the empire, white West Indians were met with little respect. These negative views had long-term consequences. One of the least recognized results of the American Revolution was that it was a disaster for West Indian planters, who loyally supported Britain.[20] Recent work by Andrew O'Shaughnessy and Christopher Brown suggests that British re-adjustments to the loss of America dramatically weakened planters' political leverage in Britain. I would like to suggest that white West Indians lost out in another way in the same period: planters lost a massive amount of cultural influence as the emerging abolitionist movement portrayed them as sex-obsessed tyrants who were fundamentally non-British in how they behaved toward their slaves, toward black women, and toward other Britons.[21]

Abolition occurred for a wide range of reasons, including changes in Britain's political climate, the rise of evangelical Christianity, and the growing awareness of the horrors of the slave trade. But distaste for West Indian planters also played a part. As Kathleen Wilson summarizes, "The fabulously wealthy Caribbean planter that emerged in fact and fiction came to represent the West Indian uncouthness, backwardness and degeneracy that inverted the acclaimed standards of civility and culture." The West Indian, she asserts, represented "that 'secret, underground Self' of English society."[22] Prominent among the deficiencies of West Indian national character was West Indian irreligiosity. Christopher Brown points out that opposition to slavery started as much from clergymen's distaste for slave owners' lack of religious sensibility as from genuine concern for the interests of Africans. As Brown comments, "If slaveholders in St. Kitts had permitted [James] Ramsay to instruct some of the enslaved men and women in his parish, his appetite for reform might have been satisfied."[23] Brown suggests that "by rejecting the ideal of Christian stewardship, [planters] forfeited the chance to present themselves as benign paternalists." The differences between the British West Indies and the American South are suggestive. The paternalist ethos established in the American South helped neutralize the antislavery movement by enabling masters to cast themselves as stewards and patrons, with slavery as a civilizing institution.[24]

The novelty of Britain's rising distaste for white West Indians after the 1780s is more obvious if one recognizes that abolitionists' values were not generally characteristic of late Georgian Britain. This was after all the age of Byron, Shelley, and Keats. West Indians had many attractive characteristics, by the lights of people who prided themselves on their modernity, liberalism, and lack of religious zeal. Defenders of the white West Indian character often pointed out that what abolitionists like Ramsay described as faults were, in fact, indicative of positive qualities in the British character. The historian Edward Long, British-born but descended from the Jamaican planter elite, affirmed that West Indian whites were good-looking, brave, good-natured, affable, generous, remarkably hospitable, and fond of enjoying themselves. In Long's telling, even some of their faults were endearing, such as their lack of attention to economy, their fondness for the other sex, and their passionate natures. That they were irreligious, keener on gaming, dogs and women than on going to church or reading books, may have offended upright evangelical Christians.

But not everyone shared such sober tastes. The cartoonists of late-eighteenth-century London illustrate that metropolitans of all conditions, especially men, were keen on bawdy and lewd laughter and were predisposed to sexual license, religious indifference, and rakish behavior.[25] If it was the age of Jane Austen and William Wilberforce, it was also the age of the Regency dandy and the Brighton Pavilion, of Lord Byron and dashing military heroes like Nelson and Wellington, each of whom was celebrated for his licentious reputation. In short, eighteenth-century London was not yet Victorian England; a culture war between puritans and libertines had begun but it had not yet decided in favor of sobriety.

Much like Franklin in the 1750s, British abolitionists in the 1780s and 1790s condemned the white West Indians in order to advance their own cause. By showing West Indian planters as deviant and un-British, abolitionists could demonstrate that their own movement represented the best elements of Britain's national character.[26] This specific historical context helps explain why white West Indians faced such fierce hostility in Britain.

But other forces were also at work in the metropolis, where in the wake of the American Revolution new understandings of imperial subjecthood and of "whiteness" were starting to take hold. These were partly based on contemporary understandings of race and climate. A common theme in descriptions of the West Indies was that the hot climate affected the very metabolism of white residents, changing the balance of the humors. Not only did this endanger Europeans as they became exposed to new diseases, it altered their very personality. Heat increased both license (in the sense of devotion to principles of liberty and self-assertion) and licentiousness (devotion to the pursuit of sensuality). People who lived in hot climates, therefore, had personalities different from people in cold climates. These "hot climate" personalities were usually considered as inferior. Hot climates made people slothful, addicted to vice and luxury, and overly concerned with momentary pleasures. Unsurprisingly, these were characteristics also assigned to Africans, preeminently the people Britons thought best suited to and most shaped by hot climates. When Europeans living in hot climates shared some of the attributes commonly given to Africans, it was a short step between showing distaste for what the climate was doing to Europeans and to thinking of Europeans as "infected" by African traits.[27]

We can see this in attitudes about two areas of white life in the West Indian tropics: interracial sexuality and the demographic failure of white West Indian society. Even their defenders acknowledged that the Achilles' heel of the white West Indian character was the frequent sexual relations that white men had with black women. There was a plenitude of evidence that white men customarily took sexual advantage of black women. Most plantations had numerous mixed-race slaves, and the white men in the islands frequently and openly lived with their black mistresses. White West Indian men waxed lyrical in print about the charms of black women. Bryan Edwards, an Englishman who inherited several Jamaican estates and became a prominent member of the Jamaican Assembly in the 1770s, may have been determined to uphold the honor of the West Indian interest. But his cause was hardly helped by his decision to publish in 1794 the Reverend Isaac Teale's 1765 "Ode to a Sable Venus," where the reverend author fetishized the erotic charms of black beauties. John Stedman's best-selling narrative of his exploits in Surinam was published in 1796 with etchings by William Blake that were dangerously close to pornographic in their depiction of black women subject to the white male gaze. Stedman's text confirmed the West Indies as a place of erotic encounter between white and black, where male desire could be satiated through forbidden erotic expression.[28]

Abolitionist attacks on white West Indians for their sexual molestation of black women struck at a particularly sore point. As Felicity Nussbaum has noted, the beginnings of the abolitionist campaign coincided with considerable cultural concern over miscegenation and racial mixing. It occurred, moreover, at a time when notions of biological racism were firming up. To be a Briton was to be white and to be white was a sign of inclusion within British society. Thus, evidence that West Indian planters were attracted more to black women than to white women not only damaged their moral reputation but suggested that they were not full members of the British nation.

Ironically, it was white West Indians themselves who first raised concerns about miscegenation. In the late eighteenth century, pro-slavery West Indians such as Philip

Thicknesse, James Tobin, and especially Edward Long warned that miscegenation resembled the crossing of different species. They claimed that racial mixture endangered the purity of the nation. Of course, these pro-slavery writers were using race to exclude black men and women from the British polity. But, in a move that not all West Indians anticipated (though Long certainly did), the image of white planters lusting after black women made those men themselves suspect, since their fondness for interracial sex showed that they were not keeping the white and nonwhite races distinct. As Nussbaum notes, "by the 1780s . . . as the movement for abolition began to gather force, the tide began to turn toward thinking that . . . mixed-race couples were as gnawingly unnatural as their American cousins had legislated them to be."[29]

The growing idea that racial mixing was non-British affected the very groups in British society that were most likely to find the white West Indian character appealing and abolitionism disagreeable. The indelible association of colonial planters with this behavior was crucial in leaching away support for white West Indians. As V. I. C. Gatrell argues, polite London society in the early abolitionist period was not very polite. It was not until the 1820s that bawdy, licentious behavior became an object of considerable social derision. The loose morality of West Indians and their tendency toward libertinism was not at odds with the prevailing culture in the 1780s: it was the abolitionist worldview that was alien and disturbing to the large numbers of men who enjoyed London's fleshpots. From the Prince Regent down to James Boswell, and further down to the low-life of the London neighborhoods of St. James and St. Giles, many Britons thought Wilberforce and his ilk were contemptible hypocrites and wanted no part of their social reform program. The amazing triumph of abolitionists in turning British opinion against slavery and against West Indians misleads us into thinking that West Indians had no body of natural supporters in Britain in the late eighteenth century. On the contrary, the wide popularity of scurrilous prints by caricaturists such as Isaac Cruikshanks and James Gillray shows that there was considerable opposition over a long period to the moral reformers of what was termed the Age of Cant. The men who flocked to see these prints should have formed a natural constituency for pro-slavery thought.[30]

To some extent, they did, of course, form such a constituency. But what is interesting to note in the prints that caricaturists made concerning slavery, the slave trade, race, and the West Indies is how often they associated West Indians with racial immorality. Gillray and Cruikshank both produced powerful plates protesting the treatment of slaves in the slave trade and in slavery, such as Cruikshank's 1792 attack on Captain Kember in *The Abolition of the Slave Trade* and Gillray's *Barbarities in the West Indies.* They also produced attacks on Wilberforce and other abolitionists that used racist images of miscegenation to accuse the abolitionists of indifference to English working-class distress. In famous prints such as Gillray's 1796 *Philanthropic Consolations after the Loss of the Slave Bill* and Cruikshank's 1819 masterpiece *The New Union Club,* the dominant mode of attack is to accuse abolitionists of promiscuous intercourse with oversexed and oversized black women. The problem for white West Indians was that what might be suggested by way of insult to Wilberforce could be suggested as fact about white West Indians—that West Indians were over familiar with black women. Gillray's images of blacks consorting with whites suggest a disapproval of what he saw as the overturning of proper order. Yet they also exhibit a prurient interest in white sexual behavior with black women, as in his 1788 engraving of the Duke of Clarence, son of the king, a prominent proslavery supporter, embracing a black mistress in a hammock.

The overwhelming sense of these prints is that while West Indians might be like other Britons in their liking for good times, their innate conservatism, freethinking, and dislike of moral hypocrisy, they were different from other Britons by dint of their fondness for black women. This aspect of white West Indian behavior alienated their natural supporters, Britons of a libertine disposition, whose racism and fear of miscegenation made them wary of identifying with people who seemed too keen on having sex and producing mixed-race children with black women.[31]

Britons also suspected that white West Indians' constant intercourse with Africans and their long residence in a debilitating tropical climate was turning them from "proper" white people into black people. What happened to the white body when exposed to hot sun and to African culture was a constant concern for white West Indians because they suspected that a long exposure to hot climates was what had made Africans themselves different from other people. Fear of Africanization is everywhere in white West Indian polemical writing. What was especially problematic for white West Indian writers was that the enormous economic triumph of sugar planting in the tropics was not matched by similar social and especially demographic success. Despite considerable white immigration into the British West Indies, the white population was barely able to sustain itself; in 1770 it was barely larger than it had been over a century earlier. The principal cause of white demographic failure was ferocious mortality among both newcomers and infant children. But white men's propensity to "riot in the goatish embraces" of their colored mistresses and their disinclination toward marriage with white women accentuated the white population crisis by keeping fertility rates very low. These demographic characteristics seemed to confirm arguments like those made by Benjamin Franklin that only in the northern American colonies could transplanted Britons reproduce and create properly Anglicized societies.[32]

Writers like Edward Long feared that the real reason the white population could not reproduce was over-fraternization with Africans. Colonists, Long believed, were deterred from coming to Jamaica—the largest British West Indian island and the island where the failure of a white population to establish itself was most obvious—because they were worried about the overwhelming presence of Africans, African values, and ultimately the degeneracy he believed inherent in the African people. His three-volume history of Jamaica was a valiant but in the end futile effort to demonstrate that the future of Jamaica was not to emulate the "mongrelisation" that he saw in the mestizo societies of Spanish America. Instead, the island should become as Anglicized and as white as Britain's colonies to the North. Long's work, in short, was an attempt to counter the slurs of writers like Franklin by asserting that white settlement in the West Indies was not ephemeral, that English-style local institutions were flourishing, and that white society was becoming ever more civilized and cultivated. But even while Long agreed with Franklin that Jamaica should be full of "lovely white" people, he realized that without black people places like Jamaica could not prosper.

Because Long wanted so much to believe that Jamaican planters were English gentlemen, he was blind to many of the deficiencies in white plantocratic behavior. His most notorious and indefensible comment was that planters were "humane and indulgent masters." He evinced a manifest prejudice not only against Africans but also against Jews, Irish, Spaniards, and Scots. Particular objects of his ire were free blacks, whom he felt were getting above themselves in their attempts to emulate whites. He approved heartily of the legislation introduced after Tacky's revolt in 1760 to limit the amount of money that free people of color could inherit from their fathers. What he wanted was for free people of color to remain in a state of poverty, able to act as a barrier between enslaved persons and whites but kept poor and barred from white professions to preserve racial boundaries. He strongly supported attempts made by white Jamaicans, emulating similar actions in neighboring Saint-Domingue, to codify racial nomenclature, making it harder for people of color to be able to pass as white.[33]

Nevertheless, even Long's willful blindness to the realities of the demographic situation of white West Indians and wishful hope that the West Indies would become places of large and anchored white populations was not sufficient to allow him to elide some of the more painful truths about white West Indian social mores. He was forced to admit that white Jamaicans were overly influenced by close contact with Africans. Significantly, he did not place the blame for such cultural closeness on the white men who could not stop themselves from frolicking with colored women, thus producing "spurious offspring." Instead, he charged white women with the most egregious cultural offenses. In a famous passage, he castigated white women for their over-closeness to black domestics, which he felt helped to explain why white men turned away from marrying them. White Creole women, he contended, "who have been bred up entirely in the sequestered country parts, and had no opportunity of forming themselves either by example, are truly to be pitied." He elaborated on a tableau of his imagining, in which "a very fine young woman" sits "dangling her arms with the air of a Negroe-servant, lolling about almost the whole day upon beds or settees, her head muffled up with two or three handkerchiefs, her dress loose, and without stays ... gobbling pepper-pot ... with her sable hand-maids around her." When roused to talk, "her speech is whining, languid, and childish" while "her ideas are narrowed to the ordinary subjects that pass before her, the business of the plantation, the tittle-tattle of the parish; the tricks, superstitions, diversions, and profligate discourses, of black servants, equally illiterate and unpolished."[34]

Much of this diatribe is standard eighteenth-century misogyny. But the adverse comments about the dress of the white women reveal a specific fear that Long had concerning white women—the markers, after all, in tropical societies of what constituted the boundaries of whiteness, as the people centrally involved in the reproduction of white children.[35] In the mid eighteenth century, racial difference was very much correlated to physical appearance. It was also correlated strongly to gender. The black body was depicted differently from the white body, meaning that if stark differences between the two, especially in regard to adornment, could not be perceived, then the cultural attributes accorded to the one could be also assumed to pertain to the other. The distinctions between the white female body and the black female body in illustrations of West Indian people were meant to be sharp. White women were dressed; black women were not. The black body was both objectified and also stripped of outside adornment. Invariably the black woman was depicted, as in *The Sable Venus* or in the paintings of William Blake that accompanied Stedman's text, or in the prints of Agostino Brunias, such as *The Washerwoman,* as naked or near naked. This nakedness indicated not just the erotic gaze of white men but also was connected with savagery and with lack of civility.[36]

All of these features of the representation of the female black body in the New World are well known. What is only sometimes appreciated, however, is how often representations of women of color slipped from depicting black bodies to saying something interesting about the female white body, as well. Felicity Nussbaum notes this in her penetrating study of changing performances of Thomas Southerne's *Oroonoko* (1695) in the eighteenth century. Southerne's play was itself a remaking of Aphra Behn's earlier (1688) play of the same name. Nussbaum shows that the "beautiful black Venus to our young Mars," Imoinda, turns white over different playings of the drama. But even when white, her whiteness is challenged by her adornment. Nussbaum displays a print of Mrs. Kemble as Imoinda in 1791. It shows how although much of her dress is unmistakably English, showing up her civilized whiteness, her headdress marks her as foreign and exotic. Moreover, to people attuned to visual depictions of black and colored women, the headdress suggested blackness and Africanness. As Nussbaum notes, "in the nineteenth century scientific racism elided differences into an increasingly rigidified division between black and white but in the eighteenth century the relationships between costume and geography, pigmentation and the faculties of the mind, bodily features and character, and social privilege and 'blood' remained inconsistent and uncertain, deemed to be both performative and foundational."[37] Nussbaum also notes that the staging of the play changed notably in the 1780s, just as the abolitionist movement got under way and at a time when fears over miscegenation were beginning to become pronounced. Whereas earlier eighteenth-century productions had treated interracial sexual relations as unfamiliar but enticingly erotic possibilities, from the 1780s the stress was on depicting interinterracial unions as deeply unnatural. As she states, "diverse theatrical representations of Southerne's *Oroonooko* ... helped negotiate attitudes towards the masquerade of race even as it remained an urgent matter to articulate the whiteness of femininity."[38] In short, the whiteness of white women became increasingly more evident in performances.

Try as they might, white West Indians were unable to erect the racial boundaries they wished for in their societies after the mid eighteenth century. The problem was that it was more difficult than theorists thought to distinguish between what was white and what was not white in West Indian social life. Despite attempts to codify racial identities more rigorously in the latter part of the eighteenth century, such identities were in fact becoming less distinct, as clothing, especially the clothing of women, illustrates. A skilled observer ought to have been able to distinguish which women belonged to which social category, by reference to their birth, color, or sense of fashion. White women dressed in one way, free colored women in another way, slaves in a third way. In the absence of sumptuary laws, such distinctions in dress were merely customary rather than prescribed. But as can be seen in Agostino Brunias's paintings of West Indian scenes, distinguishing women by dint of clothing and color is difficult. One reason for the difficulty is that all the women pictured wear headdresses or head wraps, or what Jamaicans call tie wraps. With this accessory, white women succumbed to what white observers feared most, the conscious adoption of African cultural forms. Long, for example, noted that wearing head wraps was an African custom. In all likelihood, wearing such adornment was a form of African self-identification.[39]

For Long, however, a keen observer of clothing among both whites and blacks (he devotes several pages of his history to a detailed analysis of European dress in the tropics), African use of the head wrap could be attributed to a mixture of physiognomy and climate. Africans wore head wraps, he presumed, so that they could be protected from the rain, as "perhaps their woolly fleece would absorb it in great quantities and give them a cold." But Long recognized that practicalities were also tied up with matters of style, and that women of all colors thought a headdress to be an attractive and vital component of female attire in the tropics. Free colored women, he noted, adopted and adapted the headdress to such an extent that it became a marker of their identity. They "think themselves not completely dressed without this tiara and buy the finest cambric or muslin for the purpose."[40]

White women also used the head wrap. Long thought they did so in order to avoid the sun and the damage it did to their skin. He stated that "the Creole White Ladies till recently adopted the practice so far, as never to venture a journey without securing their complexions with a brace of handkerchiefs; one of which is tied over the forehead, the other under the nose and covering the lower part of the face, formed a large helmet." It is an interesting statement, telling us much about the intersection of race, class, and identity among whites in the British West Indies. On the one hand, Long suggests that the intention behind wearing a headdress was to preserve white complexion. Male commentators sometimes tried to explain their predilection for colored women as being related to their distaste for how the tropical skin discolored white women's pigmentation. The libertine John Stedman contemptuously described white women in the West Indies as "a poor, languid generation, with complexions not much better than that of a drumskin." Brown women, he thought, were much more attractive. He waxed lyrical about the color of his "Surinam wife," Joanna, "Goddess like . . . with Cheeks through which glow'd in spite of her Olive Complexion, a beautiful tinge of vermilion when gazed upon."[41]

On the other hand, as seems clear in the prints of Brunias, when white women wore a head wrap, just as did black and colored women, the distinctions that were meant to exist between women of different colors became blurred. The distinctions that were meant to exist, in any case, did not really exist, when we compare the social and economic position of ordinary white women and their free colored counterparts. The similarities in condition and outlook, as well as appearance, of unmarried white women and free brown women, make it difficult to distinguish between them. Each group, especially in urban areas, where the majority of free women of both races congregated, had similar levels of wealth, roughly the same patterns of slave ownership, similar exclusion from political structures controlled by white men, and lived in roughly similar living arrangements. They competed against each other in similar occupations (the ownership of boarding houses and the provision of services, from providing slave seamstresses to prostitutes, being common areas of competition) and shared the same proclivity to conspicuous display. This love of display was especially obvious in their dress and love of partying. Male commentators found these similarities disturbing because they wanted white women to confine their cultural activities to their reproductive function as the progenitors of a new generation of authentically white Jamaican children. Yet white women were unable to achieve this aim, in part because so few white men chose to marry them (rates of cohabitation in Kingston between white women and white men were remarkably high by contemporary British standards) and because they produced very few surviving children.[42]

If white women were like black or brown women, then the whole project of white settlement was endangered. For this reason, as Edward Long well knew and as he articulated in his history, gender relations depicted the true nature of West Indian creolization, where whites were influenced as much by African as by British cultural inheritances. White women aping black women's mode of dress was as powerful an indictment of the failure of white colonization in the British West Indies as white men rejecting the "joys of matrimony and connubial bliss" in order to "riot in the goatish embraces" of colored mistresses. Whiteness was endangered by the dereliction of gender rules.

Notes

1. For an intriguing introduction to this question, by a sympathetic outsider to the West Indies, see Catherine Hall, "What is a West Indian?" in Bill Schwarz, ed., *West Indian Intellectuals in Britain* (Manchester: Manchester University Press, 2003), 31–50.

2. Two contrasting studies of West Indian identity in the modern world by leading Trinidadian intellectuals, both written at the same time, are C. L. R. James, *Beyond a Boundary* (London: Stanley Paul, 1963) and V.S. Naipaul, *The Middle Passage: Impressions of Five Societies—British, French and Dutch in the Wst Indies and South America* (London: Andre Deutsch, 1962).

3. A useful definition of how early American historians might understand identity can be found in Jack P. Greene, *Imperatives, Behaviors & Identities; Essays in Early American Cultural History* (Charlottesville: University of Virginia Press, 1992), 113–14.

4. For an attempt to examine what blacks thought of whites in a different colony in a slightly later period, see John Lean and Trevor Burnard, "Hearing Slave Voices: The Fiscal's Reports of Berbice and Demerara-Essequebo," *Archives* 27, no. 106 (2002), 37–50.

5. Jack P. Greene, *Pursuits of Happiness: The Social Development of Early Modern British Colonies and the Formation of Early American Culture* (Chapel Hill: University of North Carolina Press, 1988), 170–210, and T. H. Breen, *The Marketplace of Revolution: How Consumer Politics Shaped American Independence* (New York: Oxford University Press, 2004). For my thoughts on these subjects as they referred to the Chesapeake, see Trevor Burnard, *Creole Gentlemen: The Maryland Elite, 1691–1776* (New York: Routledge, 2002).

6. Kathleen Wilson, *The Island Race: Englishness, Empire and Gender in the Eighteenth Century* (New York and London: Routledge, 2003), 130. For an exploration of death in Jamaica, see Vincent Brown, *The Reaper's Garden: Death and Power in the World of Atlantic Slavery* (Cambridge, Mass.: Harvard University Press, 2008).

7. For seventeenth century barbarism, see Bernard Bailyn, *Atlantic History: Concept and Contours* (Cambridge, Mass.: Harvard University Press, 2005), 62–72.

8. For a discussion of the tensions between Enlightenment thinking and savage behavior in mid-eighteenth century Jamaica, see Trevor Burnard, *Mastery, Tyranny, and Desire: Thomas Thistlewood and His Slaves in the Anglo-Jamaican World* (Chapel Hill: University of North Carolina Press, 2004), 101–36.

9. The modernity of the West Indian slave system and planter class is made clear in Robin Blackburn, *The Making of New World Slavery: From the Baroque to the Modern 1492–1800* (London: Verso, 1997).

10. James Ramsay, "Motives for the Improvement of the Sugar Colonies," Additional MSS 27621, British Library, ff. 44, 69.

11. Benjamin Franklin, "A Modest Enquiry into the Nature and Necessity of a Paper-Currency," Leonard W. Labaree, et al., *The Papers of Benjamin Franklin* (New Haven: Yale University Press, 1959–) I: 142–56.

12. "Observations Concerning the Increase of Mankind," in *Papers of Benjamin Franklin*, 4: 225–34.

13. David Waldstreicher, *Runaway America: Benjamin Franklin, Slavery and the American Revolution* (New York: Hill and Wang, 2004), 176.

14. "Observations."

15. Ibid., 133–39.

16. James Otis, *The Rights of the British Colonies Asserted and Proved* (Boston, 1764) in Bernard Bailyn, ed., *Pamphlets of the American Revolution, 1750–1776* (Cambridge, Mass.: Harvard University Press, 1965), I: 435–36.

17. Andrew O'Shaughnessy, *An Empire Divided: The American Revolution and the British Caribbean* (Philadelphia: University of Pennsylvania Press, 2000), 10–17.

18. Samuel Foote, *The Patron* (London, 1764), 13.

19. O'Shaughnessy, *An Empire Divided*, 14.

20. O'Shaughnessy, "The Formation of a Commercial Lobby: The West India Interest, British Colonial Policy and the American Revolution," *Historical Journal* 40 (1997), 71–95, and Lillian M. Penson, "The London West India Interest in the Eighteenth Century," *English Historical Review* 30 (1921), 373–92.

21. Eric Williams, *Capitalism and Slavery*, (Chapel Hill: University of North Carolina Press, 1944); O'Shaughnessy, *Empire Divided*; Christopher Leslie Brown, *Moral Capital: Foundations of British Abolitionism* (Chapel Hill: University of North Carolina Press, 2006).

22. Wilson, *Island Race*, 130.

23. Brown, *Moral Capital*, 74.

24. Sylvia R. Frey, *Water from the Rock: Black Resistance in a Revolutionary Age* (Princeton: Princeton University Press, 1991), 243–83, and Jon Butler, "Enlarging the Bonds of Christ: Slavery, Evangelism, and the Christianization of the White South," in Leonard I. Sweet, ed., *The Evangelical Tradition in America* (Macon, Ga.: Mercer University Press, 1984), 98–112.

25. Vic Gatrell, *City of Laughter: Sex and Satire in Eighteenth-Century London* (London: Atlantic Books, 2006).

26. Ben Wilson, *Decency and Disorder: The Age of Cant 1789–1837* (London: Faber, 2007).

27. For the effect of hot climates on Europeans, see Karen Ordahl Kupperman, "Fear of Hot Climates in the Anglo-American Colonial Experience," *William and Mary Quarterly* 41 (1984), 213–40. For white understanding of African character, see

Winthrop D. Jordan, *White over Black: American Attitudes toward the Negro, 1550–1812* (Chapel Hill: University of North Carolina Press, 1968); Roxann Wheeler, *The Complexion of Race: Categories of Difference in Eighteenth-Century British Culture* (Philadelphia: University of Pennsylvania Press, 2000); and the essays in "Constructing Race," *William and Mary Quarterly*, 3rd Ser., XLIV (1997), 1–252. An important work on geo-humoralism is Mary Floyd-Wilson, *English Ethnicity and Race in Early Modern Drama* (Cambridge: Cambridge University Press, 2003).

28. Teale's poem can be found in Marcus Wood, *The Poetry of Slavery: An Anglo-American Anthology 1764–1865* (Oxford: Oxford University Press, 2003), 30–35. For Stedman, see Richard Price and Sally Price, *Stedman's Surinam: Life in an Eighteenth-Century Slave Society* (Baltimore: Johns Hopkins University Press, 1992), and Marcus Wood, *Slavery, Empathy and Pornography* (Oxford: Oxford University Press, 2003), 87–140.

29. Felicity A. Nussbaum, *The Limits of the Human: Fictions of Anomaly, Race, and Gender in the Long Eighteenth Century* (Cambridge: Cambridge University Press, 2003) 187, 250–51, 255; David Dabydeen, *Hogarth's Blacks: Images of Blacks in Eighteenth Century English Art* (Kingston-on-Thames: Dangaroo, 1985); Robert J. C. Young, *Colonial Desire: Hybridity in Theory, Culture and Race* (London: Routledge, 1985), 8; Philip Thicknesse, *A Year's Journey Through France, and Part of Spain*, 2nd. ed. (London, 1778), II:102; James Tobin, *Cursory Remarks Upon the Reverend Mr. Ramsay's Essay on the Treatment and Conversion of African Slaves in the Sugar Colonies* (London, 1785), 118; Edward Long, *History of Jamaica*, 3 vols. (London, 1774).

30. Gatrell, *City of Laughter*.

31. Ibid., 552–53; Nussbaum, *Limits of the Human*, 250.

32. Trevor Burnard, "European Migration to Early Jamaica, 1655–1780," *William and Mary Quarterly*, 3rd Ser., 53, (1996), 769–96; idem, "'The Countrie Continues Sicklie': White Mortality in Jamaica, 1655–1780," *Social History of Medicine* 12 (1999), 45–72; idem, "A Failed Settler Society: Marriage and Demographic Failure in Early Jamaica," *Journal of Social History* 28 (1994), 63–82; Long, *History of Jamaica*, II: 328.

33. Long, *History of Jamaica*, II: 289, 293–300. For the hardening of racial categories in Saint Domingue, see John Garrigus, "Redrawing the Colour Line: Gender and the Social Construction of Race in Pre-Revolutionary Haiti," *Journal of Caribbean History* 30 (1996), 28–50.

34. Long, *History of Jamaica*, II: 279.

35. Ann Laura Stoler, "Sexual Affronts and Racial Frontiers: European Identities and the Politics of Exclusion in Colonial Southeast Asia, *Comparative Studies in Society and History* 34 (1992), 514–51.

36. See Kay Dian Kriz, "Marketing Mulàtresses in the Paintings and Prints of Agostino Brunias," in Felicity Nussbaum, ed., *The Global Eighteenth Century* (Baltimore: Johns Hopkins University Press, 2003) 195–210; Kay Dian Kriz and Geoff

Quilley, eds., *An Economy of Colour: Visual Culture and the Atlantic World, 1660–1820* (Manchester: Manchester University Press, 2003); and Beth Fowkes Tobin, *Picturing Imperial Power: Colonial Subjects in Eighteenth-Century British Painting* (Durham: Duke University Press, 1999).

37. Nussbaum, *Limits of the Human,* 150, 178–88.

38. Ibid., 187.

39. Kay Dian Kriz, *Slavery, Sugar, and the Culture of Refinement* (New Haven: Yale University Press, 2008).

40. Long, *History of Jamaica,* II: 413. For an analysis of female dress, see Steeve O. Buckridge, *The Language of Dress: Resistance and Accommodation in Jamaica, 1760–1890* (Kingston: University of the West Indies Press, 2004), 60–70.

41. Price and Price, *Stedman's Surinam,* 22.

42. Trevor Burnard, "'Rioting in Goatish Embraces: Marriage and Improvement in Early British Jamaica, 1660–1780," *History of the Family* 12, no. 1 (2007), 185–97; idem, "'Gay and Agreeable Ladies': White Women in Mid-Eighteenth-Century Kingston, Jamaica," *Wadabagei* 9, no. 3 (2006), 27–49; idem, "Countrie remains Sicklie."

Illegal Enslavement and the Precariousness of Freedom in Nineteenth-century Brazil

SIDNEY CHALHOUB

A law enacted on November 7, 1831, prohibited the African slave trade to Brazil. It declared free all Africans taken to the country after that date and established legal sanctions to be applied to traffickers and to those who bought captives aware of their origins in the illegal trade.[1] The Brazilian parliament passed the bill mainly due to the pressure of the British government;[2] however, it seems that Brazilian authorities never intended to enforce such law, which faced the opposition of the planter class, soon to become even stronger as a result of the expansion of coffee cultivation in the southeastern provinces of the Empire. From the early 1830s to the early 1850s, more than seven hundred thousand Africans are deemed to have been illegally smuggled into the country. The law of 1831 abolishing the trade became a matter for derisory laughter, and it even seems to have originated a phrase still existent in Brazilian Portuguese: *para inglês ver*, that is, "for the English to see," meaning something that everyone knows is not to be taken seriously.

A Historical Problem Turned Upside Down

The lack of enforcement of the law of 1831 is thus a well-established historical fact, and that leads us to another point of entry. Robert Conrad offers a detailed description of the attempts to revoke the law of 1831 during the years immediately following its enactment.[3] He shows that the marquis of Barbacena made a conspicuous attempt in 1837, a little before the coming to power of Bernardo Pereira de Vasconcelos, who hinted unequivocally that he had no intention of enforcing that piece of antislavery legislation. Barbacena deemed the law of 1831 unenforceable and argued that its only effect had been to stimulate the energy and inventiveness of importers, who had devised sophisticated ways to avoid being caught by local officials upon arrival, to hide the Africans until they could be safely taken to plantations, and even to teach them a few words in Portuguese, so that they could pass as captives arrived at an earlier period. The marquis proceeded to say that never before had a law been disobeyed for "such plausible reasons," since planters could not be reproached for seeking the growth of their fortunes—this was a "natural," "irresistible desire" common to all humans. He thought that the planters who had been buying Africans since 1831 had done so in good faith—they were "peaceful landlords, heads of respectable families, men full of industry and virtue" who promoted the public good as they sought prosperity for themselves. Finally, the marquis said that planters were justified in buying the people offered to them as slaves because they needed laborers and could not know the origin of the Africans brought by itinerant traders.

It is clear that the marquis of Barbacena was concerned with the fact that a constantly increasing part of the slave property existent in the country was illegal, originating in contraband. Thus he advanced an astute proposal to solve the problem. The law of 1831 should be revoked and replaced by another law, surely one that would maintain the objective of stopping the African slave trade, but based on the idea that vigilance and repression should be strictly limited to the sea and harbors. In other words, the government should seek to establish an efficient apparatus to prevent traffickers from disembarking Africans along the Brazilian coast, and the Africans captured in the sea or harbors had to have their freedoms guaranteed. However, once an African had been introduced to the hinterland, he or she became a legal asset, a bona fide property to be freely bought and sold. The proposal of the marquis of Barbacena succeeded in the Senate, but stalled in the Chamber of Deputies, certainly due to the protests of the British government, which had obviously understood what was about to happen. Nonetheless, what I find most interesting in Robert Conrad's rendering of all this is his final remark regarding the practical consequences of this seemingly failed attempt to revoke the law of 1831. He says that although Barbacena's proposed bill was not approved, its public discussion provided slaveholders with a justification and a degree of legitimacy to the de facto enslavement of hundreds of thousands of people whose status as captives the marquis had attempted to confirm and legalize.[4]

If I understand this correctly, the classic historical approach to the law of 1831 must be turned upside down. Historians have emphasized the fact that the law was not enforced and have sought to understand the motives for such outcome. In contrast, Conrad suggests that there existed a bill which, despite not having been approved, was diligently enforced by slaveholders and, as we shall see, public authorities as well. The piece of non-approved legislation seemed to substantiate a practice that became increasingly a *customary seigneurial right* during the 1830s, that of randomly and massively enslaving Africans smuggled into the country and their Brazilian-born descendants as well. To achieve this, slaveholders relied on the cautious consent of successive imperial administrations and the overt cooperation of local officials. Furthermore, there became firmly established and operative in daily life the notion that blacks were to be seen and treated as slaves unless clear evidence appeared to prove otherwise. This is not to say that illegal enslavement was a new practice in Brazil. However, after the 1830s it became a critical aspect of why the planter class supported the newly established monarchical regime in independent Brazil. On the one hand, the anti-slave trade law of 1831 posed a potential threat to the planter class since it meant that a good part of the slave property held by landholders could be legally challenged at some point. On the other hand, this very same threat made coffee planters rally around the throne. The monarchical regime and its defense of large estates and slavery became the pillars of planters' dominance of Brazilian society.

Recently historians have renewed their interest in the law of 1831. Without challenging its lack of impact on the slave trade, researchers emphasized the law's enduring political and social consequences during the Empire. Eduardo Pena and Lenine Nequette show that the controversy over whether the law of 1850, which did effectively end Brazil's African slave trade, revoked the law of 1831 became an important legal question that affected planters' ability to control their slaves.[5] Indeed, the law of 1831 eventually became a decisive element in the strategies of slaves and their allies in the struggle for freedom. Elciene Azevedo[6] argues that in the 1860s the abolitionist, lawyer, and ex-slave Luiz Gama used the law of 1831 to file freedom suits in the São Paulo courts, at the same time that the British were pressuring Brazil about the fate of the *africanos livres*—that is, Africans who were seized from illegal slave ships, declared formally free, and put under the guardianship of the imperial government. All the Africans introduced after the law of 1831 were *africanos livres*, Gama maintained, not only those intercepted by British warships and given to the imperial government. Several historians—Joseli Mendonça, Keila Grinberg, Hebe Mattos, and me, among others—have found petitions for freedom in different counties and regions of the country in which the enslaved sought their liberty, claiming to have been imported after 1831.[7] More recently, Beatriz Mamigonian has concluded the best and most comprehensive study to date on the *africanos livres*, exploring the ways in which the experience of these few thousand people may have resonated in the strategies and visions of slavery and freedom of hundreds of thousands of others, whose bondage derived from the illegal trade and who were not caught by British or Brazilian authorities.[8]

The defense of illegal enslavement made freedom deeply precarious for all black Brazilians. This paper focuses on how these two themes were connected. In Brazil from the 1830s into the 1860s all Africans and Brazilian-born descendants of Africans, black or *pardo* (mulatto), freeborn or manumitted, were threatened by the customary seigneurial right to enslave people regardless of the law. I seek to observe both how public authorities enforced the seigneurial right to enslave illegally, and how Africans and their Brazilian descendants dealt with this situation. For, as Brazilian masters followed Barbacena's lead and ignored the law of 1831, they strengthened and/or created a variety of shared assumptions, daily practices, and institutional procedures that made all Africans "natural" slaves and severely limited the meaning of freedom for almost everyone else identified as carrying some degree of Africanness. One of the revelations of this paper is the ways Brazilian authorities determined what constituted "Africanness."

Assumptions about Slavery and Freedom.

I start with an episode in which public authorities themselves discussed and devised a course of action illustrating the connection between illegal enslavement and the precariousness of freedom.

Eusébio de Queiróz eventually became a prominent politician and minister associated with the Conservative Party. He led the cabinet that enacted the law of September 1850 that again prohibited the African slave trade to Brazil and this time achieved the proposed end—in fact, the bill became known as the Eusébio de Queiróz Law. For an extended period in the 1830s and early 1840s Eusébio served as the chief of police of the court—that is, the city of Rio de Janeiro—a job which put him in charge, among other things, of repressing the illegal slave trade.[9]

In November 1835, Limpo de Abreu, then minister of justice, wrote to the chief of police about how the police dealt with blacks arrested in Rio on suspicion of being runaway slaves. It is probable that the minister demanded these explanations from the chief of police because he had become aware that some blacks were living for long periods in the slave jail or *calabouço*, without their supposed masters reclaiming them or the police investigating their status. A previous regulation issued by the Ministry of Justice, dated August 12, 1834, had requested that "all slaves apprehended and held in the *calabouço* for six months and not reclaimed by their masters be sent to the Judge of Orphans and there declared *bens de ausentes*"—that is, "unclaimed property" belonging to an absent or unknown owner. The regulation stipulated that these individuals should be publically auctioned to new masters. It also established that the police should publish a monthly account of these detained but unclaimed slaves, with "names, features and other information" that might clarify their condition and aid in their identification by alleged masters.[10] In November 1835, the minister of justice wanted the chief of police to inform him of what exactly was being done to ascertain that any given black person arrested for appearing to be a runaway slave was really a runaway slave. Clearly uneasy, Eusébio de Queiróz answered thus: "I have the honor to inform Your Excellency that given the custom of most runaway blacks to declare themselves freed when they are arrested, those who are presumed to be runaways due to any circumstance are sent to the *calabouço*, regardless of the fact that they say that they are free; however, in case they present a document, or if after six months no one appears to reclaim them, even if the black does not submit his letter of liberty, he is maintained under the control of the Justice of the Peace of the 1st district of S. José, so that the judge can verify if he is free, and in this case liberate him. This is the usual practice."[11] The minister of justice surmised that the chief of police actually did nothing to investigate the status of black people arrested as runaway slaves. Eusébio de Queiróz simply waited for at least six months to see if the detained person would present a document that proved his or her liberty, or if someone would appear alleging to be his or her master. Meanwhile, the prisoner worked in government institutions or in public works. The minister expected swift action and gave the following guidelines to the official who would draft his answer: "Reply that as soon as there are blacks apprehended, that are deemed to be slaves, and runaways, [the police] must not only publish immediately in the newspapers their physical features to make it possible for the masters to appear, but also proceed *ex officio* to verify their condition in case they state that they are freed, either seeking information in the places that they say that they resided, or conducting other investigations so that it is not necessary to keep these individuals in the *calabouço* uselessly for such a long time, without the police seeking to find out the truth, and they are to be released in case the due investigations do not result in evidence regarding their captivity."[12] In other words, the minister determined that if there was no evidence confirming the bondage of a person who claimed to be free, the police should presume that he or she was free. Of course, Eusébio de Queiróz promised to follow the orders received, but he did not hesitate to offer his viewpoint on the matter: "It is my duty to remark that since it is not easy to obtain proof of slavery, when a black insists that he is free, these procedures will necessarily entail the setting free of many fugitive slaves, however cautious we are; *it seems to me that it is more reasonable, in the case of blacks, to presume their bondage,* until they present a certificate of baptism or a letter of liberty to prove otherwise; however, I assure Your Excellency that your orders will be obeyed strictly, unless others to the contrary follow suit" [my emphasis].[13] Perhaps impatient with the stubbornness of his subordinate, Limpo de Abreu answered that the execution of the new mandatory procedures would reduce the probability of releasing fugitive blacks: on the one hand, the police had the obligation to seek the publication of the names and features of the blacks under arrest; on the other hand, the answers offered by the blacks had to be checked by the police—that is, they were expected to go to the places where the supposedly enslaved said they lived to check the veracity of their stories and to talk with people who could confirm their freedom. The minister expected that the adoption of such routines would diminish the duration of the stay of captives in the *calabouço,* besides preventing the detention of free people unnecessarily or for long periods.

As it happened, nonetheless, Limpo de Abreu was soon gone from the Ministry of Justice. Other ministers came and went, but Eusébio de Queiróz remained the all-powerful chief of police of the capital of the Empire for years to come. He built a reputation punishing gangs of robbers, counterfeiters, and street fighters or *capoeiras;* he persecuted and often jailed beggars and vagrants, attacking what he saw as the "scum" of society, people "who wandered about without a job or a place to live."[14] Furthermore, he reorganized the police and structured modes of vigilance and repression that would shape the future of the institution in Rio. As a result, he came to be regarded by some of his contemporaries as a good administrator, a tough sheriff, and a talented politician. In the ensuing decades, faithful to Eusébio's legacy, the police of the capital adopted the assumption that any black person, and many *pardos* as well, were slaves until proved otherwise. Needless to say, such an assumption became instrumental in the consolidation of the customary seigneurial right to enslave people irrespective of the law. Eusébio, his peers, and subordinates would not see the thousands of recently arrived Africans, called *boçais,* that worked and endured slavery in the city and its surroundings in the 1830s and 1840s. When they arrested a black deemed to be a runaway slave, they rarely took the opportunity to make sure that he or she was not among those imported illegally and thus having the right to freedom. Moving in the city or in its hinterland, any black person tended to be regarded as valuable property, to be bought and sold at will. If captured as a supposed fugitive slave, and a master did not materialize to reclaim his property, a local judge would pronounce him or her *bens do evento,* literally "property of the wind," to be sent to public auction.

In addition, because whether someone "seemed to be a slave" or "was suspected to be a slave" depended much on the class-biased and interested eyes of the beholder, this practice of illegal enslavement reinforced the power of the planter class. Government misdeeds in the period made the experience of freedom a very precarious and uncertain one indeed, for free and freed people of color in general. This suggests another historical problem that seems turned upside down. Historians of Brazil have been describing in rich detail how slaves could attain freedom in that country. However, they may have been paying less attention than they should to the quality of that freedom. For whether an enslaved person won or was given freedom, the precariousness of that status fostered personal dependence on an ex-master. Emancipation might even lead back to slavery.

Slaves, Freed Persons, Vagrants, Conscripts

A close reading of police records in pursuit of the motives alleged for the detention of people of color in the capital in the 1830s and 1840s reveals procedures that brought together bondage and Africanness, liberty of blacks and vagrancy, vagrancy and need for compulsory labor (as prisoner or conscript).

In the 1830s, the chief of police of the city of Rio received daily reports from Rio's sixteen justices of the peace. There were usually two for each parish, though Sacramento had three and Lagoa just one. Each of these officials passed on information he received from the approximately ten neighborhood inspectors in his jurisdiction.[15] In the parish of Santana, for example, a typical case, there were two districts, each of them with one justice of the peace and ten neighborhood inspectors. The following extracts come from that parish and were forwarded from the J.P. to the chief of police, Eusébio de Queiróz.

From the inspector of the third block, to the justice of the Second District of Santana, December 12, 1835: "On the 7th of the month Vitorino dos Passos Guimarães, a freed black, whitewasher, came to reside in this block, at the house number 288, bringing with him three freed black women, and a slave woman. On the 10th of the month, the Mina black Eugênio Joaquim José Maurício and his wife left house number 276, where they had been hired."

From the inspector of the first block, Second District of Santana to the J.P., December 12, 1835: "On the 11th I inspected the whole block pertaining to the Campo de Santana, requiring that all residents who had not done so yet present their family lists within 24 hours." From the inspector of the second block, Second District of Santana to the J.P., December 12, 1835: "On the 5th the free black woman Maria Helena da Silva came to reside at house number 122 and 124; she brought a Pass given by the Justice of the Peace of the 3rd District of Sacramento on the same date, as well as a list of seven people; *she has not yet presented her letter of manumission*" [my italics].[16] While reading these passages it is important to keep in mind that neighborhood inspectors lived on the blocks they watched and reported about. Furthermore, they did this work for free, thus had other occupations to earn a living. In Santana parish some inspectors were described as "proprietor," "retired major," "captain of the defunct Veterans' battalion," "elementary school teacher," and "public employee."[17] They walked the neighborhood unarmed, supervising at least twenty-five dwellings. They were often given responsibility for a single residential street.

This kind of urban surveillance perpetuated a seigneurial politics of social control based on paternalist ideology. Police authorities accepted the private power of masters and bosses over enslaved or free workers they described as dependents. Thus the neighborhood inspector was supposed *to know personally and report on each and every person under his supervision;* he had to follow their movements and learn what happened in their homes that might affect the public order. This could include receiving guests, gambling, or allowing gatherings of slaves, ex-slaves, and other suspicious persons. Otherwise, he had *to note the presence of strangers* within his area, seek information about them, and make detailed reports to the justice of the peace. For this reason the daily reports the justices of the peace summarized for the chief of police roughly once a week, which he forwarded to the minister of justice on a monthly basis, include such apparent trivialities as the movement of freed and enslaved people in and out of the parish. In the 1830s Rio de Janeiro was not yet experiencing the intense human movement it would see in the second half of the nineteenth century, when individuals would move within city limits and back and forth from the countryside. This migration would make Rio a haven for runaway slaves, but in the 1830s, the police still practiced a personal, highly localized surveillance of individual city dwellers. By the late nineteenth century, as the city grew, Rio's police seemed to suspect the multitude rather than the individual, which of course translated into an overarching suspicion of all black and poor people.[18]

The inspector who reported that "the free black woman Maria Helena da Silva" had moved onto his block added that she still needed to submit her letter of manumission. In other words, he regarded Maria Helena as "allegedly free"—that is, as a former slave—thus imposing on her the obligation to prove her assertion. It is difficult to know precisely what led any given inspector to doubt what a person said about his or her slavery or freedom. Of course, the question did not apply to people deemed to be white. The reliability of the others—that is, people seen to be of African descent—might depend on their clothes, their speech, perhaps visible body marks. In any case, it is evident that the inspector used criteria based on social and cultural assumptions widely shared by his colleagues, since he did not think it was necessary to explain these criteria. Nevertheless, the brief and fragmented extracts sent to the chief of police do express a social logic that reveals much about the experience of freedom in this part of Brazil:

From the First District of Santana, November 11, 1835:

The black Domingos Cabinda, a slave of Mariano de tal [Mariano So-and-So] was *arrested as a runaway* and sent to the Calabouço. *Arrested for vagrants,* and sent to the Arsenal de Marinha [Navy Yard] for naval service were João Antônio da Silva, a black freedman, Antônio Correa, white, Fernando Antônio da Costa, a gypsy, Pedro Fernandes, gypsy, Justo Brum, caboclo [offspring of a white with an Indian], José Pereira Maia, pardo [a mulatto or a person whose skin is deemed brown; my italics].

From the First District of Santa Rita, November 25, 1835:

Nicolau Afonso, crioulo [a black person born in Brazil], *who says he is free,* son of Alberto Dias and Maria Redondo, was arrested *to present his letter of manumission, or proof of his release from military service, because he says that he had been a soldier* in the Brigades—and sent to the Calabouço. Domingos Pinheiro, *who says that he is free,* was arrested for throwing a stone and hitting a boy [my italics].

From the First District of Santana, November 25, 1835:

Joana Mozambique was arrested and sent to the Calabouço for wounding a black man; *she says that she is a slave of Manoel So-and-So. The black Mateus Angola, slave of Clara Maria de Jesus* was arrested and sent to the Calabouço [my italics].

From the Second District of Santana, Novmber 25, 1835:

Two Africans were seized in the house of Dona Leonarda Angelina de Castro; *there is evidence to suggest that they are free,* because of coming to Brazil after the end of the slave trade [my italics].[19]

From the First District of Santana, February 22, 1836:

Mariana, slave, was arrested as *a runaway* and sent to the Calabouço. Joaquim, *a crioulo freedman, known to be a vagrant and disorderly sort,* was sent to the Navy Yard for naval service [my italics].

From the First District of Sacramento, March 11, 1836:

Francisco Antônio da Silva and Joaquim Kassange, *who says that he is a freed man,* were seized for begging needlessly [my italics].[20]

The authors of these reports expressed different degrees of skepticism about what they had heard from the detainees. Some cases are self-evident. The black Domingos Cabinda, slave of Mariano So-and-So, was deemed a runaway and sent to the slave jail. Everything seems to be in its place in this episode: Africans (a Cabinda, in this case) are black, slaves, and in case they run away, must be caught and sent to the slave jail, to wait for the master to claim them and to receive punishment. The same keywords, the same unflinching belief, apply to Mateus, black, African, a slave, in jail. In the case of the two Africans seized in the house of Dona Leonarda Angelina, the wording appears to indicate a degree of unexpectedness. Despite the fact that they were Africans, there was evidence of their freedom. Nevertheless, the author suggests how uncommon it was to see Africans as free people.

Seemingly unusual as well is the case of Joana Mozambique, detained for injuring a black man, "who says that she is a slave of Manoel So-and-So." It is rare in these documents to find scribes that doubt Africans who declare that they are slaves. However, there appear some examples of free and freed people, *crioulos* and Africans, who say to the police or to the justice of the peace that they are slaves. Joana Mozambique had been arrested for committing a crime; in case she was really a captive, she may have declared her bondage, hoping that her master would be interested in obtaining her release from jail. If she were not a slave, saying that she was one could confuse and delay police and judicial proceedings. In the several cases of free and freed blacks and *pardos* who affirm that they are captives, they do so seeking to avoid conscription for military service.

Public scribes displayed impressive confidence about the alleged vagrancy of

many detainees. It was words like "free" and "freed" that made them uneasy and doubt-
ful. Freed blacks and *crioulos, pardos,* Gypsies, even a white individual, were held as
vagrants, with no doubt expressed about their status. Joaquim was "a crioulo freedman, *known to be* a vagrant and disorderly sort." In this passage, it is curious that
the writer does not question Joaquim's condition as "freed," as is so often the case in
these extracts, perhaps because the black man had his letter of manumission in hand.
Instead, the official chooses to emphasize that he is sure of the freed person's idleness. Thus "freed" and "vagrant" become closely related words: the uncertainty about
freedom seems resolved by the necessity of repressing vagrancy. As a consequence,
"vagrant" appears almost as a synonym for "conscript." One concept or situation often
leads to the other, as when someone deemed a vagrant must end up "a soldier," "a
marine," or must be "sent to the Navy Yard," "to the Navy," "to the Army," in sum, to
military service, if not simply to jail, to perform forced labor in public works.[21]

Hence it is not surprising to find repeated examples of resistance to conscription
in police and prison papers. Several free people or ex-slaves declared to the authorities
that they were slaves to avoid being sent to the military. Damásio Maximiano, for example, held in the slave jail in November 1836,[22] addressed a complaint to the emperor,
through his attorney, saying that "he was a free black man, a native born Brazilian
citizen, a former soldier of the extinct 4th Battalion of the 2nd Brigade of the Province
of Pernambuco, now a marine on the ship Niger." He argued that, despite being a free
man, authorities treated him as if he were a slave. Furthermore, the director of the jail
ruled the institution despotically, having "cut his flesh" with whippings and forced him
to carry water on the streets, accompanied by slaves. Maximiano asked His Majesty to
protect him, to order his release from jail, and for permission to return to the warship,
"because he is a citizen, as the Constitution guarantees him this title."

The story reached the minister of justice, Gustavo Adolfo de Aguilar Pantoja,
who wrote to the chief of police, Eusébio de Queiróz, to ask for explanations. Eusébio's
reply, dated December 11, 1836, and based on information provided by the director of
the slave jail, stated that when he was jailed, the prisoner had not identified himself
as Damásio Maximiano, a free man and a Brazilian citizen. Instead, in the presence
of the slave jail director himself, he had said he was José Crioulo, "a slave of Antônio
Tertuliano dos Santos, who lived in the city of Santos." Regarding the allegation of
cruel treatment in jail, the director retorted dismissively that it had not gone beyond
"half a dozen lashes," applied as a necessary punishment because the complainant had
been behaving badly. As for having the detainee carry water on the streets as part of
a slave gang or *libambo,* Maximiano should have thought of that before declaring he
was a slave, "which he did perhaps to escape from naval service" in the brig of war. In
sum, given two undesirable options, the black man seemed to use them strategically,
though in the end he could not avoid one of his seemingly necessary destinies: if he
remained José Crioulo, slave, it would be slave jail, lashes, *libambo;* if he chose Damásio

Maximiano, a free native Brazilian, it would be conscription, brig of war, and, for sure, lashes again.

In January 1845, the chief of police wrote to the director of the slave jail to seek information about two sailors held there.[23] The director replied that the men had been seized because they were "suspected of being slaves." One of them, Manoel Francisco, said that he had deserted from the navy; thereafter, he had been working on several commercial coastal ships. Lately, he had enrolled "as a slave" in the boat *Espadarte.* However a man named So-and-So Andrade appeared at the slave jail, showing documents to prove that Manoel Francisco had indeed been in the *Espadarte* and seeking his release. Interrogated again, the detainee declared that "he was a freed man, but enrolled as a slave [in the *Espadarte*] to escape from military service." Manoel Francisco remained in the slave jail, perhaps until authorities decided on which of his stories they would believe.

These examples suggest that police violence, prolonged and arbitrary detentions, and the threat of military service led people such as Joana Mozambique and Simão Congo, our next protagonist, however freed, to say that they were slaves, maybe to facilitate their access to a protector—that is, a *padrinho,* a supposed godfather—when in danger. They deployed this strategy to deal with particular situations, choosing bondage over freedom to avoid, for example, being deported to Africa[24] or forced to serve on a warship. Simão Congo had been seized and remained in the House of Correction in April 1845, apparently "just because he had been out on the street a little after ten o'clock at night." When arrested, he said he was "a slave of dr. José Bento da Rosa."[25] Prison officials shaved his head and assigned to him duties reserved for slaves. Soon thereafter authorities received a petition on his behalf. It argued that Simão Congo was in reality a freed person and a dependent (*agregado*) living in the house of his protector and former master, Dr. José Bento. The director of the House of Correction explained that the detainee was an African-born black—"*um preto de nação*"—who spoke Portuguese in a jumbled manner, hence officials believed him when he said that he was a slave: "poor black," he concluded, "so ignorant that, being free, he made believe he was a slave." Nonetheless, if Simão Congo, finding himself arrested and abused, thought that passing as a slave would make it more possible for him to communicate with, and obtain the protection of, his former master, it seems that he managed to use the authorities' belief in his "ignorance" to his own benefit. It took just jumbling a few words.[26]

Belonging to the National Guard brought exemption from service in the army or the navy. Although to join the Guard a man had to meet the income requirements for political rights established in the Constitution of 1824, this was apparently not difficult. Or so it seemed to the chief of police, Eusébio de Queiróz, who constantly sought to obtain army and navy recruits during the second half of the 1830s. During this time the Empire faced several regional revolts, of slave and free people alike, some of them aiming to secede from Brazil. Eusébio found it frustrating that the justices of the peace rarely produced the minimum number of recruits he demanded; the justices alleged that people hid from them. When caught, they came up with exemptions, like saying that they were married or belonged to the National Guard, or both. On December 16, 1835, Eusébio wrote to the commander in chief of the National Guard to say, "It is well-known that many members of the National Guard are far from fulfilling the requisites established by the Law for such a great honor. Since we need to exclude these people from the ranks of the institution, in order to draft them (into the Army), I urgently request Your Excellency to provide me with a list of people under these circumstances."[27]

Eusébio delivered this document to the commander in chief marked as "classified," surely because it made quite clear how far he was determined to go to ignore formally recognized citizenship rights to fill the ranks of the military. In any case, the irritation of the chief of police also suggests how effective the strategy to join the National Guard may have been to obtain protection from forced military service. Perhaps knowing this, in January 1836, "some blacks and pardos" who resided in the parish of Engenho Velho decided that "they wanted to constitute a unit of National Guards." Local and police authorities interpreted the initiative as "attempted insurrection," therefore arrested and prosecuted them. The jury found them not guilty.[28]

In June 1849, the police subdelegate of Inhaúma reported on Deolindo José de Faria, a resident of his parish who loved to pass time in taverns, to be with his girlfriend—a "black slave woman"—and to participate, with "black slaves," in *batuques,* that is, African dances accompanied by guitar and drums.[29] The subdelegate himself had appeared to disperse a *batuque* gathering, sending the slaves to their masters and singling out Deolindo for interrogation. When asked about his occupation, Deolindo replied that he was "a National Guard enlisted in the 6th Battalion." Regardless of the fact that Deolindo did not carry a document to prove this affiliation, the police official let him go, though allegedly warning him that he should obtain such a document from his commander. A few days later police officials caught Deolindo with his black slave girlfriend in a room belonging to a tavern. Because the young man was still unable to present a certificate of his National Guard status, the subdelegate kept him in the local police jail. Soon afterward, Deolindo was drafted into the navy. However, he had told the truth. The commander in chief of the National Guard wrote belatedly to the chief of police to state that "Deolindo was one of his old guards and had been serving regularly, hence requested his release." The chief of police told the commander in chief that he should address his petition to the Navy Ministry.

If neither a slave nor a citizen in the National Guard, how could a man avoid being deemed "a vagrant" and sent to military service? At times, of course, government officials themselves labeled people made available to them "unfit." In March 1848, the chief of police wrote the minister of justice that he had "personally examined" all "the vagabonds seized in the House of Correction," concluding that not one of them seemed "fit for service in the Navy or in the Army."[30] Since stories featuring poor people—free and freed—struggling to avoid the draft are so numerous, it will suffice to mention just one more that is especially revealing.

In November 1835, Eusébio de Queiróz delivered to the justices of the peace an order that displeased the minister of justice, Limpo de Abreu.[31] Informed of the situation through a petition on behalf of one of the victims, the minister demanded an explanation. The chief of police provided it on December 9: "The inspector of the Navy Yard had requested me to find people to serve in war ships. Besides other measures, I decided that it would be convenient to send to the Navy Yard all prisoners that had finished serving their sentences, since these are the kind of people that must be expurgated from this City, which is so infested with thieves; this is what I intended in my address to the Justices of the Peace." In other words, it seems that Eusébio had instructed the justices of the peace to send people who had served short sentences for petty crimes in parish police jails directly to the Navy Yard to be drafted, instead of having them released. The justice of the peace in the First District of Santana had followed the instructions promptly and sent Belisário José d'Oliveira to the Navy Yard, from where he had already been dispatched to a frigate. The minister of justice sought information about the case because he had received a letter from Thereza Joaquina, Belisário's mother, who pled to His Majesty the emperor to release the young man. The woman's letter, signed by a man on her behalf, vents the despair of a mother seeking to regain her son. It is exaggerated, dramatic, colorful, and full of spelling and grammar mistakes. The letter is untranslatable, thus it is reproduced in its original Portuguese in the endnote.[32] It argues that Belisário served a sentence of four months because he had been found a little drunk. When this time had expired his mother went to the jailhouse only to find that he had been sent to the navy. She was a widow and depended on Belisário, her only son, to support her with his work as a carpenter. His absence had left her in dire necessity and even hunger. The minister of justice, reckoning that Belisário had passed to the authority of the Ministry of the Navy, recommended that the woman petition the respective minister.[33]

In several of the extracts cited above, as we saw, justices of the peace and police authorities constructed their sentences to convey the idea that they were not convinced by detainees' statements that merely seemed to be true. In other words, their truthfulness remained to be ascertained. So we turn now to this very problem—how to determine the credibility of statements regarding slavery and freedom—when the issue consisted of evaluating claims to slave property.

Enslavement

The flimsy criteria for enslavement prevailing from the 1830s to the 1860s encouraged the growth of slave stealing, with gangs actively suborning and kidnapping free and enslaved people and taking them from Rio to other provinces, especially Minas

Gerais. Moreover, the procedures to investigate the cases of Africans deemed to be *boçais*—new arrivals—demonstrate how authorities formally recognized the illegality of importing enslaved Africans yet validated the bondage of smuggled Africans on shore. A decree of 1842, about slave registration and taxes, went so far as to include an article stipulating that "nobody may be required to present the title under which he possesses a slave."[34]

Police papers suggest that Eusébio de Queiróz sought to combat the practice of slave stealing, in contrast to his obvious lack of interest in fighting the illegal African trade. Regarding the latter, there was a significant episode in November 1837, a little after the discussion of Barbacena's parliamentary proposal to stop enforcing the slave trade laws. Two police officials in charge of inspecting the health conditions aboard ships in Rio's harbor had been accused of corruption. Eusébio told the minister that "some respectable local businessmen" had told him that, indeed, "it was possible to obtain anything from those two officials, as long as one wished to spend money." Furthermore, he discovered that the officials practiced their extortion more often when dealing with ships coming from Africa. They had established a set price for the release of such ships, and businessmen who resisted these impositions faced all kinds of obstacles. The chief of police asked for the dismissal of the two corrupt officials, observing that they had taken their audacity "to the point of hinting that they shared the profits with their superiors, thus extorting higher sums" from their victims. In other words, what irritated Eusébio the most was that these officials degraded his reputation as they perpetrated their crimes. However, he reported that he was unable to prosecute the two men because the businessmen he had talked to refused to testify in court, "for reasons that are easy enough to understand." After all, Eusébio *did not say*, his "respectable" informants were in the business of bribing public officials to smuggle Africans to the country.[35]

In August 1838, customs officials and neighborhood inspectors overseeing Rio's coastal areas accused each other of not fulfilling their obligations. In response, the chief of police wrote to the minister of justice affirming his trust in all his subordinates; moreover, he attached to his letter several documents that supposedly testified as to their probity. The British consular authorities had claimed that newly arrived Africans were openly sold on the streets of Rio. Eusébio deemed the accusations false, though he continued to remark, paradoxically, that his efforts to fight this type of crime had been "useless." According to him, "interest, customs and the involvement of a large part of our population, especially planters, contribute to protect individuals accused of this crime." He complained also that the fact that such crimes were submitted to jury trials, instead of to career judges, made it difficult to obtain convictions. He thought that "a large part of the population" opposed the idea of punishing people for smuggling Africans.[36] In June 1841, just to mention one last example among many, British consular authorities accused the justice of the peace of Santa

Rita parish of conniving with the slave trade. They said that this official had facili-
tated the entrance of ships coming from the African coast without carrying any merchandise on board—a clear indication that they had disembarked their human cargo
in some faraway location outside the bay before entering the port to load for a new
trip. The surviving papers about this case say nothing about what was done in this
matter, if anything.[37]

Although the lack of enforcement of the 1831 law is a well-known historical
fact, it is striking to see the abundance of information available to the chief of police
and successive ministers of justice about how the illegal African trade operated.
They were aware of the strategies of the slavers, they had the names of the "respectable" businessmen involved, and they knew about the local authorities who participated in the scheme. The police papers pertaining to the period in which Eusébio de
Queiróz held the post of chief of police illuminate why, as the leading minister of the
cabinet in power in 1850, he had no difficulty stopping the illegal trade once it was
decided this had to be done. His knowledge and credentials in this area were truly
astounding.[38]

It follows that Eusébio's efforts against slave stealing, a crime that appeared to
have become endemic during the period in which the contraband trade intensified,
deserve attention. It may not have been simple to reconcile procedures meant to allow
the routine enslavement of newly imported Africans with the maintenance of order
and discipline in the domestic slave labor market. After all, the contraband trade
required a constant process of forging "proof" of slave ownership so those who bought
these illegally imported men and women could appear to be bona fide slave owners.
Those who were expert in forging slave papers seem to have used their skills for other
captives, including kidnapped free and freed blacks. Let us return to the excerpts sent
by the justices of the peace to the chief of police.

From the First District of Santana, February 14–20, 1836:

We sent the *pardo* José Joaquim de Lima, a vagrant and suspect of passing stolen
slaves to the Navy Yard for naval service. . . . Francisco Cabinda, a slave of Joaquim
José de Proença, was arrested for having suborned Miguel Mozambique, a slave of
Albino Gomes Guerra; both are held in the Calabouço, for procedures.[39]

From the First District of Sacramento, August 23, 1836:

The freed black João Antônio de Souza Dutra was arrested for suborning the
black Francisco Benguela, a slave of Ladislau José de Oliveira, intending to sell
him to Manoel dos Anjos Victorino do Amaral.[40]

From the First District of Santana, October 19, 1837:

We arrested . . . Manoel Joaquim Vieira Bastos, for stealing a slave, and Antônio Mina, a slave of F. Barros, for being found in the house of Manoel Francisco da Luz Gouvêa inviting his slaves to run away.[41]

From the Second District of Sacramento, December 6, 1837:

The blacks Manoel, a slave of Father Queiróz, and Faustino, a slave of Manoel So-and-So Lima, both of the Mina nation, were arrested for suborning Joaquim, a black of the Congo Nation, a slave of José de Carvalho; the latter was detained as well.[42]

From the First District of Santana, April 19, 1838:

Joaquim Bento and José Mendes were indicted for the crime of stealing two slaves, according to article 269 of the Criminal Code and the Resolution of October 15, 1837.[43]

These few examples, again chosen among several others, suggest the diversity of situations and people allegedly involved in slave stealing.[44] Those arrested included a *pardo* deemed a "vagrant," a "freed black," "Antônio Mina, a slave" and other "blacks . . . of the Mina nation." It appears that this business often involved "suborning" or convincing the human property involved that they would have a more tolerable bondage if they allowed themselves to be kidnapped. Antônio Mina, for example, had "invited" his peers in captivity to run away. Of course, police papers carry plenty of examples of situations in which slave stealers seized blacks by force. At times these actions resulted from the work of well-organized gangs who snatched at once a number of Africans who had been found on a ship accused of contraband; in addition, there were the cases of gangs or individuals who kidnapped free or freed blacks, oftentimes children, to resell them to the interior.[45] In any case, what appears more often in the sources consulted are cases of blacks—slave, freed, or freeborn—assisting captives in moving away within slavery, that is, in seeking a new master that supposedly offered improved conditions under bondage. The agency of blacks in slave stealing explains, at least in part, why Eusébio seems to have taken a considerable interest in repressing it.

Eusébio de Queiróz regularly informed the minister of justice about the jury trials that had taken place in the city of Rio over which he presided. Defendants accused of stealing slaves were a constant presence in such reports, which led the chief of police to remark, in April 1838, that "it is noteworthy that among the 20 defendants that stood trial, 13 had been charged with the crime of stealing slaves. Fortunately, the important Resolution of October 15, 1837, will result in the decrease of this type of crime because it established more severe penalties for it and made it impossible for the offender to be released on bail." This Resolution "extended to slave stealing the penalties and other rulings pertaining to robbery."[46]

Although police papers convey the idea that "seducers" of slaves constituted a quite varied lot, free and enslaved people alike, Africans as well as *crioulos,* Eusébio alleged that Africans of the Mina nation predominated in this type of activity. Addressing the minister of justice on July 31, 1839, he argued that there existed Mina blacks in Rio who, although also engaged in petty thefts, lived almost exclusively from convincing slaves to let themselves be kidnapped. He proceeded to seek permission for the summary deportation of freed Africans accused of this crime, considering this course of action even more appropriate because they were foreigners. Eusébio mentioned the recent example of a group of Mina blacks who had decided to return to Africa voluntarily, saying that he would like to send others to the same destination. He believed that "the expulsion of twelve or sixteen of those people from the Empire" would prevent others from continuing their activities. Weeks later, in September 1839, Alexandre and Salvador, both Mina blacks, were deported to Benguela, along with other individuals who received equal punishment.[47] References to Mina blacks forcefully returned to Africa appear regularly in police correspondence pertaining to the 1830s and 1840s, and not only because of their supposed participation in slave stealing.[48]

"Suborners" of slaves would not exist without their counterparts, the receptors of stolen human property. Nonetheless, curbing the distribution of kidnapped workers through the interior of the country proved to be a formidable task. Besides the fact that it was difficult to deport guilty parties in such cases as the law required, except for some Portuguese offenders,[49] central government officials had to deal with the connivance and often the active participation of planters and local authorities. In January 1842, Eusébio forwarded to the minister of justice copies of several pieces of correspondence he had exchanged with the president of the province of Minas Gerais.[50] He remarked that the minister would give such papers "the consideration they deserved," but it is clear that the chief of police intended to inform the higher authority that he knew how the slave stealing network operated in that province; in addition, he hinted that he had encountered resistance on the part of the president of the province in his initiatives to fight it. Eusébio detailed a particular episode, which had come to his knowledge because of a correspondence that had been sent from an inhabitant of Minas to João Corrêa dos Santos, who had turned it over to the chief. He says, "As Your Excellency will see in these letters, a man named José do Carmo e Vasconcellos refers to a given captive, supposedly a runaway, but actually kidnapped from the mentioned Santos, and for this reason he is sure to buy him!" The letters contained a list of captives in similar conditions, that is, deemed runaways belonging to João Corrêa dos

Santos, who Vasconcellos proposed to purchase for a low price, seemingly confident that he would have no difficulty legalizing the stolen property.[51] On the same occasion, Eusébio had been able to trace the story of the black Silvério, carried away from her mistress, a widow resident in the city of Niterói, and taken to Minas Gerais by "the conspicuous José Vieira Novo." Despite names, addresses, and documents presented, Eusébio could not convince the president of Minas to seize the captives and send them to Rio to be identified, interrogated, and returned to their owners. The president alleged that "although I would like to engage local authorities in aiding the Police in their efforts to seize stolen slaves and return them to their masters, I understand that many troubles would result from the practice of having captives turned in under the request of the Presidency." Having forwarded the documents to the minister, it seems that Eusébio did not approach the subject again. However, he continued to prosecute and bring to jury trials defendants charged with the crime of stealing slaves.

The sources examined for this paper do not permit a proper evaluation of the effectiveness of police efforts to curb slave stealing, but they show that people involved in this type of activity had at their disposal a vast repertoire of deceit and forgery. I would argue that much of it was made possible by the ongoing necessity of legalizing the large number of enslaved people brought illegally to Brazil from Africa. The reports sent by the administration of the slave jail to the chief of police regularly describe cases of slaves who had their names changed, for a variety of reasons. On July 12, 1845, "José Crioulo, a slave," or rather, "the black Martinho, a slave," or whatever name he went by, said that he was a native of the province of Pernambuco, but "he had been kidnapped there about six years ago," and thereafter he had been sold to several masters, "always with a different name."[52] The following piece of correspondence, dated June 12, 1845, accompanied a detainee sent to be interrogated by the chief of police:

> José Antônio Roiz, who says that he has deserted the Sixth Company of the Battalion of Fusiliers. . . . This individual entered the slave jail on September 16, 1844, saying that his name was Luiz, a slave of Father José Maria, Rector of the Santa Cruz School . . . in the city of Olinda, Pernambuco. The same Father had bought him in the province of Ceará—and in Pernambuco he had been suborned by a Diogo So-and-So, who brought him to the Court, but he ran away when the said Diogo wanted to send him to the province of Minas.
>
> All this jabbering appears in the file of the mentioned detainee, who entered the slave jail because of what he first declared regarding his condition.[53]

It seems that the strategy of changing names, used by slave dealers and planters to sell stolen slaves, and to illegally enslave free people, could be used by bondspeople themselves to avoid sale to places they did not want to go, or to deny their bondage altogether. In the same bundle of documents, there appears the case of Mariana, later discovered to be Tereza, a slave of José Alves da Graça, but whose identification still did not seem right to the official in charge of the slave jail. He "remembered" that "this black woman ha[d] been here before." However, "perhaps because she changed her name then as well," it had not been possible for him "to find her promptly in the registration books" (letter dated July 12, 1845). On the one hand, manipulating names and identities was an important part of the process of reducing people to the condition of human property: newly imported Africans lost their original names immediately upon arrival;[54] kidnapped slaves had their names changed at the whim of their dealers and receptors. On the other hand, depending on the circumstances, black men and women, freeborn, freed, and enslaved, transformed the experience of losing and acquiring names into a way to defend themselves against abuse and to struggle for their own objectives.

The importance of the contraband slave trade meant that thousands of slave owners were continuously making false claims about the legality of their slave property. In many ways, this situation turned the Brazilian Empire into an inverted Land of Make Believe, built not on fairy tales but on imaginative ways of sidestepping the law in order to continue exploiting African labor, regardless of the cost in human suffering.[55] One last long tale will illustrate the situation. This is an episode Eusébio reported to the minister of justice in May 1839, attaching a wealth of documentation.[56]

It seems that the problem originated in an act of illegal enslavement that remained incomplete, thus arousing the greed of another potential perpetrator. In November 1837, Luiz, a Congo African, had "appeared" on the property of Dona Tereza Rita Loureiro, located in the distant parish of Lagoa. The *moleque* (a black boy) could not speak any Portuguese, thus Dona Tereza's slaves talked to him "in their language" (*língua*). The African was evidently a *boçal* and Dona Tereza, at least initially, decided to abide by the law, informing the justice of the peace that she held the African boy. In addition, she proposed to become his legal guardian and later follow procedures to formalize his right to freedom. Dona Tereza had only completed the procedures for the guardianship itself and nothing more when, in 1839, Francisco José Pereira das Neves came forward and claimed that Luiz, Congo, was in fact Paulo, Cabinda, a slave he had bought in 1830, who had run away. As the minister of justice and the chief of police recognized, the local justice of the peace had not investigated the question of the African boy's freedom and this allowed Pereira to claim him.

Documents attached to the report show that the contending parties sought to prove the real identity of the African, as they interpreted it, by discussing the signs inscribed on his body. People supposed to have the expertise to read such texts compared written descriptions of the signs pertaining to Paulo, Cabinda, with the ones they saw in the alleged Luiz, Congo, concluding that they were not the same person. Furthermore, the *curador dos africanos livres*—that is, the government official responsible for accompanying the cases of Africans that had a right to freedom because they had been seized in the illegal trade—interrogated the African. Speaking partly in Portuguese, partly in his native language, in the presence of a translator, Luiz recounted his arrival ashore with many other Africans, then the journey to the inland, always marching through the woods during the night, followed closely by armed men on horseback. He and four other Africans seized an opportunity and disappeared into the woods. Separated from his comrades in the escapade, Luiz reached Dona Tereza's property alone. Later in the testimony, when asked about how he had acquired his name, he explained "in his language that his name was Luiz, of the Congo nation, and that with this name he had left his land, and that here he had not been baptized yet." Thus it is possible that Luiz had been a Christian in Congo, having managed to keep his name despite the crossing of the Atlantic. Required to offer his view of the subject, the *curador dos africanos livres* said that it was obvious that Luiz had been a recently arrived African when Dona Tereza held him. He discounted the allegations presented by Pereira das Neves. The *curador* observed that Luiz spoke several words and phrases in Portuguese, but his knowledge of the language was compatible with what could be expected of someone who had been in the country for about two years, not nine or more, as would be the case if one believed in the story told by Pereira das Neves. In conclusion, the *curador* stated that "the African is indeed one of those imported against what is established in the law of November 7, 1831, therefore he should be declared free."

During this whole trial, Dona Tereza insisted that her intention had always been to guarantee Luiz's freedom. No one explained why she had not done anything on the matter for the one and a half years that she had kept him. But she could have claimed the African was her property. Instead of notifying the local justice of the peace that Luiz had "appeared" on her property, she could have included him on the list of people living in her household. In doing this, she would have counted on the discretion of the local justice of the peace not to ask her for Luiz's slave papers. Next, she could have paid slave taxes on Luiz, or have sold him promptly, preferably before a notary. That way the future owner would have the notarized record of the sale, which he or she would present to Luiz's next owner, and so on. Eventually, Luiz could be included in an estate inventory, to be inherited by a new generation of slave owners.[57] In each step, the assumption that an African found inland was "naturally" a slave, a piece of property about which no questions should be asked, remained in force. Thus we have come full circle in this paper, back to historian Robert Conrad's insight which gave us a point of entry.

Untold Stories

Despite enactment of the law of September 1850, that resulted in the actual end of the African slave trade to Brazil, the problem of the illegality of the slave property acquired after the law of 1831 continued to haunt slaveholders and state officials in the ensuing decades. They knew that they had to proceed with care on this matter. On August 5, 1854, in a "classified" letter, the chief of police, Theophilo Rezende, wrote to the minister of justice, Nabuco de Araújo, about the publication in the newspaper *Jornal do Commercio* of information regarding slaves put to auction that seemed to confirm that they had been imported illegally.[58] The chief of police referred to a particular auction, conducted by the Portuguese consulate, in which two of the supposed African slaves had been given the ages of twenty-two and twenty-three, thus suggesting that they had arrived after 1831. The minister of justice had asked the chief of police to investigate but the chief deemed this unwise. Rezende argued that if he were to investigate the stories of Africans announced for auction with ages in the early or mid-twenties, then to be consistent he would have to do the same regarding "all African captives existent among us, whatever their ages, since they could have been imported after the law of 1831 with the ages of 5, 10 or 15 years, or older." He considered the adoption of such routine procedures "not at all prudent in our present circumstances." It seems that his view prevailed.

In the same period, August and September 1854, the Brazilian parliament debated a bill proposed by João Maurício Wanderley (later the Baron Cotegipe), a deputy from Bahia, intended to curb the internal slave trade. Wanderley alleged that the end of the African trade had been followed by the intensification of the domestic slave trade, with a constant flow of captives from the northern to the southern provinces of the Empire.[59] The deputy offered several arguments in favor of his bill, such as the importance of keeping workers in the northern provinces and the risk of having the country divided on the issue of slavery in a way that would be similar to what had been happening in the United States. Although his main arguments were economic and political, Wanderley sought to strengthen his case by depicting the suffering associated with the booming internal slave trade business, "a traffic more barbarous and inhuman than the traffic on the coast of Africa was before it," resulting in "children torn away from their mothers, husbands separated from their wives, parents from their children!" In a recent and detailed study of the Brazilian internal slave trade, Robert Slenes demonstrates that many of the blacks forcefully transplanted from the northern provinces as a consequence of the domestic trade were *ladino* Africans, that is, Africans who had been in Brazil for many years, and *crioulos*, or Brazilian-born blacks, who had been enjoying a degree of stability within the paternalist practices of their masters when they were struck by the new situation beginning in the 1850s. According to Slenes, "The very real possibility that their families could be dismembered by sale was only one aspect of a general shattering of former 'rules' and expectations." These blacks found that "they were being treated, in effect, like 'new Africans.'"[60]

One is left to wonder to what extent this observation conveyed the naked truth about the internal trade. On his speech delivered on September 1, 1854, Wanderley argued that "the enslavement of free people" had "made its appearance in the north" as a consequence of the internal slave trade. There were reports of people selling the "unfortunate mulatto or black children" entrusted to them, and accounts of criminals kidnapping children and selling them. In sum, he continued, there was "the tendency to reduce free persons to slavery." As Wanderley made his point on the enslavement of free and freed black people, he had to interrupt himself a couple of times to reply to the deputy Silveira da Mota, who received these observations unperturbed, deeming such practices routine, business as usual: "Such things happen everywhere in the public marketplace. . . . There will always be slave auctions."[61] It is revealing that both deputies, although disagreeing about whether the internal slave trade was a good thing, agreed that the practice of enslaving free and freed black people was widespread and inescapable.

The reference to slave auctions in the two episodes related above, both times associated with illegal enslavement, leads us to many stories that remain untold regarding the precariousness of freedom in nineteenth-century Brazil. The surviving papers pertaining to the *calabouço*—the slave jail in Rio—register the routine arrest of black people "suspected" of being runaway slaves. Following procedures reminiscent of Portuguese colonial regulations, a person in this situation was held in jail for a certain period of time in order to let a hypothetical master come forward and reclaim his or her captive. If nobody did, the regulations, both under colonial Portuguese rule and during the Brazilian Empire, likened these unclaimed prisoners—so-called runaway slaves—to the situation of stray cattle, whose owner was unknown. That is, they were formally declared *bens do evento*, literally "property of the wind." After summary proceedings that included the interrogation of the suspected slave by a municipal judge, the usual result was the "confirmation" of bondage and the subsequent auctioning off of the human property in hand to a new owner.[62] The underlying assumption in all these procedures, of course, was that a black person deemed to be a runaway slave, and detained for this reason, remained a runaway slave unless proven otherwise. Occasionally stories of free and freed blacks who narrowly escaped the fate of being auctioned off to slavery pop up from the jailhouse books. But this suggests that many others did not have such good luck at a decisive moment. Freedom remained a very risky enterprise for blacks in Brazil at least until the enactment of the gradual emancipation law of 1871.

Notes

Part of this paper was written while I was a Tinker Visiting Professor, University of Chicago, in the winter and spring of 2007. Research in Brazil was funded by the Conselho Nacional de Desenvolvimento Científico e Tecnológico (CNPq) and the Fundação de Amparo à Pesquisa do Estado de São Paulo (FAPESP). I would like to thank professors Dain Borges, Michael Hall, Robert Slenes, and John Garrigus for their comments and corrections of my English.

1. Law of 7 November 1831, articles 1 and 4, in *Colleção das Leis do Império do Brazil.*

2. Leslie Bethell, *A Abolição do Tráfico de Escravos no Brasil. A Grã-Bretanha, o Brasil e a Questão do Tráfico de Escravos, 1807–1869* (Rio de Janeiro: Editora Expressão e Cultura, São Paulo, Edusp, 1976).

3. Robert Edgar Conrad, *World of Sorrow: The African Slave Trade to Brazil* (Baton Rouge: Louisiana State University Press, 1986), 94–97.

4. Conrad, 97.

5. Eduardo Spiller Pena, *Pajens da Casa Imperial: Jurisconsultos, Escravidão e a Lei de 1871* (Campinas: Editora da UNICAMP, 2001); Lenine Nequette, *Escravos & Magistrados no Segundo Reinado* (Brasília: Fundação Petrôneo Portella, 1988).

6. Elciene Azevedo, *Orfeu de Carapinha: A Trajetória de Luiz Gama na Imperial Cidade de São Paulo* (Campinas: Editora da UNICAMP, 1999); Elciene Azevedo, "O Direito dos Escravos: Lutas Jurídicas e Abolicionismo na Província de São Paulo na Segunda Metade do Século XIX," (PhD diss., UNICAMP, 2003).

7. Sidney Chalhoub, *Visões da Liberdade: Uma História das Últimas Décadas da Escravidão na Corte* (São Paulo: Companhia das Letras, 1990), 171–72, 233–35; Joseli Nunes Mendonça, *Entre as Mãos e os Anéis: A Lei dos Sexagenários e os Caminhos da Abolição no Brasil* (Campinas: Editora da UNICAMP, 1999); Keila Grinberg, *Liberata, a Lei da Ambigüidade: As Ações de Liberdade da Corte de Apelação do Rio de Janeiro no século XIX* (Rio de Janeiro: Relume-Dumará, 1994); Hebe Maria Mattos de Castro, *Das Cores do Silêncio: Os Significados da Liberdade no Sudeste Escravista–Brasil, Século XIX* (Rio de Janeiro: Arquivo Nacional, 1995).

8. Beatriz Galotti Mamigonian, "To Be a Liberated African in Brazil: Labour and Citizenship in the Nineteenth Century," (PhD diss., University of Waterloo, Canada, 2002).

9. Eusébio de Queiróz was chief of police from March 1833 to April 1844, with a brief interruption of five months in 1840; S. A. Sisson, *Galeria dos Brasileiros Ilustres* (Brasília: Senado Federal, 1999), I:29.

10. "Aviso" of the ministry of justice, number 274, 12 August 1834, in *Colleção das Decisões do Governo do Imperio do Brazil de 1834* (Rio de Janeiro: Typographia Nacional, 1866).

11. Correspondence from the chief of police to the ministry of justice, 25 November 1835; maço IJ6–171, "Secretaria de Polícia da Corte, ofícios com anexos, agosto a dezembro de 1835," Arquivo Nacional do Rio de Janeiro (henceforth ANRJ).

12. Annotation in pencil, probably from the minister Limpo de Abreu himself, on

the margins of the document. There is a copy of the correspondence sent to the chief of police in the same packet.

13. From Eusébio de Queiróz to Limpo de Abreu, 7 December 1835; IJ6–171, ANRJ.

14. Maço IJ6–171. About Eusébio de Queiróz as chief of police, Thomas H. Holloway, *Policing Rio de Janeiro: Repression and Resistance in a 19th-Century City* (Stanford: Stanford University Press, 1993), chapters 4 and 5; specifically regarding the repression against *capoeiras*, Carlos Eugênio Líbano Soares, *A Capoeira Escrava e Outras Tradições Rebeldes no Rio de Janeiro (1808–1850)* (Campinas: Editora da UNICAMP, 2001), chapter 6.

15. Thomas Holloway, *Policing Rio de Janeiro*, 110–11.

16. Maço IJ6–171, ANRJ.

17. Códice 45–1–24, "Inspetores de quarteirão. Freguesias de Santana e do Engenho Velho, 1831–1840," Arquivo Geral da Cidade do Rio de Janeiro (henceforth AGCRJ).

18. For social control in Rio in the second half of the nineteenth century, Sidney Chalhoub, *Visões da Liberdade*, chapter 3. For seigneurial, personal modes of dominion, Silvia Lara, *Campos da Violência. Escravos e Senhores na Capitania do Rio de Janeiro, 1750–1808* (Rio de Janeiro: Paz e Terra, 1988).

19. All excerpts so far taken from maço IJ6–171, ANRJ.

20. For the last two excerpts, maço IJ6–172, "Secretaria de Polícia da Corte, ofícios com anexos, janeiro a julho de 1836," ANRJ.

21. Fortunately, the bibliography on forced recruitment, so important to understand the experience of poor people, free and freed, in nineteenth-century Brazil, has been growing lately: Álvaro Pereira do Nascimento, *A Ressaca da Marujada: Recrutamento e Disciplina na Armada Imperial* (Rio de Janeiro: Arquivo Nacional, 2001); Peter M. Beattie, *The Tribute of Blood: Army, Honor, Race, and Nation in Brazil, 1864–1945* (Durham: Duke University Press, 2001); Hendrik Kraay, *Race, State, and Armed Forces in Independence-era Brazil, Bahia, 1790s–1840s* (Stanford: Stanford University Press, 2001). Also, Peter M. Beattie, "Conscription versus Penal Servitude: Army Reform's Influence on the Brazilian State's Management of Social Control, 1870–1930," *Journal of Social History* (1999), 847–78; Peter Beattie, "The House, the Street, and the Barracks: Reform and Honorable Masculine Social Space in Brazil," *Hispanic American Historical Review* 76, no. 3, (August 1996), 439–73; Hendrik Kraay, "Reconsidering Recruitment in Imperial Brazil," *Americas* 55, no. 1, (July 1988): 1–33.

22. GIFI, maço 6H-15, ANRJ.

23. Maço IIIJ7–42, "Registro de ofícios relativos ao calabouço, 1844–1848," ANRJ.

24. For a story, among others, of a freed person deported to Africa, see maço IJ6–211, "Secretaria de Polícia da Corte, ofícios com anexos, 1848," ANRJ. Cesário, a black

Mina, had obtained his freedom from a businessman in the city of Rio. Later, his former master deemed him ungrateful and thought the black was a threat to him. Thus the businessman asked the police to deport his former slave, who was sent to Africa in January 1848. In October of the same year Cesário reappeared in Rio, to be deported again in November.

25. Maço IIIJ7–42, ANRJ.

26. Beatriz Mamigonian mentions a similar strategy put to an altogether different use—that of passing as a "free African" (*africano livre*): in the 1850s, *ladino* slaves sought to pass as recently arrived Africans to mingle with Africans apprehended in the illegal trade, thus seeking to achieve their right to freedom in this way; "To Be a Liberated African in Brazil," 263.

27. Códice 335, volume 1, "Registro de correspondência reservada expedida pela polícia, 1835–1839," folha 1, verso, ANRJ. For an example of correspondence addressed by Eusébio to the justices of the peace demanding recruits, see, in the same book, the document dated December 13, 1835, folhas 5 and 6.

28. Eusébio de Queiróz to Limpo de Abreu, document entitled "List of crimes committed in the Court in the month of January, 1836"; maço IJ6–172, ANRJ.

29. Maço IJ6–212, "Secretaria de Polícia da Corte, ofícios com anexos, 1849," ANRJ.

30. Maço IJ6–211, ANRJ.

31. Maço IJ6–171, ANRJ.

32. "Senhor, que tristes dhis [*sic*] tem acompanhado a Suppte. Thereza Joaquina maim terna vendo a seu unico filho entranhas do seu coração a quatro mezes retido em huma prizão da correição só por que foi encontrado hum bocado fora do seu Juizo! concluido os quatro mezes procurou a Suppte. naquela casa de correição ao dito seu filho Belizario Joze de Oliveira visto ter-se acabado o tempo foi então que soube ter hido para bordo da Fragata de guerra. Quem hade valer a Suppte. em tal dezamparo! Aquele filho e unico q. a Suppte. tem hé quem a socorre pelo seu officio de carpinteiro: as nescecidades a estão perceguindo; amanhece o dia não tem o pão para o comer; valhame o Magte mandando-lhe intregar o seu filho para matar a fome a sua maim por ser esta ação do agrado de Deos socorrendo V. Mgte. deste modo a huma viuva necessitada que vem pedir seu filho por cuja esmola

E R Mce.

Signal de Thereza Joaqna [cruz]

Joze Machado Tores Homem."

33. For another letter of a mother seeking to liberate her son from naval service, see maço IJ6–211, ANRJ; the episode happened in 1848 and the mother's name is Ana Rosa de Jesus.

34. Decree number 151, chapter 1, article 6th, April 11, 1842; *Colleção das Leis do imperio do Brasil*.

35. Maço IJ6–185, ANRJ.

36. Maço IJ6–190, ANRJ. For evidence regarding support to slave dealers in certain sectors of society, see Jaime Rodrigues, *O Infame Comércio: Propostas e Experiências no Final do Tráfico de Africanos para o Brasil (1800–1850)* (Campinas: Editora da UNICAMP, 2000), chapters 3 and 4.

37. Maço IJ6–196, ANRJ.

38. For a quite different perspective on Eusébio de Queiróz, see Jeffrey Needell, *The Party of Order: The Conservatives, the State, and Slavery in the Brazilian Monarchy, 1831–1871* (Stanford: Stanford University Press, 2006). According to this author, Eusébio had "remarkable personal attributes" and was "an acclaimed prodigy" (p. 67); "celebrated as the prestigious voice of saquaremas [members of the conservative party] in the Chamber of 1848," he had "garnered considerable national prestige for the precision and acuity of his speeches" (p. 135); he "had won praise" for his work as chief of police (p. 68), a "crucial position" in which he had a valuable "apprenticeship" (p. 135), and so on. All these statements may be debatable, if one chooses to depict Eusébio merely reproducing what his political peers and accomplices in the Conservative Party said of him. Moreover, Needell's account is unknowledgeable regarding Eusébio's deeds as chief of police.

39. Maço IJ6–172, ANRJ.

40. Maço IJ6–173, ANRJ.

41. Maço IJ6–185, ANRJ.

42. Maço IJ6–185, ANRJ.

43. Maço IJ6–186, ANRJ.

44. For a pioneering article on the subject, see Marcus J. M. de Carvalho, "'Quem Furta Mais e Esconde': O Roubo de Escravos em Pernambuco, 1832–1855," *Revista do Instituto Histórico e Geográfico Brasileiro* 150, no. 363, (April/June 1989): 317–44.

45. For example, on May 19, 1839, Eusébio wrote to the minister of justice to discuss measures to prevent the stealing of Africans held in ships accused of participating in the slave trade; IJ6–191, ANRJ. For a specific case, see the report on the attempted stealing of Africans seized in the brigantine Ganges; IJ6–194, ANRJ. Here the pioneering work is by Judy Bieber Freitas, "Slavery and Social Life: Attempts to Reduce Free People to Slavery in the Sertão Mineiro, Brazil, 1850–1871," *Journal of Latin American Studies* 26, no. 3, (October 1994), 597–619. For a possibly telling example, of a Portuguese man accused of kidnapping and selling a freed girl (*crioulinha forra*), see IJ6–172, ANRJ.

46. Decree n. 138, October 15, 1837, *Colleção das Leis do Imperio do Brazil*.

47. Maço IJ6–194, ANRJ.

48. For an example of Mina blacks deported in 1839 for suspected insurrection, see IJ6–191. In 1844, a member of the prominent Nabuco de Araújo family sought and obtained from the government the "re-exportation" of the free African (*africano livre*)

Felício, Mina, who appeared to have moved from being a faithful gardener to a black runaway (*negro fugido*) and a threat to the family; he was sent to Angola; maço IJ6–202. Similar examples appear regularly in the documentation. João José Reis refers to the summary deportation of freed people to Africa following the Bahian insurrection of 1835; *Slave Rebellion in Brazil: The Muslim Uprising of 1835 in Bahia* (Baltimore, Johns Hopkins University Press, 1993), 207–208.

49. For the deportation of a Portuguese man accused of being a "well-known slave stealer," in 1838, see IJ6–190, ANRJ.

50. Maço IJ6–199, ANRJ.

51. For similar episodes in Pernambuco, see Marcus J. M. Carvalho, 327–28.

52. Maço IIIJ7–42, Registro de ofícios relativos ao calabouço (1844–8), ANRJ.

53. Maço IIIJ7–42, ANRJ.

54. Jean Hébrard, "Esclavage et dénomination: Imposition et appropriation d'un nom chez les esclaves de la Bahia au XIXe siècle," *Cahiers du Brésil Contemporain* 53/54 (2003): 31–92.

55. For evidence of increased suffering in the crossing of the Atlantic during the period in which the slave trade continued illegally, see the documents collected in Robert Edgar Conrad, *Children of God's Fire: A Documentary History of Black Slavery in Brazil* (University Park: Pennsylvania State University Press, 1994), 28–48.

56. Maço IJ6–191, ANRJ.

57. These examples of ways to produce documents regarding slave property derive from the general observation of cases that appear in police records and prison books in which there was dispute for the possession of a supposed slave. Other types of documents that appear in this context are baptismal records, passports issued for slaves traveling with their masters, depositions in judicial cases. Baptismal records, deemed relevant in the case of litigation regarding the freedom or bondage of blacks born in Brazil, did not seem important for the case of newly arrived Africans, who generally were not baptized after 1831. For a packet which contains several rich examples of such disputes, see IJ6–203 (police papers for 1845). For a telling case about the importance of baptismal records regarding the status of a black Brazilian at birth, see Conselho de Estado, pareceres, seção Império, códice 783, volume 2 (1876–7), document 2, ANRJ; I addressed this story in Sidney Chalhoub, "The Politics of Silence: Race and Citizenship in Nineteenth-Century Brazil," *Slavery and Abolition* 27, n0.1, (2006), 71–85.

58. Maço IJ6–218, ANRJ.

59. *Annaes da Câmara dos Deputados*, 1854, volume 4. The speech delivered by João Maurício Wanderley on September 1, 1854, is the most important piece for our purposes here, and most of it appears translated in Conrad, *Children of God's Fire*, 343–50.

60. Robert Slenes, "The Brazilian Internal Slave Trade, 1850–1888: Regional Economies, Slave Experience, and the Politics of a Peculiar Market," in Walter Johnson, ed., *The Chattel Principle: Internal Slave Trades in the Americas* (New Haven: Yale

University Press, 2004), 325–70; the quotes are from pp. 355–56. For stories of northern captives uprooted by the domestic slave trade and found in the city of Rio, sometimes seeking to find their way back north, see Sidney Chalhoub, *Visões da Liberdade,* chapter 1.

61. The quotes in this paragraph are from Conrad, *Children of God's Fire,* 349–50.

62. For this summary, I have relied on a wealth of documentation on the subject, to be used in a future paper about slave auctions and the precariousness freedom in Brazil from the 1840s to the 1870s. The main series pertaining to the *calabouço* is the III J7, "Registro [sometimes "Minutas"] de ofícios relativos ao calabouço," ANRJ.

Rosalie of the Poulard Nation

Freedom, Law, and Dignity in the Era of the Haitian Revolution

REBECCA J. SCOTT AND JEAN M. HÉBRARD

For Marie Louise (Loulou) Van Velsen, kin-keeper

On December 4, 1867, the ninth day of the convention to write a new post–Civil War constitution for the state of Louisiana, delegate Edouard Tinchant rose to make a proposal. Under the Congressional Reconstruction Acts of 1867, the voters of Louisiana had elected ninety-eight delegates—half of them men of color—to a constitutional convention charged with drafting a founding document with which the state could reenter the Union. Edouard Tinchant was a twenty-six-year-old immigrant to New Orleans, principal of a school for freed children on St. Claude Avenue. Having made something of a name for himself as a Union Army veteran and vigorous proponent of equal rights, he had stood for and won election from the multiracial Sixth Ward of New Orleans.[1]

In this speech on the floor of Mechanics' Hall, Tinchant proposed that the convention should provide "for the legal protection in this State of all women" in their civil rights, "without distinction of race or color, or without reference to their previous condition."Over the next weeks, Tinchant plunged into additional debates on voting rights and public accommodations, staking out a position in favor of a wide suffrage and the same "public rights" for all citizens. Then, in the last days of the convention, he returned to the topic of women's rights, and particularly the recognition of conjugal relationships that had not been formalized by marriage. He proposed that "to prevent concubinage in this State, the General Assembly shall enact such laws that will facilitate all women, without distinction of race or color, to sue for breach of promise [of marriage]. The General Assembly shall also provide to compel to marriage upon application of one of the parties, such persons who may have lived together not less than one year consecutively."[2]

This eagerness to compel men to marriage is surprising in a twenty-six-year-old male, and his implicit call to formalize interracial unions is notable for its boldness.[3] Who was this brash young man? Tracing the French-born Edouard Tinchant back through the surviving archival record, we find him studying in public schools in the city of Pau in the south of France during the 1848 revolution and then emigrating with his parents to Belgium after Louis-Napoléon Bonaparte's 1851 coup d'état. Drawing on experience from New Orleans, Edouard's older brothers developed an international cigar-trading business based in Antwerp. Edouard himself turned up in New Orleans in early 1862, in the midst of the Civil War, ostensibly to work with his brother Joseph, a tobacconist there. After the city was taken by Union forces in April, Edouard made his abolitionist beliefs public, and volunteered to serve in a newly constituted Union Army regiment of men of color. Demobilized in August of 1863, he returned to the cigar trade, but wrote exuberant letters to the editor of the *New Orleans Tribune* laying out his vision of citizenship and equality. These youthful experiences help to explain the intensity of Edouard Tinchant's refusal of legalized caste distinctions and of what he called "aristocratic tyranny."[4]

But there is more. In addition to building on his political education in Europe, and invoking his service in the Union Army, Tinchant also described himself in a letter to the editor in 1864 as a "son of Africa," and he later referred to himself as of "Haitian descent." These hints led us to the French colonial archives in Aix-en-Provence, where we located documents that reveal a still-deeper story, that of Edouard Tinchant's enslaved grandmother, a woman first called "Rosalie of the Poulard nation," and later Rosalie Vincent.[5]

Examining each of the surviving documents in which Rosalie Vincent intervened, one discerns her efforts to achieve freedom and to protect her sons, her daughters, and her grandchildren. Edouard Tinchant's conceptions of citizenship and of women's rights can from this perspective be anchored in three generations of experience, with enslavement and the Haitian revolution as the points of departure. This family's story, in turn, becomes part of a history of vernacular concepts of rights and dignity in the Atlantic world, concepts rooted in the awareness of individual and family vulnerability. The family's multiple encounters with administrative and legal writings—including manumission papers, baptismal records, wills, and marriage contracts—suggest some of the dynamics of engagement with law they sought to assert and document freedom and to secure its full benefits. Their story also suggests the importance of citizenship to those who had known statelessness in its starkest form, that of enslavement and deportation.[6]

Jérémie, Saint-Domingue

Our first documentary trace of the woman called Rosalie of the Poulard nation is a 1793 notarized contract from Jérémie, on the northern coast of the southern peninsula of the French colony of Saint-Domingue. In this document, a free black woman

named Marthe Guillaume [Aliés], a *marchande* (female merchant), sold a slave designated "Rosalie nation Poulard" to a *mulâtre* freedman named Jean-Baptiste Mongol, a
butcher. Despite its geographical isolation from the colony's sugar-producing centers of
the north and west, the district of Jérémie held a substantial population of slaves, most
of them employed in the production of coffee, others working in town or as domestics.[7]
The term "Poulard" following Rosalie's name referred to speakers of Pulaar, and by
extension to the group generally called Peul in French and Fulbe in English. She had
evidently been made a captive years before, somewhere in the broad area across which
the Peul had migrated, extending from the Senegal River valley to the upper Guinea
coast and inland to Mali and beyond. She may have been purchased in the Galam
trade, the annual convoy of boats that traveled upriver from the West African island
port of Saint-Louis du Sénégal to exchange textiles, paper, and other merchandise for
gum Arabic (used in textile processing) and captives.[8] It is possible that she had been
brought to the Americas on an English slaver, for a vigorous contraband trade through
Jamaica to southern Saint-Domingue had flourished before the French Revolution.
Given her age, however, it seems more likely that she came on a French ship leaving
the port of Saint-Louis at the mouth of the Senegal River at some point between the
early 1780s, when the French took Saint-Louis back from the English, and 1792, when
the direct trade was interrupted by revolution in Saint-Domingue and in France.[9]

Ethnonyms designating Senegambian origins were relatively infrequent in Saint-
Domingue. Most African-born slaves appeared in the records with the designation
Congo, Arada, or Nagó, suggesting origins further south in Africa. Even among the
approximately 10 percent of African-born slaves who were from Senegambia, the
labels Bambara, Sénégal, or Mandingo, rather than Poulard, were the most common.
Thus while a name like Jean Congo could refer to any of several people in a particular
neighborhood, the name Rosalie de nation Poulard, applied to a young woman living
in the relatively small community of Jérémie, can reasonably be assumed to refer to a
single individual.[10]

By the date of the first appearance of Rosalie of the Poulard nation in the archival
record, France had been in revolution for three and a half years, with reverberations
throughout its colonies. Free men and women of color knew that this was the moment
to push for rights that had previously been denied them.[11] In the enormously complex
web of events that we now refer to as the Haitian Revolution, struggles in the district
of Jérémie were particularly convoluted. Following the slave uprising in the Northern
Plain in August of 1791, some slaves and free people of color in the southern peninsula
pushed to break the monopoly on power of their white neighbors. In December of
1791 the town council of Jérémie faced attacks from men they characterized as "brig-
ands," and the councilors implored the revolutionary government in France to send
help. In the councilors' view, it was the *gens de couleur* (free people of color) who had
triggered an uprising of the *ateliers* (the slave work forces) in the outlying districts.[12]

Although some families of mixed ancestry owned large coffee plantations and dozens of slaves, thus sharing the economic interests of their white counterparts, others simply worked in the countryside as farmers or in town as artisans, and were closely tied to those still in slavery. It was in this milieu that Rosalie of the Poulard nation had been held in the early 1790s, by a man named Alexis Couba, who had himself been freed from slavery in 1778. Couba had first acquired a slave named Anne, whom he married in 1781. Under the Code Noir that formally governed in such matters, Anne became free by virtue of the marriage. Alexis Couba had gone on to acquire at least one more slave: Rosalie de nation Poulard, whom he had subsequently transferred to the *marchande* Marthe Guillaume.[13]

Marthe Guillaume owned several properties in the center of town, and had married one of her daughters into the family of Noel Azor, himself an activist man of color closely involved with the ongoing political struggles. Marthe Guillaume's business dealings regularly took her before the local public notaries, where she was required each time to display her own proof of freedom in order to have standing to make a contract. As of the early 1790s, then, Rosalie of the Poulard nation was held as a slave in the extended household of an entrepreneurial free woman of color, a household linked through marriage to additional free families of color in the countryside, and led by a woman adept at dealing with law and formal writing. The ties between Rosalie and Marthe Guillaume seem to have been sufficiently close that in a January 1793 draft of her will, Marthe Guillaume planned to grant Rosalie her freedom. But a few days later she changed her mind, selling Rosalie to the butcher named Jean-Baptiste Mongol.[14] Events in the colony were evolving rapidly, however, bringing the whole structure of hierarchy, color privilege, and the ownership of persons into question. Hoping to forestall further revolt by placating free people of color while temporizing on the question of slavery, in April of 1792 the National Assembly in Paris had eliminated formal legal distinctions of color among free people in the colony. Alarmed white planters, however, had no desire to relinquish these social distinctions, and their recalcitrance led to further confrontations with their neighbors. When the municipal council in Jérémie was seated without any members of color, protests among the people "formerly known as colored" began again, followed by uprisings in the countryside.[15]

The civil commissioners sent by the French Republic to try to manage the crisis could see that this kind of impasse would further undermine order on the island. By June of 1793 the commissioners were persuaded that the only way to retain the colony for France was to ride the crest of the wave of claims made by slaves and free people of color, in order to use those energies to thwart white counterrevolution or incursions by the Spanish who controlled the other half of the island of Hispaniola. The commissioners had formed armed Legions of Equality from among the population of color, and took the key step of declaring the abolition of slavery in the north. These decrees were to be extended to the south in October of 1793. Officially, slavery would soon be gone in places like Jérémie, and the law would recognize no claims to property in men and women.[16]

Faced with the prospect of losing control over those whom they held as slaves, a group of wealthy white property-holders, including men from Jérémie, had been seeking help from the British. By the autumn of 1793, the British were willing to step in, aiming both to humble the French and to grab a piece of the still-rich colony. Redcoats dispatched from Jamaica landed at Jérémie in late September of 1793. The presence of British troops from 1793 onward shielded slaveholders in the district of Jérémie from the direct legal effects of the abolition of slavery won by the rebels. The British were nonetheless faced with continuing pressure from General André Rigaud, a man of color fighting throughout the south in the name of the French Republic. By the end of 1794 Republican forces had regained control of Léogane to the east and Tiburon to the south. At the same time, the British confronted what one colonist described as "une masse de Canaille attachée à la République" (a rabble still attached to the Republic), that is, a population of non-elite whites and other citizens unwilling to shift their loyalty to the British occupiers.[17]

Despite Republican attacks on a fort near the outlying coastal settlement of Les Abricots, the British were still in control of Jérémie in December of 1795, when we find Marthe Guillaume back in possession of Rosalie. This time, however, Marthe Guillaume came to a notary not to sell or to buy, but to register the *affranchissement* (individual manumission from the bonds of slavery) of Rosalie, designated *négresse de nation Poulard* (black woman of the Poulard nation). The text of the document spoke only of Rosalie's fidelity, and made no reference to any payment by Rosalie or anyone else—though such payment could well have occurred surreptitiously outside the view of the notary. The document granted full liberty to Rosalie, and enjoined her to follow all the laws governing freedmen and freedwomen in the colony. Marthe Guillaume promised to seek the necessary formal ratification of Rosalie's freedom from the British authorities in Jérémie.[18]

The relationship between law and slavery, however, was in a state of flux. With antislavery Republican forces pressing at the edge of the area of British control, and the British governor promising freedom to some black men in order to persuade them to enlist in support of the occupation, it was not easy to maintain the social subordination essential to bondage. At the same time, the governor's advisors among the planters exhorted him to block all non-military manumissions—in their view, the colony held too many free men of color already, and manumissions of individual women entailed a loss of the labor power of their future children as well.[19] Rosalie's status would thus have been thoroughly ambiguous. No longer claimed by her former owner, but probably without a properly ratified manumission paper to prove her freedom, she would have been mobile but vulnerable.

Attacks against the British occupation of the colony gained strength in the years that followed, and by 1798 the British withdrew their forces.[20] The Republicans took control, and General Rigaud was acknowledged by the French to be the ruler of this portion of Saint-Domingue, though to the north General Toussaint L'Ouverture sought to extend his own forces southward. The formalities of full abolition could now in principal be observed in the region around Jérémie, with all of those who had been enslaved henceforth designated *affranchis, cultivateurs,* or simply *nègres* and *négresses libres.* Rosalie of the Poulard nation was, along with everyone else, now legally free.[21]

She next appears in the written record the following year, this time designated Marie Françoise *dite* Rosalie *négresse libre*—Marie Françoise, called Rosalie, free black woman. The reference to a baptismal name—Marie Françoise—and to her familiar name of Rosalie is intriguing. This was a sacramental record, so perhaps a neglected baptismal name was being recalled for the purposes of the church.[22] The event was an important one: the parish priest of neighboring Cap-Dame-Marie, which served the rural district of Les Abricots, was recording her as the mother of a "natural child," whom he baptized with the name Elizabeth Dieudonné.[23] The term "natural child" indicated that the parents were not married. The baby's father, however, was present and acknowledged paternity.

The father's name was given simply as Michel Vincent, without a courtesy title. (As a European and a property owner, Vincent might have expected the title Sieur). From other records we learn that his full name was Michel Étienne Henry Vincent, and that he owned a small farm in the coastal community of Les Abricots. Son of a notary from Le Mans, in France, he had migrated to Saint-Domingue around 1770, acquiring a monopoly privilege on the sale of meat in the district of Les Cayes, and marrying a rich widow. But with the 1789 revolution in France, and its counterpart in the colonies, a royal monopoly became less and less useful. His wife, moreover, had adroitly secured her own property for her children by a previous marriage. Apparently ruined financially, Michel Vincent started over in the coffee country around Jérémie. The town of Jérémie had held only 180 houses in 1789—several of them owned and rented out to Europeans by the *marchande* Marthe Guillaume. Michel Vincent was not a man of much property, though he occasionally went to the notary to sell off small pieces of his land in Les Abricots to his neighbors, including the citizen Jean called Tomtom and the citizen Olive, both designated *cultivateurs,* the term often used for former slaves in the countryside. By the mid-1790s, his wife had died. It is not difficult to imagine circumstances under which this widowed Frenchman slipping down the social ladder might have met Rosalie of the Poulard nation.[24]

Under *ancien régime* rules, Michel Vincent's presence as the father at the 1799 baptism fell short of full legitimation of the child through marriage. Under much-contested French revolutionary rules, however, natural children could under certain circumstances make inheritance claims alongside those of legitimate children. It was anyone's guess what rules might hold by the time Michel Vincent died, but he seems to have been making some effort to secure the baby Elizabeth's future in the face of uncertainty, giving her a recognition of paternity and a godmother and godfather to whom she might turn for assistance in an emergency. The baby's godfather was le Sieur Lavolaille, a ship's carpenter. The baby's godmother was Marie Blanche widow Aubert. Like the father, the godmother carried neither a courtesy title nor a color qualifier. She apparently had sufficient status to discourage the priest from attributing a color marker to her, though documents drawn up some years later in Louisiana refer to her as a *femme de couleur libre* (a free woman of color).[25]

By 1799 the sedimented layers of respect and disrespect that characterized *ancien régime* slaveholding society had been thoroughly churned up by the Haitian Revolution, but the crucial fact of freedom remained insecure. As Napoléon Bonaparte consolidated power in Europe, he moved to subordinate the long-free and the recently freed in Saint-Domingue and secure his vision of an American empire. In late 1801 Bonaparte sent an expedition under his brother-in-law, General Victor-Emmanuel Leclerc, to wrest power away from the black and brown men who had come to hold the title of general in Saint-Domingue. The district commander in Jérémie attempted to resist, but troops from France succeeded in entering the town in early 1802, and then received reinforcements by sea. In May of 1802 the consuls in Paris reauthorized the Atlantic slave trade and reasserted slavery in the French colony of Martinique, signaling Bonaparte's ultimate intention to restore slavery in Saint-Domingue as well.[26]

Black soldiers in Saint-Domingue who had been loyal to the French Republic could see the growing risks of a French reoccupation under Napoleonic auspices. French commanders in turn became more suspicious of black men who remained in their ranks, and their hostility to their own black troops triggered still further defections to the opposition. By October of 1802 General Leclerc reported that insurrection had broken out in Jérémie, and that plantations there had been burned. The last letters written by General Leclerc before yellow fever carried him away convey something of the situation in the colony: "All of the blacks are persuaded by the letters coming from France, by the law reestablishing the slave trade, and by the decrees of General Richepanse which reestablish slavery in Guadeloupe, that we want to turn them into slaves." "These men," he wrote, "do not want to give up." The rumor was spreading that the French would soon be forced to leave. The remaining black troops who had fought under the French moved quickly to shift to rebel lines, pulled by events and pushed by the murderous contempt shown for them by Leclerc and his brutal successor General Donatien Rochambeau.[27]

In the last weeks of March 1803, Rochambeau ordered a coordinated attack by French forces and Polish legionnaires on the rebel-held cities of the south, but to no avail. Some plantation laborers from Les Abricots joined the insurrection as black revolutionaries advanced rapidly toward Jérémie from the south, besieging and starving out French garrisons along the way. The revolutionaries used fire as their most frightening weapon, burning fields and hillsides as they advanced.[28]

It was on May 10, 1803, that the next document in which Rosalie appears was created. As unbridled war approached, Michel Vincent made plans to leave for France—but without Rosalie or her children. Rosalie now faced the prospect of becoming a solitary mother and a refugee of war in a countryside literally in flames. Under the circumstances, Michel Vincent was apparently persuaded—probably by Rosalie herself—that if he was going to abandon them he owed her an effort to give additional written force to her legal freedom and that of her children. Without the aid of a notary, but apparently using an earlier manumission document as a model, Michel Vincent covered a sheet of paper with improvised legalistic language. (He was, after all, still a notary's son, and such language may have come easily.) This was a document drawn up in a moment of great danger, a shield designed to ward off the worst. It was something between a text and a talisman, an unofficial declaration intended to have the force of a notarized document, but which lacked the signature of a notary.[29]

This 1803 text begins by identifying Marie Françoise called Rosalie as *négresse de nation Poulard.* In the next lines of the document, Michel Vincent declared—altogether falsely—that Rosalie and her four children were his slaves. He enumerated the children: "Juste Theodore Mulatre, Marie Louise dite Resinette Mulatresse, Etienne hilaire dit Cadet mulatre, et Elisabeth dite Dieudonné Mulatresse." Étienne, the younger boy, had been given Michel Vincent's own middle name. Elizabeth had been recognized as his at baptism. All were designated as *mulâtre* or *mulâtresse,* implying mixed African and European parentage. It seems quite possible that Michel Vincent was the father of all of Rosalie's children.[30]

Michel Vincent then declared that he granted freedom to Rosalie and her four children, using the conventional language of gratitude for Rosalie's loyal services, "in sickness and in health." He promised to exact no further services from her, except those that she might provide of her own good will, and for which he would pay her wages. She was free to go wherever she wished and to pursue her own affairs. He declared that the document was to have as much force as if it had been authenticated by a notary. In view of his possible departure for France, he gave the bearer of the document the power to "pursue its ratification before the chiefs of this colony, or in whatever other country allied to France the said *négresse* might go and establish herself."[31]

The form of this 1803 manumission document is quite odd. We know that four years earlier, Rosalie had already been designated a *négresse libre* when Michel Vincent went to baptize their daughter Elizabeth Dieudonné, and that Elizabeth had been born free. Rosalie herself had been provisionally freed through manumission by Marthe Guillaume in 1795, and then definitively freed by virtue of the edicts of emancipation passed by the French National Assembly. So in what sense did she and her children need to be freed once again?

The answer may have to do with the power of paper in a situation of uncertainty, and the symbolic and juridical potential of documents, even unofficial ones. With war raging around them, it was difficult to know what was going to happen next, and whether the abolition of slavery in Saint-Domingue would hold. Moreover, conditions in Les Abricots were becoming so dangerous that Rosalie might herself need to flee to one of the nearby Caribbean islands—and nearly everywhere else in the Americas slavery was still in place. Even the most rigid slaveholding societies nonetheless generally acknowledged the right of a slave owner to relinquish a claim to his or her own particular "property" in another human being, subject to varying degrees of government regulation.[32] So an individual grant of freedom signed by a white man declaring himself to be a slave owner was likely to travel a good deal better than a French Republican decree (or than the private document created by the black woman Martonne under a now defunct British occupation force). And Michel Vincent would have to declare them all to be his slaves in order to have the authority to free them.[33]

Michel Vincent's plan to leave for France never materialized. In the turmoil of May and June of 1803, he may have been unable to find a passport, money for passage, or a willing captain. Perhaps his health worsened; perhaps he lost heart when the moment came to leave his children; perhaps he simply ran out of time. A bitter eyewitness account of these weeks written by a French planter and officer named Peter Chazotte enables us to envision something of what happened next.

Chazotte writes that in June of 1803, in the face of the advance of black rebels from the south, the French general Sarrazin ordered French troops and the Polish legions accompanying them to withdraw from the rural districts around Jérémie. Chazotte was enraged at what he perceived as a cowardly decision, but rode from plantation to plantation conveying the order and warning civilians to flee. Reports soon reached him that "the country . . . over our mountain *was all on fire.*" As flames approached, people struggled to find some path of retreat and refuge. In the bay at Les Abricots "there being but two small vessels, it was agreed to embark first the white women and children, and after the colored ones." Those who could not make it on board trudged on foot along the dirt highway toward Jérémie, a mass of the displaced, black, white, and brown, with only what they could carry with them. "We abandoned the small town of Abricots at the moment when a column of a thousand blacks rushed in it, with flaming torches in their hands."[34]

The town of Jérémie, however, offered no permanent refuge. France and Britain were again at war, and the French troops could not hope for supplies or reinforcements from metropolitan France. Within days the town would be evacuated by the French commander, whose besieged French and Polish troops were near starvation. Some civilians went over to the lines of the revolutionaries, hoping for the best; others tried to escape by boat. Hostile English ships hovering in the vicinity captured some of the departing boats, both military and civilian, but many passengers eventually made it to the nearest safe haven, Santiago, on the eastern coast of the Spanish colony of Cuba.[35] Michel Vincent, Rosalie, and at least one or two of the children were among them.[36]

Santiago de Cuba

The Cuban port city was staggered by the arrival of boatloads of refugees from various ports in Saint-Domingue, eventually numbering close to eighteen thousand. White refugees, women of color, children, and loyal "domestics" were permitted to land; the ragged French troops were generally not allowed into the city.[37] Out of fear of revolutionary contagion the authorities ordered all men of color over the age of thirteen among the refugees to be held offshore, and deported to the mainland (*Tierra Firme*) at the first opportunity. In the eyes of Spanish administrators, former slaves who had witnessed or participated in the Haitian revolution were an unequivocal threat—though a few could perhaps be trusted if they accepted reenslavement and showed proper subordination to those who had been their masters.[38]

Michel Vincent and Rosalie made their way ashore, separately or together, and their daughter Elizabeth landed as well. Rosalie's daughter Marie Louise seems to have made it to Cuba, but Rosalie's sons Juste Théodore and Étienne Hilaire vanish from the record. Perhaps they had remained behind in revolutionary Saint-Domingue, soon to become Haiti, or were trapped on the boats held offshore by order of the Spanish governor. It is possible that they entered Cuba surreptitiously and stayed out of view of the list makers and record keepers.[39]

For a time, Michel Vincent apparently worked as a *mareschal,* a farrier, attending to horses, and he and Rosalie raised pigs and chickens. With so many French citizens in refuge in Cuba, the officers of the Agence des Prises de la Guadeloupe, men charged with adjudicating the property of ships seized by French corsairs, improvised a temporary response to the problem of dealing with the émigrés' affairs. Neither a consulate nor an embassy, this office did not legally have the authority to notarize documents or to undertake diplomatic tasks. Their main goal was to gain revenue from the sale of prize ships, and channel it into the maintenance of the remaining French colonies, now largely isolated by British control of the seas. But these bureaucrats unofficially served the "functions of a chancery," and copied or took deposit of relevant papers that the French refugees might give them. By 1804 Michel Vincent had apparently become ill, and on March 14 he submitted a last will and testament to their office in Santiago, where it was *homologué* (validated).[40]

Three days later Rosalie herself came to ask the same officials to register the freedom papers that had been drawn up in Les Abricots ten months earlier. With Michel nearing death, Rosalie seems to have hoped that by causing this text to be written into a French register she could give it greater legal force, leveraging up the authoritativeness of her fragile proof of freedom. As Rosalie could see from events around her, other women arriving from Saint-Domingue, as free as she was under the French Republican decrees, were treated in Cuba as slaves, and sold from one putative owner to another. Indeed, there was no guarantee that the revenue-hungry French officials would be immune from the same temptation. But she took the chance.⁴¹

The French scribe in Santiago began his task as if it were a slave owner who stood before him, writing, "Registration of freedom by—"Then he stopped, inserted a period, and began again with a different preposition, clarifying that this text dealt with the freedom *of* the woman named Marie Françoise called Rosalie. At this crucial moment Rosalie was, in effect, authorized to attest to her own liberty. In a last gasp of revolutionary-era practice in France and Saint-Domingue, the official gave her the courtesy title *citoyenne* (citizen) as he transcribed her text into his records. He also provided her with a copy of the new document with his own signature added. In truth, the courtesy title *citoyenne* carried almost no legal content; the Agence des Prises was not a true consulate; and acts registered by the agent would not necessarily be respected by Cuban colonial courts. For the moment, however, with this hybrid text in hand, and the man who claimed to be her former master acting in accordance with it, Rosalie apparently retained her freedom in Santiago. But within days, Michel Vincent was dead, and an executor was named to carry out the terms of his will.⁴²

The report of the executor has survived in the registers of the French officials in Santiago, a vivid record of the way that the direct intrusion of a somewhat more formal proceeding could disrupt the arrangements negotiated in the legal limbo of war and revolution. The executor, François Vallée, a tailor and fellow émigré from Saint-Domingue, began by explaining what he had done with the moveable goods belonging to the estate. He had sold "the little pigs" as well as the "*serpes et haches*" (billhooks and axes), yielding a modest seven and a half gourdes, equivalent to an equal number of Spanish piastres. He had given the red horse, along with the chickens and the *chaudières* (kettles), to Citizen Rosalie, who was described as the *légataire particulière* (individual legatee) of Michel Vincent. So far, so good. Then the executor reported that he had been about to give Marie Louise Désir to Rosalie as well, as called for in the will. This may well have been Rosalie's daughter, elsewhere designated Marie Louise *dite* Resinette. Michel Vincent had apparently tried to ensure that Rosalie could keep custody of Marie Louise, even if the manumission document failed to hold, by specifying this arrangement. But the executor testified that given the debts that encumbered the estate, he had not delivered Marie Louise to Rosalie. The implication was that she would be retained by the executor as a servant or sold as a slave in order to pay off Michel Vincent's creditors.⁴³

Rosalie's second daughter, the freeborn Elizabeth Dieudonné, was apparently in the care of her godmother, the widow Aubert, who had also fled from Les Abricots to Santiago. Counting on more prosperous Saint-Domingue refugees for help, however, was a risky strategy, for many of them were busily converting the people of color who had fled with them back into slaves. The widow Aubert may have taken protective custody of Elizabeth, but she hardly eschewed slaveholding. Whether she treated Elizabeth as a daughter, as a servant, or as a combination of the two, is difficult to discern.[44]

In the era of the Napoleonic wars, moreover, all of the Saint-Domingue refugees in Cuba were vulnerable to shifts in European politics. When Bonaparte's forces marched into Spain in 1808, the relationship between Spain and any French subjects in the Spanish colonies was suddenly cast into doubt. Once Spaniards in the Iberian peninsula rose up against Napoléon's forces in May of 1808, France came to be widely perceived as an enemy in the colonies as well. In earlier years, the Spanish colonial government had offered some refugees in Cuba the possibility of swearing allegiance to the Spanish crown, and local authorities had been pleased with the rise of coffee plantations developed by émigré planters. But after the uprisings in the peninsula there was strong pressure to expel the French from Spain's colonies, forcing the hand even of their protectors. In April of 1809 the governor ordered all French citizens to leave the island.[45]

For Rosalie and her daughters, the situation had become untenable. They were not protected by the 1793–94 general abolition, which no French official would any longer enforce. Moreover, they were part of a refugee population whose wealthier members had quickly resumed the habits of a slaveholding society, but whose host community was now ready to expel them. Those ordered to depart would again have to try to find boat, money for passage, and passports. Once again, the family would be fractured: Elizabeth accompanied her godmother, the widow Aubert, to New Orleans. Rosalie—an African woman whose status as a free person was utterly insecure in any slave society—seems to have remained in Santiago, and then found her way back to now-independent Haiti. Marie Louise disappears from the written record.[46]

New Orleans

In the spring and summer of 1809 dozens of ships filled with French-speaking refugees from eastern Cuba arrived in the port of New Orleans, and Territorial Governor William C. C. Claiborne faced an immense political problem. Many of the men and women on board those ships claimed that others among the passengers were their slaves. These "slaves" included men and women freed in Saint-Domingue, some of whom had been reenslaved in Cuba, as well as others purchased as slaves in Cuba itself. But the U.S. Congress had very recently outlawed the international slave trade, and no one was legally permitted to bring slaves into the country from abroad. One logical solution would have been to give formal recognition to the French abolition decrees of 1793–94, and declare all those who had come from Saint-Domingue to be free. But this was not the kind of solution that the governor of the slaveholding territory of Louisiana was likely to contemplate. Instead, Claiborne took the circumstances to be extraordinary, and eventually allowed the passengers to land, some as free men and women, others as slaves.[47]

The widow Aubert, godmother of Rosalie's daughter Elizabeth, had made the passage successfully from Santiago to New Orleans. The widow's companion, Jean Lambert Détry, a Belgian innkeeper turned carpenter, bought two plots of land in Faubourg Marigny, close to the river, on Rue Moreau. Détry began to work as a contractor, employing several slave sawyers. The widow quickly became an active businesswoman, buying and selling plots of land and slaves. It was in her household that the young Elizabeth Dieudonné would be raised, with the widow serving as a surrogate mother—and perhaps also as taskmaster.[48]

When Jean Lambert Détry died in 1821, he left a "mystic testament"—that is, a will prepared privately and left under seal with a notary. He left most of his property to two young women of color who were the natural daughters of his friend and executor François Xavier Freyd, but he gave the widow Aubert the usufruct of most of this property during her lifetime—and as it turned out, she lived to be ninety. He specified that two of his slaves were to be freed as soon as they attained "the age required by the law for manumission."[49] Détry also designated a bequest of $500 for the widow Aubert's goddaughter Elizabeth Dieudonné, the child of Michel Vincent and Rosalie of the Poulard nation. Détry explained the bequest by referring to her as his own goddaughter, though this was not technically accurate. Perhaps the years of living with the widow Aubert had given him this status de facto.[50] In effect, from his long conjugal relationship with the widow Aubert, Lambert Détry had developed an extended network of dependents, most of them free people of color. Détry made no mention in his will of potential heirs-at-law who might be back in Belgium, but after his death a group of those kin hired a lawyer and tried to invalidate the will, invoking Détry's open "concubinage" with the widow Aubert. They quickly settled, taking a share of the proceeds.[51]

With the promise of the bequest from Détry in hand, Elizabeth Dieudonné (who was also sometimes called Marie), now twenty-three years old, became engaged to marry a young man named Jacques Tinchant, the son of a Saint-Domingue émigrée woman of color, Suzette Bayot. At the moment when the marriage contract was drawn up in 1822, it was the widow Aubert who appeared with the prospective bride at the notary's, claiming that she had been like a mother to her since she was a child, and asserting that the bride's actual mother was currently living not in New Orleans but in what the widow still called "Saint-Domingue." Elizabeth's mother had taken on the surname of the man who never married her, and was now referred to as Rosalie Vincent.[52]

Over the years from 1799 to 1822, the web of kin and fictive kin woven around Rosalie Vincent's children had been a source of both danger and security. Marie Louise was apparently remanded into some form of servitude at the time of Michel Vincent's death, and we do not know whether she obtained her freedom again in Santiago, or perhaps came as a slave to New Orleans with one or another free person. Rosalie's other daughter Elizabeth had achieved freedom at birth, been separated from her mother to come under the patronage of the widow Aubert, and had her path to marriage smoothed by the promise of a bequest from the widow's companion Lambert Détry.[53]

A year or so after their marriage, Elizabeth Dieudonné and Jacques Tinchant took their distance from the widow.[54] Jacques went on to develop a flourishing business as a carpenter and a builder, and in 1835 he went to a notary to constitute a formal *société* with his half-brother Pierre Duhart, with the goal of buying land, building houses, and reselling. They acquired one or two slaves whose labor supplemented their own.[55] As Jacques and his wife ascended into the ranks of property owners, and began a family, some of the documents they had signed along the way seem to have troubled them. In November of 1835 they went to a notary to "rectify" Elizabeth's name as it had appeared on their marriage contract. The couple now held out a copy of her baptismal record, in which her father Michel Vincent had recognized his paternity, and they asked that her name be corrected to Elizabeth Dieudonné Vincent.[56]

The sudden and quite convenient appearance of the baptismal record—thirty-six years after its creation and thirteen years after Elizabeth's marriage—is puzzling. There is one clue: the document they proffered was not the 1799 original, but a copy made by a Haitian official in the 1820s. Given what we now know about Rosalie Vincent, a hypothesis emerges. In Les Abricots, Saint-Domingue, with the production of the manumission document signed by Michel Vincent, and then again in Santiago, with the recopying of that paper by a French official, Rosalie of the Poulard nation had shown a keen awareness of the importance of official paper. It is possible that as a girl in the Muslim society of the Senegal River valley, the woman later called Rosalie might already have learned the importance of the words written in ink on paper, and of an amulet or talisman that could protect one from harm.[57] But whether Rosalie brought this awareness with her from West Africa, or learned it in the house of the trader Marthe Guillaume on the Place d'Armes in Jérémie, or saw it for herself in the household of Michel Vincent in Les Abricots, the lesson had taken hold.

One function of official documents is to make the putative facts behind them irrelevant. Their official nature itself makes the words on paper peremptory—they supersede the complicated history behind them.[58] "Rosalie is my slave and I hereby declare her free." With an official signature, these words could become the kind of "freedom paper" that an African-born woman in the slaveholding city of Santiago would need to be able to show if stopped and questioned, or if she had business of her own to carry out at a notary. It would not matter that she had not been a slave when she left Saint-Domingue, and that Michel Vincent had in fact probably never been her master. Slavery was the creation of positive law, and that positive law had been abolished in Saint Domingue. But in slaveholding societies like Cuba, freedom too was a creation of positive law for persons of African descent, for the presumption might be slavery. So Rosalie, free in one polity, had to find a way to become free in another; and she did.

Rosalie's daughter Elizabeth faced a different challenge. Her freedom was not questioned, but her legitimacy and her standing were, for she was a "natural child," bereft of a surname of her own. Even a recognized sacramental marriage to Jacques Tinchant could not expunge that stigma. But maybe Rosalie could. In April of 1835, a two-masted ship, the brig *Ann*, landed in New Orleans after a journey from Port-au-Prince, Haiti. On its passenger list we find the name Rosalia Vincent. The Spanish form of the name Rosalie may date back to the time in Cuba; we know where the sur-name Vincent came from. It seems a good bet that Rosalie herself had obtained a copy of Elizabeth's baptismal certificate from the authorities at Jérémie, perhaps shortly after the marriage in 1822, and held it for safekeeping. She could then climb aboard a ship with that paper on her person, in order to bring it to New Orleans, where its power could be amplified by taking it before a cooperative public notary.[59]

With the notary willing to view the document as sufficient proof of paternity, Elizabeth Dieudonné now laid claim to the surname Vincent by birth from her father, and the surname Tinchant by marriage to Jacques. Given the distinction made in the Louisiana Civil Code between recognition and legitimation, it is not entirely clear that Michel Vincent's name on the baptismal record actually conferred on his "natural daughter" the legal right to adopt his surname. But the New Orleans notary, who had for years handled many of Jacques Tinchant's business dealings, assented.[60] When Elizabeth Vincent's name appeared in subsequent records, it no longer resembled that of a child born to a former slave mother, but was instead indistinguishable from the names of those born to families who had always been free.[61]

We have a final confirmation that Rosalie Vincent, now in her late sixties, had indeed made her way to New Orleans. In 1836, Jacques Tinchant and Elizabeth Vin-cent brought their most recent child to be baptized in the Cathedral of Saint-Louis, in the heart of the Vieux Carré. They gave the child the name Juste—that of his mother's brother, Rosalie's son, lost from sight in the course of the evacuation of Jérémie over thirty years earlier. It had taken three generations to reach this point, but like his older brothers, the baby Juste was designated a legitimate child, not a natural child. Alfred Duhart—the son of the New Orleans freemason and teacher Louis Duhart and of Jacques Tinchant's mother Suzette Bayot—stood as godfather. The woman they chose as godmother made no mark of her own on the sacramental record, but the priest recorded her name: Rosalie Vincent.[62]

Epilogue and Conclusion

By 1836 slavery was hardening in Louisiana, and soon the state legislature would try to block the ascent of free people of color on nearly every front. Jacques Tinchant's mother, Suzette Bayot, had already left the United States altogether, sailing for France and settling in the Basses-Pyrenées, where she was able to legalize her union with Louis Duhart.[63] A few years later their son Pierre, Jacques Tinchant's half-brother and business partner in New Orleans, followed them to the town of Gan, where he married a young Frenchwoman. In 1840 Jacques Tinchant and Elizabeth Vincent, accompanied by four of their five children, made the same journey. (Their eldest boy remained in New Orleans.) The story of their life in France, the birth of their son Edouard, their family's establishment of a cigar business in Belgium, and their sons' lives in Gan, Pau, Veracruz, New Orleans, Mobile, and Antwerp, is far too long to recount here.[64] But we might conclude by returning briefly to that extraordinary moment in the history of Louisiana with which we began this essay.

Rosalie Vincent's grandson Edouard Tinchant—the youngest of Jacques and Elizabeth's children—arrived in New Orleans from Antwerp in 1862 at the age of twenty-one. Born in France, he was coming to the city that his parents had left, as he later recalled, because his father refused to raise his sons in a New Orleans characterized by "infamous laws and stupid prejudices." After volunteering in the Union Army, Edouard drew upon his political eloquence and his polished French to make a name for himself, writing letters to the editor of the *New Orleans Tribune* to explain and advance his equal-rights credo, and becoming principal of a school for freed children when the war ended. With suffrage now open to nearly all adult males, he was elected to represent the Sixth Ward of New Orleans in the constitutional convention of 1867–68.[65]

In the end, only a portion of Edouard Tinchant's ideals would make it into the final draft of the 1868 Louisiana Constitution, and enforcing the equality of "civil, political and public rights" guaranteed in the state's new Bill of Rights turned out to be no easy task.[66] Moreover, after the convention ended, Edouard Tinchant found himself without employment. With his wife and young children, he spent the remaining years of Reconstruction in Mobile, Alabama, building his own modest cigar manufactory. When Reconstruction ended, and white supremacy emerged triumphant, Edouard and his wife Louise Debergue, like his parents in 1840, boarded a ship for another shore. They would raise their own children in the northern European city of Antwerp. If they could not thus entirely escape what Edouard called "stupid prejudices," they could at least get out of the reach of "infamous laws."[67]

Just before they left the United States, Louise gave birth to a girl. They named her Marie Louise, perhaps recalling her great-aunt Marie Louise who had been freed once by French law in Saint-Domingue in 1793–94, and again by her father's action in 1803, only to be remanded into servitude in Santiago de Cuba in 1804 as a result of the debts on her father's estate. And in the generations that followed, their descendants would continue the name, down to Edouard's great-granddaughter Marie Louise Van Velsen, who today lives in Antwerp.[68]

Edouard Tinchant's life history and his political imagination were Atlantic in scope. At different moments he claimed French citizenship, American citizenship, and Haitian ancestry. When we go back another two generations and trace the woman who was first denominated Rosalie of the Poulard nation, briefly called Citizen Rosalie, and finally called Rosalie Vincent, we can see that the family's Atlantic perspective swept even further, to the middle valley of the Senegal River, to the town of Jérémie on the southern peninsula of Saint-Domingue, to the crowded city of Santiago, Cuba, and finally to independent Haiti. Edouard Tinchant's convictions had been built on his awareness of the histories of the men and the women in his family who had faced the multiple "infamous laws" that accompanied slavery. Along with the intergenerational transmission of trauma there had also been the development of habits of engagement with writing and with the law. When Rosalie of the Poulard nation faced a crisis of war and potential abandonment in Les Abricots in 1803, she knew that the situation called for the creation of a powerful piece of writing. And she knew, as Michel Vincent was approaching death in 1804, that she needed to make sure that the manumission document he had penned was recopied into the papers of the French authorities in Santiago. Decades later, even after her younger daughter Elizabeth was herself married and a mother, Rosalie traveled from Haiti, apparently carrying a copy of the baptismal record that would belatedly confer a surname on Elizabeth. Elizabeth, in turn, would with her husband Jacques abandon their apparently successful business in New Orleans and move with their children to France, to a country where the boys could attend public schools.

In Edouard Tinchant, these habits of engagement with writing, reinforced by his study of French and Latin rhetoric at the *lycée* in Pau, would expand once he reached Louisiana into eloquent public letters and vigorous legislative initiatives. Refusal of racial hierarchy was for him a matter of first principles, as was the question of equal rights for women. Edouard could not change the past, in which the freedom of Rosalie of the Poulard nation was denied, and his mother's claim to the surname Vincent required such effort. But when the moment arrived he, like Rosalie before him, seized the opportunity to write freedom into the present.

Acknowledgments

We wish to express our gratitude to the many colleagues who have discussed ideas and helped us locate documents. The generosity of John Garrigus and David Geggus has been simply extraordinary, and we are very much in their debt for research leads, insights, and timely corrections. We also thank Orli Avi-Yonah, José Luis Belmonte, Sueann Caulfield, Myriam Cottias, Natalie Z. Davis, Mamadou Diouf, Laurent Dubois, Sam Erman, Ada Ferrer, Eric Foner, Sylvia Frey, Lindsay Ann Gish, Valérie Sega Gobert, Jane Guyer, Marial Iglesias Utset, Martha S. Jones, Jochen Kemner, Martin Klein, Paul Lachance, Dawn Logsdon, Jorge Macle, Fernando Martínez Heredia, María de los Ángeles Meriño, Mary Niall Mitchell, Vernon Palmer, Aisnara

Perera, Esther Pérez, Rebekah Pite, Lawrence Powell, David Robinson, Sylvain San-kalé, Judith Schafer, Scott Shapiro, François Weil, and Michael Zeuske. The staffs of the Archivo Nacional de Cuba in Havana, the U.S. National Archives in Washington, the Special Collections of the Library of the University of Florida-Gainesville, the Archives Départementales in Pau, the Archives du Sénégal in Dakar, the Archives Nationales in Paris, and the Centre des Archives d'Outre-Mer in Aix-en- Provence have been generous with their time and effort. Ann Wakefield, Howard Margot, Charles Johnson, and the staff of the New Orleans Notarial Research Center have gone beyond the call of duty, as have John Lawrence, Alfred Lemmon, and John Magill of the Historic New Orleans Collection, and Wayne Everard, Greg Osborn, and Irene Wainwright of the Louisiana Division, New Orleans Public Library. We owe particular thanks to Keith Manuel of the Department of History at the University of Florida, who has photographed additional documents for us in the Jérémie Papers at the University of Florida libraries. Descendants of Jacques Tinchant and Elizabeth Vincent now living in France and Belgium, particularly Philippe Struyf and Marie Louise Van Velsen, as well as genealogists Raymond Bulion, Augusta Elmwood, Andrée-Luce Fourcand, Philippe and Bernadette Rossignol, and Barbara Snow, have shared leads and ideas of various kinds. We also thank Martha S. Jones, Peter Railton, Anne F. Scott, Thomas Scott-Railton, and William Scott, who have taken time from their own work to read or listen to various early drafts. Along the way, we have presented this work at the École des Hautes Etudes en Sciences Sociales in Paris, at the Barnard Center for Research on Women in New York City, at the Program in Latin American Studies and the Department of History at Princeton University, at the Centro Juan Marinello in Havana, at Rice University in Houston, at the 2006 conference "The Reluctant Archive" at the University of Michigan, at the Université Cheik Anta Diop in Dakar, and at various smaller workshops. We are very grateful to those audiences for their comments and suggestions. A much earlier version of this essay appeared in *Genèses* (Paris) 66 (March 2007), 4–29, under the title "Les papiers de la liberté: Une mère africaine et ses enfants a l'époque de la Révolution Haïtienne."

Notes

1. On Edouard Tinchant's life history, see Rebecca J. Scott, "Public Rights and Private Commerce: An Atlantic Creole Itinerary," *Current Anthropology* 48 (April 2007), 237–49. Evidence on Tinchant's service as principal, and on his commitment to integrated schools, is in the minutes of the September 16, 1867, meeting of the Orleans Parish School Board, now held in Special Collections, Earl K. Long Library, University of New Orleans.

2. *Official Journal of the Proceedings of the Convention for Framing a Constitution for the State of Louisiana* (New Orleans: J. B. Roudanez & Co., 1867–68), 35, 116–17, 192.

3. The issue of marriage across what white supremacists saw as a "color line" arose

in other state conventions as well. See the discussion of the Arkansas debates in Hannah Rosen, *Terror in the Heart of Freedom: Citizenship, Sexual Violence, and the Meaning of Race in the Postemancipation South* (Chapel Hill: University of North Carolina Press, 2009).

4. In a letter to his parents in October of 1863, Edouard described the tension of concealing his political sympathies from those he described as the "confédérés les plus endiablés" (the most furious Confederates) who gathered at the Tinchant tobacconist on St. Charles Avenue. Edouard referred to himself, with a mild degree of self-mockery, as "le plus enragé abolitionniste de la Nouvelle Orléans" (the most fanatical abolitionist in New Orleans). See Edouard Tinchant to Mes chers parents, 28 Octobre 1863, in the family papers of the Tinchant family; a transcription of this letter was courteously provided to us by Philippe Struyf, Brussels.

5. For a discussion of the language of Edouard Tinchant's letters of 1864 and 1899, see Scott, "Public Rights and Private Commerce."

6. On slavery as statelessness, see Linda K. Kerber, "The Stateless as the Citizen's Other: A View from the United States," *American Historical Review* 112 (February 2007), 1–34; especially pp. 16–17.

7. The sale to Mongol is in "Vente par marthe Guillaume a mongol de la N^esse Rosalie," 14 January 1793, Notary Lépine, File 6C-119, Jérémie Papers, Special Collections, University of Florida Libraries (hereafter SC, UFL). Mongol's circumstances are described in detail in his 3 November 1787 marriage record. Freed himself in 1782, he married his slave Lisette, thus freeing her and legitimating their two children. St. Domingue, Etat Civil, Jérémie, 1783–1786, SOM 5Mi/60, Centre d'accueil et de recherche des Archives nationales (CARAN). The classic description of the individual parishes of the colony is Méderic Moreau de Saint-Méry, *Description topographique, physique, civil, politique et historique de la partie française de l'isle de Saint-Domingue*, reprint ed. ([1797] Paris: Société Française d'Histoire d'Outre-Mer, 2004).

8. On the history of the Peul, see Oumar Kane, *la Première hégémonie peule: Le Fuuta Tooro de Koli Tenella à Almaani Abdul* (Paris and Dakar: Karthala and Presses Universitaires de Dakar, 2004). See also Frédérique Dejou, Roger Botte, Jean Boutrais, and Jean Schmitz, eds., *Figures peules* (Paris: Karthala, 1999).

9. In view of the age attributed to her in a later notarial record, we estimate her birth to have taken place around 1767. On the slave trade to Saint-Domingue, see Jean Mettas, *Répertoire des expéditions négrières françaises au xviiie siècle*, ed. Serge and Michèle Daget, (Paris: Société Française d'Histoire d'Outre-Mer, 1984); Boubacar Barry, *Senegambia and the Atlantic Slave Trade* (Cambridge, Eng.: Cambridge University Press, 1998); Martin Klein, *Slavery and Colonial Rule in French West Africa* (Cambridge, Eng.: Cambridge University Press, 1998); and David Geggus, "Sex Ratio, Age and Ethnicity in the Atlantic Slave Trade: Data from French Shipping and Plantation Records," *Journal of African History* 30 (1989) 23–44.

10. Geggus, "Sex Ratio," explores the demographics of the enslaved population in Saint-Domingue, with particular attention to the distribution of ethnonyms. We have also found Poulard to be quite rare as a descriptor in the notarial records of Jérémie.

11. See most recently Florence Gauthier, *L'Aristocratie de l'épiderme. Le combat de la Société des Citoyens de Couleur. 1789–1791* (Paris: CNRS Edition, 2007).

12. See the letters from the mayor and council in dossier 13, DXXV/65, CARAN. See also Carolyn Fick, *The Making of Haiti: The Saint Domingue Revolution from Below* (Knoxville: University of Tennessee Press, 1990), especially Part Three, "The South."

13. The marriage of Alexis Couba and Anne, which makes reference to his *affranchissement* (manumission), is dated 9 January 1781, in SOM 5Mi/59, CARAN. The transfer of Rosalie from Alexis Couba to Marthe Guillaume is referred to in the first draft of Marthe Guillaume's last will and testament, dated 8 January 1793, Notary Lépine, File 6C-116, Jérémie Papers, SC, UFL.

14. The sale of Rosalie is "Vente par marthe Guillaume a mongol de la N^esse Rosalie," 14 January 1793, Notary Lépine, File 6C-119, Jérémie Papers, SC, UFL. The 28 February 1783 marriage of Marthe Guillaume's daughter Marie Anne [Aliés] to Jean Baptiste Azor dit Fortunat is on SOM 5 Mi/60, CARAN. For a fuller discussion of Marthe Guillaume, see Rebecca J. Scott and Jean Michel Hébrard, "Servitude, liberté et citoyenneté dans le monde atlantique des XVIIIe et XIXe siècles: Rosalie de nation Poulard," *Revue de la Société Haïtienne d'Histoire et de Géographie,* 83 (July–September 2008) : 1–52

15. See "Addresse a tous les citoyens chargés des autorités civils & militaires, & à tous les citoyens de la Colonie," dated Jérémie, maison commune, le 7 mars 1793, l'an second de la république française," copy in dossier 895, DXXV/113, CARAN.

16. Laurent Dubois, *A Colony of Citizens: Revolution and Slave Emancipation in the French Caribbean, 1787–1804* (Chapel Hill: University of North Carolina Press, 2004), especially 162–65.

17. The quotation is from Bérault de Saint Maurice, transcribed in David Geggus, *Slavery, War, and Revolution: The British Occupation of Saint Domingue, 1793–1798.* (Oxford: Clarendon Press, 1982), 62–68.

18. "Affranchissement de la négresse Rosalie par Martonne," 2 December 1795, Notary Dobignies, File 9–218. Marthe Guillaume's other dealings with the British appear in her list of creditors and debtors in Notary Lépine, File 6C-210, both in Jérémie Papers, SC, UFL.

19. See the discussion under the heading *affranchissement,* p. 69, "Copie des lettres écrites par le Conseil privé," File T81/15, British National Archives.

20. On the complexity of their departure, see Geggus, *Slavery, War, and Revolution,* 373–381.

21. Rigaud's efforts to assure agricultural production, however, were built on renting out lands to men and women able to pay the price, which often left former slaves

working almost as before on the lands of others. See Dubois, *Avengers of the New World*, 197–98.

22. Perhaps, though this is more speculative, her baptism was very recent, connected in some way with the relationship with the baby's father. The absence of a surname, by contrast, is unsurprising. The taking by a freed person of any surname used by a white family had been prohibited in late colonial Saint-Domingue, and recently freed people often appear in the records without a surname at all. The designation *négresse libre* (free black woman) was by 1799 an anachronism: everyone in Saint-Domingue was now legally free. Its use could either evoke the stigma of previous slave status—or be an echo of the pre-abolition term that signaled possession of valid proof of individual manumission. A copy of the baptismal certificate is in "Rectification de noms d'épouse Tinchant dans son contrat de marriage," 16 November 1835, Act 672, 1835, Notary Theodore Seghers, New Orleans Notarial Archives Research Center (henceforth NONARC). For the 1773 *ordonnance* concerning surnames, see Moreau de Saint-Méry, *Loix et Constitutions des colonies françoises de l'Amérique sous le vent* (Paris, 1784–1790) 5: 448–50.

23. This inclusion of the nickname Dieudonné in a baptismal record is puzzling; generally only a saint's name would be given at the moment of baptism, though nicknames were widely used afterward. For a detailed discussion of the document, see Scott and Hébrard, "Servitude." On naming practices in the French Antilles, see John Garrigus, *Before Haiti: Race and Citizenship in French Saint-Domingue* (New York: Palgrave Macmillan, 2006), and Myriam Cottias, "Le Partage du Nom," in Jean Hébrard, Hebe M. Mattos, and Rebecca J. Scott, eds., *Écrire l'esclavage, écrire la liberté*, Special issue of *Cahiers du Brésil Contemporain* 53/54 (Paris, 2003): 163–74.

24. At the time of his marriage, Michel Vincent had been identified as the *fermier de boucherie* in the southern town of Les Cayes. See the parish registers of Les Cayes du Fond (1698–1782) in SOM 6Mi/37, CARAN. His marriage to Nicole Catherine Bouché Widow Randel is on p. 177, year 1772. Vincent's rare trips to the local notaries in Jérémie were to sell off portions of his land, and he showed little of the buying, borrowing, and loaning of his more prosperous planter neighbors. See, for example, the sale document dated 13 pluviose an 7, in Joubert 4–13, Jérémie Papers, SC, UFL. The description of the region and count of houses is in Moreau de Saint Méry, *Description topographique*, 2: 762–816. Marthe Guillaume's business dealings are abundantly recorded in the papers of the notary Lépine, both those held in the Centre des Archives d'Outre-Mer in Aix-en-Provence (henceforth CAOM), and those in the Jérémie Papers, SC, UFL.

25. On the use of the term "sieur" in Saint-Domingue, see John Garrigus, "Colour, Class and Identity on the Eve of the Haitian Revolution: Saint-Domingue's Free Coloured Elite as Colons Américains," *Slavery and Abolition* 17 (1996): 19–43, especially pp. 25–29. Throughout the eighteenth century, many children were born to unions of

French colonists and African women, and as adults they often established themselves as artisans, traders, entrepreneurs, and in some cases landowners. In the latter decades of the century, these men and women and their descendants had been increasingly stigmatized by whites seeking to monopolize power and civic standing. See Garrigus, *Before Haiti*. For the widow Aubert's activities in New Orleans, see below. By the time Michel Vincent actually died, the revolutionary-era rules on inheritance had been replaced by the Napoleonic Code Civil, which reduced the claims that natural children could make. See Jean-Louis Halperin, "Le droit privé de la Révolution: Héritage législatif et héritage idéologique," *Annales historiques de la Révolution française* 328 (2002).

26. Carolyn E. Fick, *The Making of Haiti*, 210–13; Beaubrun Ardouin, *Études sur l'histoire d'Haiti*, Vol. e (Port-au-Prince: Chéraquit, 1930); Yves Benot, *La Démence coloniale sous Napoléon* (Paris: Éditions La Découverte, 1992); Laurent Dubois, *Colony of Citizens*, 368–70.

27. See the letters of Leclerc in Paul Roussier, ed., *Lettres du Général Leclerc, Commandant en Chef de l'Armée de Saint-Domingue en 1802* (Paris: Société de l'Histoire des Colonies Françaises et Librairie Ernest Leroux, 1937), 200, 201, 255. On the tumult of 1802–1803, see also Dubois, *Avengers*, and Ardouin, *Études*.

28. See Jan Pachoński and Reuel K. Wilson, *Poland's Caribbean Tragedy: A Study of Polish Legions in the Haitian War of Independence, 1802–1803* (Boulder: East European Monographs, 1986), chaps. 4 and 5; Fick, *The Making of Haiti*, 234–35.

29. "Enregistrement de liberté ...," 26 ventôse an XII, folio 25 verso, register titled "Actes déclarations & dépots divers, 10 Pluviose An XII- 12 Avril 1809," in the volume "Registre Comprenant du 10 Pluviose an XII au 10 Vendémiaire an XIII," 6supsdom/3, Agence des Prises de la Guadeloupe, Dépôt des Papiers Publics des Colonies, (hereinafter APG, DPPC), CAOM.

30. "Enregistrement de liberté ...," 26 ventôse an XII. The nickname Résinette may be an affectionate diminutive from raisiné, a grape jam (a suggestion courtesy of Valérie Sega Gobert). We have not located baptismal information for the other three children, though some fragments in the Jérémie Papers are suggestive, listing the baptism in 1795, apparently in the same parish of Cap-Dame-Marie, of "Marie Louise *mulatresse*" and "Jean Théodore Mulatre." See the untitled pages, apparently the continuation of a répertoire, located in Folder 12, Box 5, Jérémie Papers, SC, UFL.

31. "Enregistrement de liberté ...," 26 ventôse an XII. See Scott and Hébrard, "Servitude," 28–30, for the text of this document in French.

32. Manumissions could be regulated in terms of the age and conduct of the slave in question, and the competing rights of the owner's heirs and creditors. Louisiana, where Elizabeth Dieudonné would eventually end up, imposed greater and greater restrictions over time. See Judith Kelleher Schafer, *Becoming Free, Remaining Free: Manumission and Enslavement in New Orleans, 1846–1862* (Baton Rouge: Louisiana State University Press, 2003).

33. For parallel documents created in a situation of comparable uncertainty in Guadeloupe, see Dubois, *Colony*, chap. 2.

34. Peter S. Chazotte, *Historical Sketches of the Revolutions, and the Foreign and Civil Wars in the Island of St. Domingo* (New York: Wm. Applegate, 1840), 32–35.

35. Pachoński and Wilson, *Poland's Caribbean Tragedy*. The descriptions of the evacuation of Jérémie found in the Rochambeau Papers, SC, UFL, are equally vivid. See, for example, the report by a ship captain in item 2021, "Copie du Rapport du Citoyen Pruniet Capitaine de la falouche la Doucereuse venant de Jérémie."

36. Michel Vincent, identified as a *mareschal* (farrier), appears in the reference to "Testament de Michel Etienne Henry Vincent Mareschal dem^t ordin^t au Bourg des Abricots," Actes Déclarations et Dépôts Divers, St Yago de Cuba, 1806–1809, Vol. II, 6supsdom/2, APG, DPPC, CAOM. For Rosalie's presence, see the discussion below.

37. Gabriel Debien, "Les colons de Saint-Domingue réfugiés à Cuba (1793–1815)," *Revista de Indias* 54 (1953): 559–605, especially 590, 593; Alain Yacou, "Esclaves et libres français à Cuba au lendemain de la Révolution de Saint-Domingue," *Jahrbuch fur Geschichte von Staat, Wirtschaft und Gesellschaft Lateinamerikas* (Cologne) 28 (1991): 163–97; Laura Cruz Ríos, *Flujos inmigratorios franceses a Santiago de Cuba (1800–1868)* (Santiago de Cuba: Editorial Oriente, 2006).

38. Some refugees circumvented customs formalities by landing on the shore without reporting to the commandant at the port. Evidence of both official and clandestine landings is scattered through the records in the Fondo Correspondencia de los Capitanes Generales, including Legajos 63, 445, and 471, in the Archivo Nacional de Cuba, Havana (ANC).

39. We can confirm the presence of Elizabeth from the later evidence that she went on from Santiago to New Orleans with her godmother. (See Scott, "Public Rights and Private Commerce.") The presence of Marie Louise is less certain, but see the discussion below of Michel Vincent's will.

40. The official who transcribed the report of Vincent's succession by François Vallée was Bascher Boisjoly, who had been a member of the tribunal of the Sénéchaussée in Jérémie (6supsdom/3, APG, DPPC, CAOM). No copy of Michel Vincent's will has yet come to light, though reference is made to it in Vol. II, 6supsdom/2, APG, DPPC, CAOM. On the French refugees in Santiago, see also Debien, "Colons"; Yacou, "Esclaves"; and Olga Portuondo Zúñiga, *Entre esclavos y libres de Cuba colonial* (Santiago de Cuba: Editorial Oriente, 2003), 58–97.

41. See, for example, the sale of another woman, coincidentally also named Rosalie. The seller claimed to have lost his proof of title, but asserted ownership based on a brand on her body. Sale, Brebion to Marsand, 12 fructidor an 12, in Archives coloniales, Saint Domingue, Agence des Prises de la Guadeloupe, Correspondence, Actes, declarations & dépôts divers St. Yago de Cuba, An XII-An XIV. This volume, now in

the CAOM [and cited above], was microfilmed as film #960762, Genealogical Society of Salt Lake City. This citation is from the microfilm edition.

42. "Enregistrement de liberté . . . ," 26 ventôse an XII.

43. "Remise de Succ[n] par Vallée," 9 floréal an XII, 6supsdom/3, APG, DPPC, CAOM. Changes of this kind in a name were common, particularly in the case of someone whose circumstances of birth precluded adoption of the father's family name. See the interpretation of naming practices in Jean Michel Hébrard, "Esclavage et dénomination: imposition et appropriation d'un nom chez les esclaves de la Bahia au XIXe siècle," in Hébrard, Mattos, and Scott, eds., *Écrire l'esclavage, écrire la liberté*, 31–92. No mention is made in the executor's report of any heirs-at-law in France. In 1827, when France agreed to recognize independent Haiti in exchange for a massive indemnity, Michel Vincent's remaining legitimate kin and heirs, including a grand-nephew living in France, appealed to the French government for a portion of the indemnity. See V 141, Vincent (Michel Étienne Henry), 1390, Indemnités traités, in 7supsdom/97, DPPC, CAOM.

44. The widow Aubert later claimed to have been like a mother to Elizabeth since her early childhood. See the 1822 marriage contract of Elizabeth with Jacques Tinchant, discussed below. On reenslavement by émigrés, see above and Martha S. Jones, "'I Was Born in . . . Croix-des-Bouquets': Slavery, Law, and 'French Negroes' in New York's Era of Gradual Emancipation," manuscript cited with the permission of the author. On reenslavement as a process in Brazil, see the essay by Sidney Chalhoub in this volume.

45. The intrigues and politics surrounding these expulsions were very complex. See Portuondo, *Entre esclavos*, 78–82.

46. The departure from Santiago was in practice a halting, incomplete, and negotiated process. Its complexity can be glimpsed in the correspondence, passenger lists, and registers in the Fondos Asuntos Políticos and Correspondencia de los Capitanes Generales, ANC.

47. On the flight of refugees from Santiago to the United States, see the essays in Carl A. Brasseaux and Glenn R. Conrad, eds., *The Road to Louisiana: The Saint-Domingue Refugees 1792–1809* (Lafayette: Center for Louisiana Studies, University of Southwestern Louisiana, 1992); and the work of Paul Lachance, including "Repercussions of the Haitian Revolution in Louisiana," in *The Impact of the Haitian Revolution in the Atlantic World*, edited by David P. Geggus (Columbia: University of South Carolina Press, 2001), 209–30. See also Nathalie Dessens, *From Saint-Domingue to New Orleans: Migration and Influences* (Gainesville: University Press of Florida, 2007). For the day-to-day drama, and the governor's difficulties, see Dunbar Rowland, ed., *Official Letter Books of W. C. C. Claiborne*, Vols. 4 and 5 (Jackson, Miss.: State Department of Archives and History, 1917).

48. The land purchase document is "Vente de terrain par B^d Marigny à Lambert Détry," 20 Juillet 1809, pp. 348r, 348v, 349r, Notary M. de Armas, Acts No. 2, NONARC. On the Louisiana Schedules of the Third Census of the United States [1810], Lambert Détry appears as the eighth entry on Rue Moreau, in a household containing one white man, three "other free people," and thirteen slaves. See U. S. National Archives (USNA) Microcopy M252, Roll 10, Page 272. Détry and the widow appear in adjacent records of slave purchases in the notarial acts of Philippe Pedesclaux, 8 March 1817, NONARC.

49. One of these slaves was named Blaise; the other was called Marie Louise in the executor's report, and Marie Joseph in the copy of the will filed with the judge. It is remotely possible that she was Rosalie's older daughter, Marie Louise *dite* Résinette, who seems to have been remanded into slavery in Santiago, and could have been purchased by Lambert Détry. The age and birthplace given in the record do not seem to match, however, and Marie Louise was a common name. Liquidation & partage de la Succ^{on} Lambert Détry, aux termes de la transaction judiciaire passée entre les héritiers & les légataires de feu Lambert Détry, File D-1821, Inventories of Estates, Court of Probates, Orleans Parish, Louisiana in City Archives, New Orleans Public Library (hereinafter NOPL).

50. See Liquidation & partage, cited above. Détry referred to this legatee as Marie Dieudonné, f. de c.1., but the executor later identified Marie Dieudonné as the wife of Jacques Tinchant, making it clear that this is indeed Rosalie's younger daughter, Elizabeth (who seems to have acquired the name Marie along the way). See also the 1822 reference to "Marie Dieudonné f. de couleur et Libre demeurant par [illeg] en cette ville faubourg marigny chez marie Blanche V^v Aubert, f de c et qui l'ayant recueillie des sa plus tendre enfance lui a constamment tenue lieu de mere; née a Saint Domingue, fille naturelle et majeure de rozalie vincent qui réside en ce moment à Saint Domingue. . . ." Marriage contract, Jacques Tinchant and Marie Dieudonné, 26 September 1822, p. 31, Vol. 22, Notary M. Lafitte, NONARC.

51. The group presenting themselves as the "lawful heirs," Jean Joseph Détry, Marie Françoise Détry widow of Jean Georges Paternot, Marie Thérèse Détry wife of Antoine Bauman, Joseph Germain Détry, and Thérèse Détry wife of Pierre Joseph Guiotte, hired P. Derbigny as their attorney, and charged that the will was null and void "because it is not clothed with the formalities required by our law and also because it contains dispositions which are prohibited by these." Moreover, they claimed that the clause under which the widow made her claim "is void, because it is a legacy by universal title, which legacies are forbidden between persons who lived together in a state of open concubinage, as these defendants aver that the plfff and the late F. L. Détry did live, and were living at the time of the said Détry's death." The case file is listed as Marie Louise Blanche, widow Aubert, fwc vs. Détry Jean (François X. Freyd, testamentary executor of) Year 1822, case number 206 in Court of Probates (Numbered

Series). The original is now filed with the "flattened records" in the Louisiana Division, NOPL. We owe special thanks to Irene Wainwright of the NOPL for having located this document, which was not microfilmed with other court records of this kind.

52. See the marriage contract cited above. The manuscript sacramental record of the wedding lists the bride's mother ("la expresada Madre de la contrayente") as one of the witnesses, but it is hard to know whether Rosalie Vincent herself was present at the marriage, or whether the priest simply took the widow Aubert for the bride's mother. (The surviving manuscript record is a copy, and the copyist seems to have skipped a line, thus garbling the first reference to the bride herself.) See Act 328, 28 September 1822, in Saint Louis Cathedral, Marriages of Slaves and Free Persons of Color, Vol. 1, 1877–1830, Part 2, in Archives of the Archdiocese of New Orleans (hereafter AANO). A summary transcript appears in Charles E. Nolan, ed., *Sacramental Records of the Roman Catholic Church of New Orleans*, Vol. 15 (New Orleans: Archdiocese of New Orleans, 2000), 368.

53. For a powerful evocation in fiction of the complexity of relationships of this kind, on into the twentieth century, see Maryse Condé, *Victoire: Les saveurs et les mots* (Paris: Mercure de France, 2006).

54. Jacques sued to try to extract the promised bequest from the widow. She countered that the couple's room and board had in fact consumed the equivalent of the bequest, and that she owed him nothing—indeed, that he owed *her* $103.20. In the course of this unseemly quarrel, the widow Aubert compiled a written record that revealed the importance to each of these households of the labor of an enslaved woman named Gertrude, aged around twenty-two, who had been given as a gift to the bride. The hiring-out of Gertrude yielded $140 annually—a sum larger than the food expenses of the couple for an entire year. See Jacques Tinchant vs. Marie Blanche Widow Aubert, docket #3920, Parish Court, Orleans Parish, Louisiana Division, NOPL.

55. See "Société entre Jacques Tinchant et Pierre Duhart," Act. 62, 1835, Notary Théodore Seghers, NONARC. Their business affairs are documented through the volumes of Seghers. Pierre Duhart was the son of Jacques Tinchant's mother Marie Françoise *dite* Suzette Bayot and Louis Duhart, a white schoolteacher and freemason. Because of Louisiana's ban on marriage across the color line, the relationship of Bayot and Duhart was technically "concubinage," though Suzette Bayot was sometimes referred to as Suzette Duhart. Bayot and Duhart migrated to France in the 1830s, and married there. See the death certificate of Marie Françoise Bayot, 8 November 1840, in Gan, Décès 1821–1853, 5Mi 230 R6, in Archives Departementales des Pyrénées Atlantiques, Pau (ADPA).

56. See "Rectification de noms d'épouse Tinchant dans son contrat de mariage," 16 November 1835, Act 672, 1835, Notary Theodore Seghers, NONARC.

57. During the eighteenth century, one of the primary items of trade along parts of

the Senegal River was paper, and in the Islamic culture of northern Senegambia reading was prized and writings were known to hold power. See P.-David Boilat, *Esquisses
sénégalaises,* reprint ed. ([1853] Paris: Éditions Karthala, 1984); James F. Searing, *West
African Slavery and Atlantic Commerce: The Senegal River Valley, 1700–1860* (Cambridge, Eng.: Cambridge University Press, 1993); and Boubacar Barry, *Senegambia and
the Atlantic Slave Trade* (Cambridge, Eng.: Cambridge University Press, 1998). We
thank Mamadou Diouf, Boubacar Barry, Martin Klein, Ibrahima Thioub, and Rudolph
Ware for discussions of Senegal in the late eighteenth and early nineteenth centuries.

58. Many thanks to Scott Shapiro, Yale University, for this observation.

59. Rosalia Vincent appears on the passenger list with an estimated age of fifty—
which seems to be an underestimate by about eighteen years; Rosalie de nation Poulard was said to be twenty-six years old in 1793, hence born in 1767. But there appears
to be nothing very precise about the ages scrawled on the passenger list, and there is
subsequent confirmation (see below) that Rosalie Vincent, mother of Elizabeth, was
indeed in New Orleans in the months that followed. The ship's manifest is reproduced
in "List of all Passengers taken on board the Brig Ann whereof Charles Sutton is
Master at the Port of Port Au Prince and bound for New-Orleans," arriving April 20,
1835, microfilmed as part of Passenger Lists of Vessels Arriving at New Orleans, 1820–
1902, USNA Microcopy 259, Roll 12.

60. By 1825, Louisiana law had made legitimation difficult, and narrowed even the
mechanisms for the lesser act of recognition: See *Civil Code of the State of Louisiana*
(New Orleans: J. C. de St. Romes, 1825), Book I, Title VII, Chapter 3, Section 1, Art.
217, and Section 2, Arts. 220 and 221.

61. By 1839 she was signing documents as Elizabeth Vincent, dropping the infor-
mal Dieudonné altogether. See Échange d'immeubles, 6 August 1839, Act 646, Notary
T. Seghers, NONARC. On the ways in which women of color in Brazil shaped their
names in successive encounters with secular and religious authorities, see Hébrard,
"Esclavage et dénomination." Efforts to gain the surname of a father could also be
related to hopes of inheritance. Michel Vincent was long dead, but the indemnities
for former property holders from Saint-Domingue being granted by France may have
been under discussion in New Orleans as well. Elizabeth Vincent's claim, however,
would have been a very weak one—natural children were far down on the list of those
authorized to inherit from their fathers.

62. The baptismal record—which repeats the error from the original marriage
contract in which Marie [Elizabeth] Dieudonné is confused with her mother-in-law
Suzette Bayole [Bayot]—is Act 326, St. Louis Cathedral, Baptisms of Slaves and Free
Persons of Color, Vol. 25, Part I, in AANO. On the formal requisites for serving as a
godmother, see Virginia Meacham Gould, "Henriette Delille, Free Women of Color,
and Catholicism in Antebellum New Orleans, 1727–1852," in David Barry Gaspar

and Darlene Clark Hine, eds., *Beyond Bondage: Free Women of Color in the Americas* (Urbana: University of Illinois Press, 2004).

63. Under the 1808 *Digest of the Civil Laws Now in Force in the Territory of Orleans,* "marriages contracted by free white persons with free people of color" could not be celebrated and were void in Louisiana. See Title IV, Chapter II, Article 9, of the *Digest* (Baton Rouge: Claitor's Publishing Division, 2008). On Bayot and Duhart, see note 55 above.

64. On conditions for free people of color, see Joseph G. Tregle Jr., *Louisiana in the Age of Jackson: A Clash of Cultures and Personalities* (Baton Rouge: Louisiana State University Press, 1999), 304. On the subsequent history of Edouard Tinchant, see Scott, "Public Rights and Private Commerce."

65. Scott, "Public Rights and Private Commerce."

66. For a discussion of the concept of public rights, and its echoes in the later *Plessy* case, see Rebecca J. Scott, "Public Rights, Social Equality, and the Conceptual Roots of the *Plessy* challenge," *Michigan Law Review* 106 (March 2008): 777–804.

67. Scott, "Public Rights and Private Commerce." For their departure, see the passport application of Edward Tinchant, issue date 29 May 1878, New Orleans, in Passport Applications, 1795–1905, General Records of the Department of State, RG 59, reproduced on USNA Microcopy M1372 [accessed through Ancestry.com 23 April 2008].

68. For the name of their daughter, see the 3 July 1878 entry for the family of Edouard Tinchant with the Administration de la Sureté Publique No. 148, in M.A., Vreemdelingendossiers 1878, Stadsarchief, Antwerp. Their youngest child is listed as Marie Louise Julie, born in New Orleans on 14 March 1878. (We have not yet located the actual baptismal record, which should be in one or another church record in New Orleans). For information on the subsequent generations, we thank Marie Louise (Loulou) Van Velsen, who has generously shared photographs, letters, documents, and memories of her great-grandfather Edouard Tinchant, her grandmother Marie Louise Tinchant, and her mother, also named Marie Louise. We also thank the Struyf and Van Velsen families very warmly for their assistance and hospitality in Belgium.

In Memoriam, Evan Anders (1946–2008)

This volume is dedicated to the memory of our colleague, Professor Evan (Buzz) Anders, who died on April 5, 2008. Professor Anders, a member of Phi Beta Kappa, received his PhD from the University of Texas at Austin in December of 1978. While at the University of Texas he won a Walter Prescott Webb Fellowship and worked with Lewis L. Gould in Progressive Era history. A month after receiving his PhD, he joined the history department at the University of Texas at Arlington as a visiting assistant professor and took a tenure-track job here in 1982. For nearly thirty years he taught introductory courses in U.S. history, along with upper-division sections in the history of Populism, Progressivism, the 1920s, the Great Depression and the New Deal, and the history of film. In addition he offered a graduate course titled Issues and Interpretations in U.S. History. Professor Anders took teaching very seriously and was good at it. He memorized his well-crafted lectures and poured an enormous amount of time into class preparation.

He also had some impressive publications. In 1979 the University of Texas Press published his *Boss Rule in South Texas: The Progressive Era,* a well-received book that went into paperback in 1987. He also wrote an award-winning article in the *Southwestern Historical Quarterly* and published an important article on Thomas Watt Gregory as well as another on the treatment of Lyndon Johnson by his biographers.

During much of his tenure in history at UT Arlington, Professor Anders was actively involved in departmental politics and service. This modest man had a keen mind and was widely read in a variety of topics and always willing to share his insights and opinions. He was passionate about his opinions, whether on his beloved University of Texas Longhorn football team, the state of U.S. politics, or the shortcomings of the American Academy. Now he is gone, but in a department of historians he will not be forgotten.

Bob Fairbanks

About the Contributors

TREVOR BURNARD teaches American and Caribbean history at the University of Warwick. He has taught at universities in England, New Zealand, and the West Indies. He is the author of *Mastery, Tyranny, and Desire: Thomas Thistlewood and His Slaves in the Anglo-Jamaican World* (Chapel Hill, 2004) and is working, with John Garrigus, on a book comparing Saint-Domingue and Jamaica, 1748–1791. He is also writing a book on the state of early American history in the twenty-first century.

SIDNEY CHALHOUB is professor of history at the University of Campinas, Brazil. He has published three books on the social history of Rio de Janeiro: *Trabalho, lar e botequim* (1986), on working-class culture in the early twentieth century; *Visões da liberdade* (1990), on the last decades of slavery in the city; and *Cidade febril* (1996), on tenements and epidemics in the second half of the nineteenth century. He also published *Machado de Assis, historiador* (2003), about the literature and political ideas of the most important nineteenth-century Brazilian novelist, and coedited four other books on the social history of Brazil.

JOHN GARRIGUS is an associate professor of history at the University of Texas at Arlington. He is the author of *Before Haiti: Race and Citizenship in Saint-Domingue* (2006) and coeditor, with Laurent Dubois, of *Slave Revolution in the Caribbean, 1789–1804: A Brief History With Documents* (2006).

REBECCA ANNE GOETZ is assistant professor of history at Rice University. Her interests include religion and race in early North America.

JEAN M. HÉBRARD has worked for many years on the cultural history of southwest Europe, focusing on the history of writing (scribal and personal practices). He participated in the large-scale enquiries on the history of reading and writing carried out in France in the 1980s and the 1990s, and published numerous articles and books in this field, particularly *Discours sur la lecture, 1880–2000* (Paris: Fayard, 2000) with Anne-Marie Chartier. Recently he has extended his research area to the colonial world of Iberian and French Empires (particularly Brazil and Saint-Domingue). Professeur associé at the Ecole des Hautes Etudes en Sciences Sociales, and visiting professor at the University of Michigan, he is a member of the Centre de Recherche sur le Brésil Contemporain (EHESS) and of the Centre International de Recherche sur les Esclavages (CNRS). He is the 2009–2010 Norman Freehling Visiting Professor at the Institute for the Humanities, University of Michigan.

FRANKLIN W. KNIGHT is Leonard and Helen R. Stulman Professor of History at Johns Hopkins University. A past president of the Latin American Studies Association and the Historical Society, he has written, edited, or coedited nine books, including *Slave Society in Cuba during the Nineteenth Century; The Modern Caribbean;* and *Contemporary Caribbean Cultures and Societies in a Global Context.*

CHRISTOPHER MORRIS of the University of Texas at Arlington is a historian of slavery, race, and the natural environment in the U.S. South. He is the author *of Becoming Southern: The Evolution of a Way of Life, Vicksburg and Warren County, Mississippi, 1770–1860,* and of the forthcoming *Big Muddy: An Environmental History of the Mississippi and Its Peoples, from Hernando de Soto to Hurricane Katrina.*

REBECCA J. SCOTT is the Charles Gibson Distinguished University Professor of History and Professor of Law at the University of Michigan. Her 2005 book, *Degrees of Freedom: Louisiana and Cuba after Slavery,* received the Frederick Douglass Prize and the John Hope Franklin Prize. She works on both Latin America and the U.S. South, and her most recent articles include "Public Rights, Social Equality, and the Conceptual Roots of the Plessy Challenge," *Michigan Law Review* 106 (2008); "Microhistory Set in Motion: An Atlantic Creole Itinerary," in Aisha Khan, George Baca, and Stephan Palmié, eds., *Empirical Futures: Anthropologists and Historians Engage the Work of Sidney W. Mintz* (Chapel Hill: University of North Carolina Press, forthcoming); and "'She ... refuses to deliver up herself as the slave of your petitioner': Émigrés, Enslavement, and the 1808 Louisiana Digest of the Civil Laws," *Tulane European and Civil Law Forum* 24 (2009).

Index

Other Titles in the Walter Prescott Webb Memorial Lectures Series: